THE SILVERING SCREEN
Old Age and Disability in Cinema

Popular films have always included elderly characters, but until recently, old age only played a supporting role onscreen. Now, as the baby boomer population hits retirement, there has been an explosion of films, including *Away From Her*, *The Straight Story*, *Barbarian Invasions*, and *About Schmidt*, where aging is a central theme.

The first-ever sustained discussion of old age in cinema, *The Silvering Screen* brings together theories from disability studies, critical gerontology, and cultural studies to examine how the film industry has linked old age with physical and mental disability. Sally Chivers further examines Hollywood's mixed messages – applauding actors who portray the debilitating side of aging while at the same time promoting a culture of youth – as well as the gendering of old age on film. *The Silvering Screen* makes a timely attempt to counter the fear of aging implicit in these readings by proposing alternate ways to value getting older.

SALLY CHIVERS is the chair of and an associate professor in the Department of Canadian Studies at Trent University.

THE SILVERING SCREEN

Old Age and Disability in Cinema

Sally Chivers

UNIVERSITY OF TORONTO PRESS
Toronto   Buffalo   London

© University of Toronto Press Incorporated 2011
Toronto   Buffalo   London
www.utppublishing.com
Printed in Canada

ISBN   978-0-8020-4079-5 (cloth)
ISBN   978-0-8020-1104-7 (paper)

Printed on acid-free, 100% post-consumer recycled paper
with vegetable-based inks

Library and Archives Canada Cataloguing in Publication

Chivers, Sally, 1972–
The silvering screen: old age and disability
in cinema / Sally Chivers.

Includes bibliographical references and index.
ISBN 978-1-4426-4079-5 (bound)   ISBN 978-1-4426-1104-7 (pbk.)

1. Aging in motion pictures. I. Title.

PN1995.9.A433C55 2011   791.43'654   C2011-900557-3

University of Toronto Press acknowledges the financial assistance
to its publishing program of the Canada Council for the Arts
and the Ontario Arts Council.

 Canada Council   Conseil des Arts
for the Arts   du Canada

 ONTARIO ARTS COUNCIL
CONSEIL DES ARTS DE L'ONTARIO

This book has been published with the help of a grant from
the Canadian Federation for the Humanities and Social Sciences,
through the Aid to Scholarly Publications Program, using funds provided
by the Social Sciences and Humanities Research Council of Canada.

University of Toronto Press acknowledges the financial support
for its publishing activities of the Government of Canada through
the Book Publishing Industry Development Program (BPIDP).

This book is dedicated to Chris Bell and Gabrielle Helms,
who didn't live long enough.

Contents

Contents

Acknowledgments

Disability studies changed my thinking and my life. Special thanks to Mike Gill, Michelle Jarman, Eunjung Kim, Robert McRuer, Nicole Markotić, John Marris, David Mitchell, Sharon Snyder, Rosemary Garland Thomson, Sara Vogt, and Cindy Wu for their comments on this work. I also owe an enormous debt of gratitude to the work of feminist cultural gerontologists for helping me to understand age as a category of analysis, and I would like to thank Suzann Campbell who told me about the Botox cartoon.

I have the support of amazing colleagues at Trent and am inspired by my students' unmatched enthusiasm for and interest in the world in which they live. My thanks to all members of the Canadian Studies, English, and Women's Studies departments. Extra thanks are due to Dimitry Anastakis, Suzanne Bailey, Martin Boyne, Dana Capell, Jeannine Crowe, Richard Dellamora, Finis Dunaway, Laura Dunbar, Charmaine Eddy, Michael Epp, Julia Harrison, Stephen Katz, Deborah Kennett, John Milloy, Janet Miron, Orm Mitchell, James Neufeld, Bryan Palmer, Zailig Pollock, Beth Popham, Joan Sangster, Kevin Siena, Margaret Steffler, James Struthers, and John Wadland.

I have also been fortune to work with the members of the Hidden Costs, Invisible Contributions research team who made me think differently about care. Special thanks to Pat Armstrong, Emily Bruusgard, Sherry Ann Chapman, Tamara Daly, Donna Dosman, Janet Fast, Norah Keating, Bonnie Lashewicz, Maggie Quirt, Carole Roy, and to SSHRC for their funding through that team as well as through a standard research grant.

I had a number of impressive research assistants working with me on this project. Thank you to Lynette Schick for literature searches that took me in new directions, to David Hugill for his work on the filmography, and to Hugill and Patrick Scott for tracking down reviews and beginning work on the images, and to Meaghan Beaton for tirelessly obtaining permissions for the images, most of which she also located. University of Toronto Press has been wonderful to work with, especially Leah Connor, Frances Mundy, Ryan Van Huijstee, and Siobhan McMenemy.

My family, as always, deserves my deepest thanks. Thank you to Peter, Sue, and Tris Chivers, Kim Schreck, and John and Jill Matthews. Above all, I thank Wade Matthews for his love, friendship, and critical acumen.

Chapter 2 is a version of my previous article 'Baby Jane Grew Up: The Dramatic Intersection of Age with Disability,' *Canadian Review of American Studies* 36/3 (2006): 211–27. The materials are reprinted by permission of the Canadian Association for American Studies (www.utpjournals.com).

Sections of chapter 1 and 3 are reprinted from my previous article '"Move! You're in the Way": Disability and Age Meet on Screen,' *Canadian Journal of Film Studies* 17/1 (2008): 30–43. The materials are reprinted by permission of the Film Studies Association of Canada.

Introduction:
The Silvering Screen

As Hollywood movies take down a brick from one part of the wall of dominant ideology, they put back another elsewhere.

Dennis Bingham, *Acting Male*

Setting the Stage

In 2008 the fourth Indiana Jones movie, *Kingdom of the Crystal Skull* (USA, Steven Spielberg), became the second highest grossing film of the year, capitalizing on its audience's nostalgia for a younger Harrison Ford. At the age of sixty-six, Ford insisted that explicit mention of the character Indiana Jones's advanced age be added to the script, while also undertaking an excessive fitness regime in order to be able to perform many of his own action hero stunts. In interviews, Ford adamantly stated his desire to display rather than hide his and his character's aging:

> What astonishes me is that people can't imagine Indiana Jones aging at all. Why expect any character to be frozen in time? The appeal of Indiana Jones isn't his youth but his imagination, his resourcefulness … My ambition in action is to have the audience look straight in the face of a character and not at the back of a capable stuntman's head. I hope to continue to do that, no matter how old I get.[1]

Ford is happy to 'look' old as long as he is seen to 'act' young (by Hollywood's definition: that is, imaginatively and resourcefully). In doing so, he appears to be contesting the dominant cultural meaning of youth, suggesting that imagination and resourcefulness are not determined by age. However, he still insists not only on portraying a character who powerfully wields a bullwhip but also on being an actor who does the whipping himself. His insistence demonstrates that, to him, aging successfully means continuing to achieve physical feats not common even for the average younger person.

By contrast, Melanie Griffith, who turned only fifty-five in 2008, struggles to find any screen work at all. She admits to having had some plastic surgery – collagen injections and breast enhancement – and considers herself to be a quintessential aging star. She complains that she suffers the consequences of the ageist assumptions circulating in contemporary culture. When she accepted a Broadway part, for lack of film work, she told the *New York Times*, 'I wish that I could make more movies. The fact that I have some lines on my face, that's it. It's not because I lost my talent or I became deformed. It's only because I'm older.'[2] Her slightly younger husband, actor Antonio Banderas, expresses sympathy for her plight, going so far as to describe her as 'a victim of aging' and explaining, 'When you have wrinkles, it seems you stop being an actress … In the future, they'll remove wrinkles digitally, so you may see Melanie on screen anyway!'[3] For Ford, an active body offsets an aging face, but for Griffith, facing the audience seems impossible without youth-enhancing technologies beyond plastic surgery. The difference between the actors' claims clearly has to do with skewed gender expectations, but it also has to do with what aging means socially and culturally. Both Ford and Griffith have to declare that they are still capable and not 'deformed,' as Griffith puts it. Ford can look audiences in the eye because he is still physically fit, and Griffith cannot, even though she too is still physically fit. These actors could not make the claim that they are still capable if a visible disability accompanied their later lives because physical fitness and physical appearance are the base of each of their careers.

In this book, I examine contemporary film to ask why claims of physical and mental ability are necessary for older actors – and older people more generally. Further, I point to what the necessity of making those claims says about cultural views of growing old at a time when the global population is aging. Because cultural attitudes toward old age intensely reveal broader cultural mores – to summarize Simone de Beauvoir, what a culture says about old age says even more about the culture – my argument expands to consider what the necessity for Ford and Griffith to declare their fitness says about contemporary culture more broadly.[4] While their utterances are most relevant to American[5]

Harrison Ford wielding Indiana Jones's bullwhip. © Terry O'Neill/Terry O'Neill/
Getty Images

Melanie Griffith, 'a victim of aging.' © Steve Granitz/WireImage/Getty Images

culture, the phenomenon extends beyond the United States, and this book is relevant to much of the global north.

Booming Hollywood

Hollywood receives and deserves much blame for a broader cultural shift to 'youth' as an object of desire, a shift evident in everything from the explosion and domestication of cosmetic surgery to the cult of celebrity, represented on the body and in the way the body is often portrayed onscreen. Corresponding with the age of a nascent art form, early Hollywood was powered and muscled by young workers, and Hollywood's most dominant discourse has always included an insistence on what is now called youth.[6] In addition to young workers on- and off-screen, scripts generally feature youthful roles, so that to stay onscreen and at work as an older actor has been uncommon.[7] This social practice has conditioned the stories told by Hollywood, in the press and in the cinema, so that audiences are assailed with tales of young romance (think *50 First Dates* and the Brangelina phenomenon) and youthful folly (think *American Pie* and Lindsay Lohan). But, times are changing even in Hollywood.

The ongoing influence of the famous among aging boomers – and the latter's demographic weight – has resulted in a growing number of notable actors, like Ford, remaining onscreen later into their lives, unafraid to look if not act their ages, and changing the 'face' of Hollywood. The continued presence of some boomer actors does not indicate a complete social transformation any more than strong female characters in 1930s cinema marked a permanent improvement in the lot of women. While some older actors are as brazen as Ford and others are happy to look *and* act older, many not-so-young actors who remain in the spotlight (if not on the screen) work hard to hide their age (usually only highlighting it) through increasingly drastic cosmetic – usually surgical – means. Other actors make the choice to exaggerate the decline that their aging appearance implies. Older actors present Hollywood with a potential challenge – as Ford puts it, 'we've got a great shot at breaking the movie demographic constraints.'[8] At the same time, they present a narrative problem because they do not fit into the plots that Hollywood has long produced; by insisting on central roles, they test those plots by exceeding what has formerly been the norm for aging U.S. residents, in turn creating higher expectations that are promoted by the film industry and associated anti-aging outfits.

While actors such as Ford, Jack Nicholson, Judi Dench, and Julie Christie will not go gently, the roles they play have changed to be primarily focused on aging. Perhaps when Melanie Griffith is old enough, parts will appear for her again. The screen presence of aging actors has significantly transformed Hollywood, even if only to reveal repeated claims of the value of youth to be suspiciously shallow. Gradually, the stories that Hollywood tells are also changing.

The Silvering Screen

At the end of the twentieth century, millennium celebrations both marked and generated a heightened awareness of time passing. In addition, this millennial shift was accompanied by increasing alarm about the 'greying' of the population because of the perceived age and size of what has been labelled the baby boomer generation. Social anxiety about old age, heightened by frightening demographic predictions, has yet to abate and is reflected in a set of films I call the 'silvering screen'. The silvering screen features aging prominently: not just as a background concern to make youthful plots more virile and fascinating, but as a central premise that drives the film.

Films focused on aging, especially on becoming old, appear periodically throughout film history within and outside of Hollywood. Ingmar Bergman's *Wild Strawberries* (Sweden, 1957) sets the stage for the most dominant characteristics of the silvering screen: a retrospective plot that omits middle age, a road trip in time and space, and the portrayal of aching regret.[9] Its seventy-six-year-old protagonist, Dr. Isak Borg, spends the day that he is to receive the highest honour for his successful career nightmarishly reflecting on his personal and professional failures. Haunted by a handless clock and shattered spectacles, he stops to sample the wild strawberries of his youth, literally and metaphorically.

Silvering screen films value and evaluate the present primarily in relation to a distant past, with the intervening years meaning little. From their perspective, middle age is uninteresting material for a narrative and remembrances typically gloss over it as a banal stage of life. Silvering screen films illuminate time – continually featuring clocks, visually noting seasons, including birthdays in the plot – and in order to do so they often exaggerate space by illustrating travel on the part of the aging characters. Most agonizingly, and most difficult for me to reckon with while conducting this research, these films usually look back on a somehow unfulfilling life, rarely resulting in a satisfied sense of accomplishment on the part of the aging protagonist. There is thus often a tension within these films whereby a sense of loss of youth is accompanied by a deep sense of youthful failures. Rarely would a character want to relive the same youth, and rarely are these characters content in their late life. Rather, they typically wish to be young again, but under different circumstances, making different choices.

Backstage dramas such as *All about Eve* (USA, Joseph Mankiewicz, 1950), *Sunset Boulevard* (USA, Billy Wilder, 1950), and *Whatever Happened to Baby Jane?* (USA, Robert Aldrich, 1962) form an early subset of films about aging. These films openly highlight the agonies facing thespian women who desire central performance roles after their youth has 'faded.' The question about the mental capacity of aging spinsters (with money) found in these three films continues in the film *Hush ... Hush, Sweet Charlotte* (USA, Robert Aldrich, 1965), and this theme has become increasingly prevalent in more recent years with Alzheimer's becoming an unwieldy, expensive, and heartbreaking cinematic figure of old age. Collectively, the earlier films introduce the idea that old age, particularly for women, is always a horror story, and in doing so they distance senescence from audience members.

In its own category, *Harold and Maude* (USA, Hal Ashby, 1971) rejects the horror-story role for older women and pushes the normative tenets of May-December romance by imbuing a young man with requited sexual desire for a seventy-nine-year-old woman. To thrive, this film had to be classified as 'black comedy,' and not only because of Harold's repeated suicide attempts. The more typical May-December romance escapes particular notice (i.e., old men mating with young women onscreen and off without much being made of it), and in the 1980s the heteronormativity of the silvering screen became especially acute. Long marriages are figured as key to identity and mourning in old age, as is particularly evident in *On Golden Pond* (USA, Mark Rydell, 1981) and *Cocoon* (USA, Ron Howard, 1985). In more recent times, these relationships have become explicitly vital to late-life care, which has been downloaded onto the 'family.'

Though these few films feature late life prominently, old age has more typically played an auxiliary role on the big screen. Film scholar Martine Beugnet draws attention to past tendencies for cinema to relegate aging to a bit part, emphasizing the scope of this pattern and demonstrating that not only Hollywood is to blame: there is a popular tendency towards 'hackneyed characterizations of old women,' but old women rarely appear in non-mainstream cinema either.[10] The pattern, albeit limited, of cinematic depictions of old age, especially of old women, has been demeaning, and the available roles have been minor, belying any sense of social progress in attitudes towards women and aging in which the public may wish to believe. Sociologist Elizabeth Markson relates social roles to film roles, arguing that for more than sixty years, despite myriad social advances, older women have been presented as exaggeratedly maternal or monstrous in cinema.[11] The big screen offers a cultural repository of regressive and outmoded beliefs about aging femininity that should long be out of vogue. The silvering screen offers a potent site for the production of cultural knowledge and requires critical attention because it has a strong influence on popular thinking about late life.

The patterns of representation that Beugnet and Markson note, and the films I have mentioned, indicate that the topic of aging is not at all new to the cinema. It is then all the more intriguing that the proportion and types of age-focused plots have increased so that in the late twentieth and early twenty-first century a multitude of such films have aired in both mainstream and non-mainstream cinemas,[12] featuring large numbers of older actors who are familiar to audiences because of their past youthful fame.

The silvering screen flourishes by tapping into the concerns of an aging audience and portraying issues frequently associated with aging, ranging from the apparently humorous 'Am I really still sexy?' to the apparently tragic 'Why can't I remember my name and, especially, my husband?' Gerontologists C. J. Gilleard and Paul Higgs argue that it should no longer be possible to imagine a homogenized status or situation for 'the old' or 'any common cultural position that can be popularly represented as "ageing."'[13] Despite an economic fragmentation and social change over time in how different groups of older people acquire and maintain different social statuses, the silvering screen not only features old age but also attempts, like Botox, to homogenize the face of aging (often into the face of *not* aging). Films, especially those made in Hollywood, try to construct a common social identity for older people and try to imagine as universal not just the fact but also the manner of aging.

In this book, I focus on the stories that films in Hollywood and beyond tell about aging. I'm interested in the ways that, even with the increased visibility of old age and prevalence of age-centred plots, recent mainstream films try to reduce old age to a manageable and controllable set of representations. Though the plots have changed, the idea that age is physical, and physically demeaning, has not. A crow's foot still signifies the passage of time and symbolizes decay rather than improvement.

Thus, the control of physical decay – imagining more successful care models, for example – offers a reassuring potential future to audience members. On the silvering screen old age appears to be, if not avoidable, at least manageable. I suggest that the recurring stock appearance of old age in film obscures a more varied and meaningful representation of aging, particularly aging into senescence. Some independent films come close to a more fruitful depiction, but they struggle against the monolith. Amidst the recent proliferation of representation, I look at what old age comes to mean in film, and I track patterns of representation that dictate a cultural shorthand for understanding late life.

Speaking of a related form of shorthand, disability studies scholars David T. Mitchell and Sharon L. Snyder argue of visible disabilities in *Narrative Prosthesis*, 'Film narratives rely upon an audience's making connections between external "flaws" and character motivations in a way that insists upon corporeal differences as laden with psychological and social implications. We refer to this production of disability as a visual indicator of *fathomless* motivations as film art's "new physiognomy."'[14] Similarly, I argue that silvering screen narratives rely on audience members reading such visual markers as grey hair and wrinkles to signify the more obvious decay, decline, and imminent death of the characters (and sometimes actors), as well as a less obvious social anxiety about identity, self, and meaning. The physical signs are the abbreviated symbols that connote decay, decline, and death. To play on Mitchell and Snyder then, films about old age offer visual indicators of fathomable (knowable) rather than fathomless motivations on the silvering screen. That is, while Mitchell and Snyder consider disability to offer a visual figure that obscures simple interpretation, old age on film offers a visual figure whose motivations – including an intended response – can be clearly understood. Whereas wrinkles and ailments appear as shorthand, the long-hand of what these visual markers connote betrays the shorthand as insufficient for the complexity of what it connotes. Put simply, there is more to old age than wrinkles and grey hair, which are only scribbles on the page until viewers bring a broad set of assumptions about what it means to grow old to their interpretations of those signs.

Images of Aging

Perhaps it is obvious that aging affects all of us. Each of us grows older every minute and, in the best-case scenario, each of us will become old, eventually. As literary gerontologist Kathleen Woodward puts it, 'Our disregard of age is all the more curious because age – in the sense of *older* age – is the one difference we are all likely to live into.'[15] But because age is always relative, we can almost always find someone further along the age continuum to comfort us about our own comparative youth. Further, we all live in relation to our current age and other people's interpretations of it. Age studies scholar Margaret Morganroth Gullette explains: 'no age class exists in a capsule, insulated from whatever is impinging on the other age classes – younger *and* older.'[16] In this view, a thorough explication of 'old age' requires an understanding of 'youth' and 'middle age' as similarly false signifiers and heterogeneous cultural positions. Markson explains how cinema contributes to the illusion of age distinctions:

> The disintegrating ill or dying female body provides a model against which spectators can perform a self-assessment, reassuring themselves of their own wholeness by projecting their fears of ageing and death outward. One's own mortality is kept at bay, perhaps one reason that the portrayal of the ageing female body as a tomb or a candidate for entombment is a prevalent movie theme.[17]

Although the topic of aging is relevant to each of our lives, most of us comfort ourselves by believing that we really are not old ... yet. Film images of decrepit elderly figures help to reassure us in that belief, particularly of our own putative yet impossible immortality.

While film studies has quietly shied away from the aging body, not a difficult task given the marginality of older actors until recently, gerontologists frequently reference the importance of cultural representations to understandings of late life, and most of them explicitly refer to the role of film in that process.[18] The argument generally involves a claim that the lingering meanings created from the big screen affect what people believe they ought to do and ought to be in relation to what they have the means and opportunities to do and be.[19] To an extent, images of aging on the silvering screen could allow for a broader acceptance of the inevitability of becoming old (barring death) in a culture that is not hospitable to older, inconvenient bodies. More likely, however, such optimism is not merited because the disproportionate wealth of film stars gives them access to a form of aging that is quite different from that of the average citizen. Also, the plots that concern aging to date generally do not celebrate its possibilities but rather, as I will demonstrate in the chapters of this book, revel in its disadvantages.

Feminist age theorists Margaret Cruikshank and Gullette, following de Beauvoir's claim, explain that we learn how to be old and become old in relation to culture.[20] Markson explains this training with explicit reference to film: 'Although cinematic representations permit spectators to play active roles in constructing and interpreting their meanings, the very act of watching a film fosters new modes of behavior and consciousness.'[21] Accordingly, recent films about caregiving are likely to foster a mode of care work that is highly advantageous to the state (in countries where the state is still thought responsible for health care) in that spouses will very likely want to emulate the sacrifices projected on screen in order to age properly. The repeated imaginings about old age that appear on film signify a larger cultural ethic.

It is of course possible to transcend the uniformity of silvering screen depictions of aging to create a complicated and generative view of late life. Speaking of both performativity in a social sense and performance more broadly, literary gerontologist and playwright Anne Davis Basting stresses the importance of critical engagement with pervasive images of aging in order to assert constructive 'modes of behavior and consciousness.'[22] In this book, I engage critically with film images of aging with the goal of asserting such modes. As Gullette argues, 'Revealing hidden ideologies is one of the most amazing faculties of recent critical literary and social theory.'[23] Without presuming to be 'amazing,' I seek in this book to bring out and analyse the hidden ideologies that cohere in representations of old people on the silvering screen.

Filming Age

Film studies has a substantial (and as yet untapped) contribution to make to rethinking age on the silvering screen. One relevant strand is the critical tradition of examining the effect that camera shots have on character identification, later also referred to as engagement.[24] In claiming that the camera angle, when it simulates the sight-lines of a particular character, literally puts viewers in the position of the character and therefore makes those viewers more likely to identify with the character they seem to be standing beside (or – more properly – on top of), film theorists stand to illuminate how a new focus on aging characters thinking through their own aging processes could elicit sympathy for and empathy with aging people. Though I am not interested here in delineating the precise imaginative faculties or the exact processes of perception involved (that is, I am not preoccupied with whether sensory or cognitive processes are supreme), I trace the cultural imagination as captured in filmic representations of old age in order to think about what such films can spark in the imaginations of audiences, mindful that audiences are varied and not likely to be composed even primarily of the normative subjects assumed by most film theorists.

Ambivalence about which character is right or wrong and about the best case scenario for the central character frequently holds film aloft, and, on the silvering screen, that ambivalence often thereby supports otherwise tired and repetitive plots in their futile attempts to homogenize oldness. As a result, engaging critically with cinematic visions of late life could allow people to imagine alternate, even opposing, perspectives vicariously – to witness, emulate, reject, invite the heteroglossia of old age. In their introduction to the *Oxford Book of Aging*, Thomas Cole and Mary G. Winkler point to a cultural illiteracy about aging, a point that Kathleen Woodward stresses twice in the introduction to her vital volume *Figuring Age*, arguing that the lack of literacy 'can have devastating consequences.'[25] Because of the emerging prominence of age on screen, cultural literacy about late life is likely to increase, but we must question the type of popular literacy that could develop. In particular, as older actors take on more meaningful roles, the potential for new models of aging to arise increases. The upsurge in the number of films that engage with late life indicates a social preoccupation with the perceived greying of the population. What is more, bringing this topic into the public sphere sparks an awareness that – while not necessarily progressive – is a start towards a changed perception of growing old.

As Gullette points out, however, a move towards late life plots does not solve anything: 'fictions of the later life course per se are not only *not* solutions to problems of generations, aging, and the future, but may misstate the problems and distract us from our real cultural quandaries.'[26] In what follows, I'm interested in the form, narrative, and influence of these distractions as they appear in film. Most importantly, I seek to uncover and examine the hidden 'real cultural quandaries' – the wrinkles feebly smoothed by the silvering screen.

THE SILVERING SCREEN
Old Age and Disability in Cinema

Chapter one

Same Difference? Gerontology and Disability Studies Join Hands

Old age is not something gratefully put on in order to gain a seat on the bus.

John Mortimer[1]

'Move, You're in the Way'

Navigating old age in the public sphere poses an intriguing and worrying set of practical and theoretical questions. I begin this chapter – in which I lay out the theoretical stakes of my project – with a story that brings such questions to the forefront. When I was a postdoctoral fellow living in Vancouver, I took the bus to and from the University of British Columbia a few times a week. Literary scholar Celeste Langan argues that

> the bus has a history of enabling and extending participation in the public sphere ... Having usually a greater number of points for access and departure along its fixed route, the bus is more irregular in keeping its appointments; it is this openness to contingency that makes it, finally, not only a portion of the public sphere, but also a figure for the transitivity or *progressive* aspect of that public sphere.[2]

Vancouver had the pretence of a physically accessible bus system that, while emulating the progressiveness mentioned by Langan, also dramatically contributed to the irregularity of the bus schedules. If someone in a wheelchair, for example, wanted to take the bus she could wait where she imagined the front end of the bus would stop and hope that the many other people lined up would not block her from the driver's view so that she could signal to the driver. The driver would then shut down the bus, push back the line of other travellers waiting to get on, lower a ramp, which had the stigmatizing addition of flashing lights and loud beeping noises (presumably a safety feature), 'help' or encourage her to wheel up the ramp, clear the front end of the bus to make room, strap her into the spot, go back outside, raise the ramp (complete with flashing lights and bells), and allow the rest of the travellers to fill up the back of the packed bus, leaving the front completely clear except for the person in the wheelchair.

This was the express route, but the process would stretch what otherwise was about a thirty-second stop into anywhere from a ten-minute to a twenty-minute stop, depending on the competence of the driver and the cooperation of fellow passengers. As disability arts practitioner Simi Linton points out in her memoir *My Body Politic*, this type of situation is an improvement for physically disabled people, many of whom depend upon even more segregating and unreliable 'special' forms of transportation.[3] While she acknowledges that the process can be cumbersome and stigmatizing, she argues, picking up on Langan's optimism, that a new collectivity is formed through the inclusion of disabled people on the public bus: 'I and other disabled passengers, alongside the non-disabled, going to work, to shop, to the movies, to the doctor's, or to a friend's house. So natural.'[4]

One day, as I was returning from the university, the bus stopped for a person in a wheelchair, and the entire conspicuous process began in a manner that threatened the inclusiveness of the collectivity Linton proposes and impeded Langan's sense of progress. The bus driver was at the stage of asking people in the front of the bus to move back. His request consisted of yelling and a small amount of shoving. Most passengers conceded, but two older riders remained in the seats clearly marked 'reserved for seniors and people with disabilities.' Since the accessibility procedure is not clearly spelled out anywhere on the bus, these venerable passengers did not seem to understand that *they* were being asked to move. They may well have thought that the driver was clearing the space that had been reserved for them, as seniors. However, the driver did not allow them to think that for long. Instead, he shouted, 'MOVE! YOU'RE IN THE WAY.'

The recipients of this verbal salvo looked bewildered and struggled towards the back of the bus. Imagine actually telling members of a segment of the population that too often invites criticism for supposedly being a burden that they are in the way! Still, though the driver was clearly at the very least having a bad day, the situation was not exactly his fault. The system was faulty, and he was trying to rearrange privilege, which is probably not what he thought he was signing up for when he took the job. The driver's statement, 'Move! You're in the way,' articulates quite clearly a widespread attitude towards old people – that is, they are burdensome and in the way of the efficiency of contemporary capitalist society. His statement articulates a common attitude towards people with disabilities, and the woman in the wheelchair in this example was hardly liberated by the exclamation made on her behalf. The statement tidily crystallizes competing interests within the space. Who deserves the reserved space more: the older bus-riders or the rider in the wheelchair? Who is more in the way? Who should get out of the way? And, how does 'being in the way' set one group against another?

Cinema as a Booming Business

For now, at least, resisting age rather than ageism greases more palms, oils more deals, and turns more dollars.

Gilleard and Higgs, *Cultures of Ageing*[5]

The turn of the most recent century brought with it a concomitant awareness of time passing and a raft of films that interrogate or at least display old age prominently. Age has long been Hollywood's nightmare, but attention to the progress of time in the late 1990s and early 2000s invites many light-hearted and light-witted images of aging that do little to challenge common attitudes towards growing old, but do offer work to aging actors. Just as the number of kitchen implements with grips friendly to arthritic hands subtly increases in mainstream consumer venues, so too does the number of greying baby-boomer-friendly plots, without being named as such. Alfonso Cuarón's *Great Expectations* (USA, 1998) previewed this focus by presenting forty-something Miss Havisham as a seventy-something Ms Dinsmoor (an aged Mrs Robinson, played by Anne Bancroft), who not only goes outside (as Miss Havisham never does) but, to emphasize her age, loves cats. David Lynch's odd pairing with Disney brought *The Straight Story* (USA, 1999), offering a straightforward American-family-driven road-trip narrative, but Alvin Straight's journey is slowed down to accommodate the apparently inevitable decline of the aging baby-boomer population. In *About Schmidt* (USA, 2002) Alexander Payne takes a fairly reasonable Louis Begley novel and makes it an unreasonable and sexist commentary on the burden of aging. On the Hollywood big screen, growing old is often funny, moving, manageable, and is often portrayed as a disability that can be overcome.

Aging with a disability does not take centre stage in this effort to smooth away the wrinkles caused by anxiety about late life, but the threat of the declining body plays a key role on the silvering screen. The aches and pains of growing older replace Jack Nicholson and Anne Bancroft's past onscreen suave and smooth sexualities, for example, but the all-too-familiar visual metaphoric shorthand of disability that invites pity or fear does not obtain. The tragic disabled heroine overcoming her inconvenient bodily difference (such as Suzy [Audrey Hepburn] in *Wait until Dark*) and the disabled supervillain manipulating his deviant bodily form to cause more evil (such as Blofeld [played by eight different actors], the Bond antagonist with the most appearances) collectively move over to make room for the representation of concerns about who will take care of 'our helpless elderly.' Filmmakers develop a new set of strategies for enforcing normalcy that hinges increasingly on able-bodiedness combined overtly with youth and not just with virtue (though caregivers are certainly portrayed as virtuous).[6]

In the face of the burden imposed by an aging population bound to need care, audience members need comforting assurances that they are not yet old, and they need reassurance that they will not individually bear responsibility for the burdensome, increasingly elderly population. This is not to argue that all members of contemporary film audiences are 'young' or 'able-bodied,' but rather to point to the work cinema does to convince audience members that they ought to – and can – be 'normal,' regardless of age, and that there are a range of freeing 'solutions' to the threatening demographic bulge.

Many seniors have money to spend; this is a new facet of the aging population that makes it a lucrative niche market in the global north.[7] However, generalizations about age cohorts are misleading. Like any age-related designation, the cohort of the baby boomers is an arbitrary yet powerful invention, often wielded for particular capitalist ends. The seeming power of the boomers is mythic in nature and imagined to be epic in scope.[8] Highlighting the problem particular to false conceptions of so-called baby boomers, critical gerontologist Stephen Katz points to the contradiction in discourse about the supposed children of affluence in that they appear ridiculously rich and powerful but unspeakably needy. As he sums it up, 'In either case they are seen as taking a disproportionate share of society's resources and disrupting intergenerational relations in the process.'[9] Age studies scholar Margaret Morganroth Gullette spells out in *Aged by Culture* how age cohort definitions serve to fracture social structures, pitting 'boomers' against 'Xers' and, as 'Xers' themselves age, 'Xers' against members of 'Generation Y.' Accordingly, I argue that the aging of the world population, popularly perceived as catastrophic because of the perceived burden this will place upon 'Xers,' and the resulting need to maintain youth at all costs have led to significant social disquiet about the presence, appearance, and ongoing infestation of the aged, despite exaggerated tales of their monetary wealth. This anxiety visibly unfurls on the silvering screen where aging can seem to be managed.

In order to sell products, the powerful and prominent anti-aging industry reduces old age to newly appearing facial lines that it then promises to minimize. On the big screen, different reductive methods – including and beyond wrinkles and grey hair – prevail. Despite the growing prevalence of age-based plots in the cinema, the unreal, tangibly constructed, youthful visages projected in the most dominant big-screen films persist next to the aging faces on the silvering screen. The increased number of older characters has not noticeably reduced the focus on youth. Mainstream film does not *always* try to make late life look like youth in the way that Botox might. However, films that focus on aging tend to coalesce social concern around a set of common middle-class anxieties about what it might mean for both individuals and societies to age into late life. In this way, mainstream cinema especially, like cosmetic surgery, attempts to unify the experience of aging. The 'ailing' body's effect on work, use-value, beauty, and consumer power figures most prominently. What is more, the silvering screen invites attention to the potential losses *caused* by aging infirm bodies even while often featuring actors who undergo procedures such as Botox injections in order to appear to be aging 'well.' Even Dame Judi Dench, so frequently praised for her insistence on a natural aging appearance and on not being afraid to look old, reportedly admits that she has turned to Botox for a little help around the eyes. In foregrounding age while trying to erase its visible appearance, silvering screen films transform representations of aging into an understandable and consumable product, fitting well into an era in which identity is tied to consumer practices and status. Film audiences can buy into positive and negative models of growing old, with little in between to contemplate.

Disability Makes Room for Old Age

This chapter presents a context for both silvering screen films and my analysis of them. The anti-aging business guides popular images of aging as well as individual practices associated with the aging body. The crude

progeny of current economic values, this industry benefits from the anxieties produced by the portrayal of aging onscreen as well as fuels the
need for criticism of those portrayals. After the next section, in which I
discuss the significance of hiding the aging face as dictated by the anti-
aging industry, I turn to the significance of displaying age. *Growing* old
means one thing in contemporary culture and *looking* old means another;
for the anti-aging industry and on the silvering screen, the distinction
between the two is elided. Looking old means *being* old, which, in this
discourse, means being ill. To age visibly means to admit ill health. By this
logic, healthy aging is an imitation of youth and so images that reveal
wrinkles suggest ill health. As a result, silvering screen films rely on illness
or disability narratives to convey the social burden of growing old. While
illness and disability arguably differ, age, disability, and illness are tightly
linked in most popular interpretations of late life. On the silvering screen,
old age is believed to indicate (at the very least) ill health, and ill health
often visually appears in the form of a disabled body. As a result, the scholarly fields that interrogate both aging and disability – namely gerontology
and disability studies – are vital critical frameworks for my analysis.

As my opening story about the bus ride indicates, encouragement to
automatically associate growing old with having a disability appears in
odd and sundry spaces, such as the ubiquitous signs that reserve spots for
'seniors and the disabled' – one of many dubious wordings. In fact,
rather than conflate disability and aging, these signs designate two separate groups and yet imagine that they belong together in a shared space,
segregated from others (presumably the young and non-disabled).

In this book I examine cinema as exemplary of the navigation of
old age and disability in the public imagination. I argue that 'old age'
requires disability to be legible within an 'efficient' capitalist society.
Without disability as what disability studies scholars David Mitchell and
Sharon Snyder might call the narrative prosthesis of old age – the crutch
that stories require in order to seem complete – old people are simply 'in
the way,' excessive or illegible within contemporary society.[10] I am not
trying to suggest that the front of the Vancouver bus should have been
ceded either to the person in the wheelchair or to the seniors. I am also
not trying to argue that they should have happily made room for each
other and become friends. I am turning to film to suggest that, in the
public imagination, disability exists separately from old age, but old age
does not ever escape the stigma and restraints imposed upon disability;
as such, the popular perception of old age could benefit from some of
the power, excitement and creativity of a disability perspective.

Similarly, rethinking old age could contribute to the productive re-thinking of social strictures that define and confine a range of 'problem bodies.'[11] Gerontologists ought to take into account the insights offered by age studies discourse, especially at this historical moment of concern about a greying population and the 'burden' it seems to impose on younger people contributing to pensions they fear they may not receive. Gerontologists ought also to take into account the insights offered by disability studies. As the population ages and many people acquire disabilities, new forms of accessibility are likely to emerge, and these ought to make space for both seniors and people with disabilities.

Social gerontology, the study of human dimensions and demographics of aging, touches on the topic of disability as acquired by the elderly, usually without fully recognizing the critical and cultural potential of a disability perspective. To practitioners and scholars studying age, disability is most often a negative category, and one that older people risk falling into. By contrast, the field of disability studies aims to recognize the full critical and cultural potential of a disability perspective; that is, scholars studying disability see that different ways of being in the world can be sources of knowledge, satisfaction, creativity, and happiness. But disability studies scholars rarely consider late life and focus much more on youth, early adulthood, and, perhaps, middle age.

There are clear commonalities between the issues faced by older people and the issues faced by disabled people (and of course some disabled people are also old). There are also clear commonalities between gerontological knowledge and disability studies knowledge, despite their attempts to ignore each other. The newer field of critical gerontology infuses data-based social gerontology with theoretical insights from critical theory and focuses on interpretation as much as on materiality. Especially compared with the broader field of social gerontology, critical gerontology has similar goals, methods, and politics to those of disability studies in that it seeks to revise a set of interpretations of late life against the grain and for the political benefit of older people, but scholars in the fields have not yet fully engaged with one another's work. Because of the commonalities, I lay out here what I perceive to be promising about the combination of critical gerontological perspectives with disability studies perspectives on contemporary aging. These foundational arguments provide me a critical lens for my ensuing analysis of silvering screen films.

Though my primary focus is on the relationship between old age and disability, especially as portrayed in film, other social preoccupations appear on the silvering screen. I conclude this theoretical framing chapter with a look at the identity discourses that accompanied the 2008 U.S. presidential race and that continue to haunt America. While ageism and the silvering screen are by no means geographically limited to the so-called Land of Liberty, race is a different issue in the United States than it is in other countries represented in this book. The idea of the American Dream – and its focus on a career model – infiltrates most of the films I discuss (whether filmed in the United States or not). The relationship of the American Dream mythology to aging as it intertwines with race, class, and gender informs the final sections of this chapter. This book is focused on a privileged subset of the world's population in that it discusses those who not only hope to age but also have the luxurious freedom to fear growing old because of what will diminish from their previously rich lives. Gerontology is not particularly interesting or relevant to those who do not expect and are not expected to live long.[12] The silvering screen is not entirely about money, but – tied as it is to anti-aging – its significance would greatly dwindle or its content transform in a world of greater economic equality.

Hiding the Aging Face

The booming business of anti-aging accompanies the much ballyhooed aging demographic bubble of the mythic baby boomers.[13] The pressure to remain young and vigorous as an ironic form of successful aging permeates everyday life. While claiming to preserve health in old age, anti-aging products (mostly creams, hair dyes, and energy drinks) and anti-aging procedures (surgical and non-surgical) tend to target superficial aspects of age that are only imaginatively linked to health because ubiquitous images make potential consumers anxious that they will never look young enough without help. According to this way of thinking, the most successful way to age is to appear not to age at all.[14] As a result of this paradox, anti-aging targets younger people with disposable income as much as the elderly without.

To offer an example of this marketing, I turn to my own experience. When I began my first tenure-track job, I was frequently assessed as looking too young. Granted, my research into aging and its cultural effects may seem to invite such commentary, but these reactions also happened independent of any knowledge of my field of inquiry: students blurted out, 'You don't look old enough to be a doctor'; colleagues mistook me for a student and, intriguingly, did not reply to my greetings as a result; secretaries remarked that they could not recognize me because of my

young appearance. Co-workers openly speculated on how many repro-
ductive years I had left, and revered visiting speakers, upon learning that
I was a faculty member, told me I looked sixteen years old. The exaggeration of the description of my age appearance makes clear that this is not
meant to be a compliment, as people so often urge me to interpret these
insults. While some people in their thirties may yearn to look twenty
again, few desire to look like a teenager or to return to the days of acne
and curfews.

Just prior to beginning my job, I had the opposite experience. A
vendor at a bridal show thought I was aging rapidly enough to merit
some attention, or at least thought I seemed likely to pay for what seems
to me to be a drastic procedure. This woman offered me a US$200 dis-
count on Botox injections. To this entrepreneur, a potential bride past
her twenties must want to look more youthful, as must any other woman
heading to a public event. Weddings, to the vendor, are about potential
– the potential for attendees to look young and for the vendor to make
money. The women attending the bridal show offered an ideal way to
combine the two.

This story could be used to argue that age identity is highly contextual,
which of course it is, and which of course these almost simultaneous, opposite interpretations of my appearance demonstrate. However, even
more intriguingly, a face too young to feasibly represent knowledge and
authority in the academy is still a face that could use a little Botox boost.
Certainly the fear of what aging means – individually and collectively –
motivates marketing to many age cohorts. Similarly, the silvering screen
attempts to target boomers' wallets, but fortuitously appeals to other age
cohorts as well, cohorts that are similarly afraid of aging and worried
about – if not yet experiencing – its personal relevance.

Botox is just one of many examples in a series of technologies developed since the beginning of the twentieth century in order to help
people – especially Hollywood actors – not face aging or even convey
aging faces. In popular discourse, Botox has come to stand in for the
other anti-aging methods. Distinct from private and secretive plastic surgery clinics that have long dotted Los Angeles' landscape, Botox is widely
available and even adopted at parties, both by and in the public eye.
Almost synonymous with anti-aging and high society, Botox has spread
throughout not just the Hollywood elite but also vast reaches of upper-
and middle-class social climbers. Signs of aging show up on other parts
of the body, and there are anti-aging interventions developed to reduce
the appearance of old hands, the sound of old voices, and the greying of

hair, but the face accrues particular symbolic value in the visual culture of old age. Culturally and socially, the meaning of an aging face is sometimes good but usually bad.

Botox has the obvious supposed upside of making people's faces look younger, but has been found to have a downside as well. Actresses think twice about using Botox because its temporary paralysis of facial muscles makes them incapable of the finer expressions necessary to good acting, which is sometimes a criterion, that along with their looks, determines casting decisions.

A cartoon from the *New Yorker* illustrates the significance of reducing aging to the maintenance of a youthful face. Two masks (presumably comedy and tragedy) with identical expressionless faces whose mouths are completely straight appear on a highly stylized stage framed by curtains and illuminated by obtrusive footlights – the caption 'Botox Theatre' appears almost as a title on a marquee. Placing these two masks that defy aging on stage recognizes that age identity is a performance. Besides the obvious idea that actors are compelled to remain unfeasibly young, the image comments upon the aging body's contribution – here again symbolized by the face – to cultural production. The 'purified toxin' Botox temporarily eradicates eye and forehead wrinkles, making facial expression difficult to discern. But the bacteria are not usually injected around the mouth because doing so would impair 'normal mouth function.' The straight-line mouths in the *New Yorker* cartoon mask exaggerate Botox's already exaggerated eradication of expression. That is, they portray Botox as a complete erasure of facial expression (mouth and eyes) instead of the partial one (eyes) that the technology actually achieves. The implication is that the compulsory youthfulness of the performing and performative[15] body deadens expression and flattens artistic production. Conveying youth is more valuable by this logic than conveying emotion.

The framing of the overtly false faces here points to a theatrical avoidance of not just aging, but also of the aging body, and, in doing so, raises questions about what exactly is at stake in hiding or revealing age. As gerontologist Simon Biggs explains of the performance of age more generally, 'the very act of hiding alerts the performer and audience that something is being hidden … The fact that we almost always go along with the performance of agelessness, or active or productive ageing, fools no one.'[16] The barely hidden cultural anxieties cut to the heart of the impetus of the anti-aging industry. Gullette explains, 'Using prosthetic youtheners to defy aging as early as midlife proves that youthfulness is

Comedy matches tragedy, thanks to cosmetic procedures. Cartoon by Roz Chast © 2008 The New Yorker Collection from cartoonbank.com. All Rights Reserved.

symbolic capital.'[17] These methods serve to highlight cultural fears of aging, even if they momentarily succeed in smoothing wrinkles. As gerontologists Chris Gilleard and Paul Higgs explain, 'age-resisting technologies require the spectral presence of old age.'[18] To hide signs of aging (believing that it is possible and desirable to remain young, vital, and active) is to smother the expression that is fundamental to artistic production. Ironically, in the absence of visible old age, mortality is still terrifyingly present. As such, the covert act of hiding age is deeply meaningful in revealing fissures where the wrinkles once lay.

Facing Age

Attempts to *hide* signs of aging reveal anxieties about suffering and mortality as well as smothering expression (cultural and physical). But *exposing* old age is thought of as tantamount to admitting – ushering in, even – ill health and mortal disease. Despite clichés about honouring elders and appreciating the wisdom that comes with experience, aging faces overtly signify disease, which in turn signifies decline, decay, death, and other horrors. A visibly aging figure is more likely to meet accusations of forgetfulness due to dementia than assumptions of the wisdom that accrues over time. As film scholar Martine Beugnet explains, 'In the context of a late capitalist culture old age *is* a disease, equivalent to the categories of low consumer value and low productivity; a social stigma that is acutely reflected in its status in terms of representation.'[19] Sociologists Toni Calasanti and Kathleen Slevin elaborate the many actions people feel compelled to take because old age implies ill health:

> Besides ingesting nutritional supplements and testosterone or human growth hormones, increasing numbers of people spend hours at the gym, undergo cosmetic surgery, and use lotions, creams, and hair dyes to erase the physical markers of age. Such is the equation of old age with disease and physical and mental decline that visible signs of aging serve to justify limitation of the rights and authority of old people.[20]

Though anti-aging texts refer to the plausible argument that good health is possible into old age, they frequently target such physical signs as wrinkles and grey hair in their promotion of the fight against any visible marker of senescence. Because of the widespread availability of interventionist products (such as wrinkle-smoothing creams), the individual becomes responsible for his or her own age status (i.e., health).

This suspect formula – wherein showing old age equals succumbing to ill health – materializes on the silvering screen as much in depictions of disability as in depictions of illness. Films can quickly convey the frailty assumed of an ill body through the depiction of a disabled body in need of care. While the relationship between disability and illness is tenuous, the distinction between them is similarly fragile so that, by smudging the line, the silvering screen inadvertently supports a fairly sophisticated perspective on the relationship of illness to disability. Both age and disability are unnecessarily treated as though they are entirely medical. Accordingly, in my analysis of the silvering screen, I want to thoroughly explicate the thorny relationship between the pathologization of age and the pathologization of disability.

'Age, redefined and deconstructed':
Critical Gerontology and Age Studies

In order to investigate the meaning that older characters offer to the silvering screen, this book engages with the insights and advances brought by interdisciplinary work in gerontology and the related field of age studies. Gerontology has long had a wealth of data but lack of theory. My interest is in developing the theoretical side, and my exploration builds on theoretical work accomplished recently, especially in the sub-field of critical gerontology.[21] Many studies of the economic and physical implications of late life exist, and social gerontology is a well-developed field. However, cultural gerontology that focuses specifically on the cultural meanings that accompany old age, and especially cultural gerontology which captures the social, political, and cultural imagination (i.e., critical gerontology), needs increased attention. Speaking of his main field of interest, Stephen Katz describes critical gerontology as a 'promising new genre whose authors challenge the limitations of mainstream gerontology' and explains that 'critical gerontologists admonish gerontology for its narrow scientificity, advocate stronger ties to the humanities, endorse reflexive methodologies, historicize ideological attributes of old age, promote radical political engagement, and resignify the aging process as heterogeneous and indeterminate.'[22] Combining debates about political economy with identity-based scholarship and cultural studies approaches, critical gerontology seeks to transform popular thinking about the elderly into insights about the untapped potential of late life as a stage of empowerment.

Situating herself in relation to critical gerontology, Gullette promotes a newer field: age studies. Age studies differs from aging studies in that it is not restricted to a focus on older people but wields 'age' more broadly as a conceptual tool: 'Age studies method, foregrounding age, justifies itself by noticing how our culture increasingly foregrounds "life time."'[23] In this way, age studies offers a way to think about all of the cohorts (Xers, boomers, boomers' parents) that the silvering screen targets without losing sight of the critical category of age. As Gullette explains, 'Age, redefined and deconstructed, is what age studies foregrounds – what makes it a field.'[24]

In this book, I focus on what imaginative deliberate visions of oldness on the silvering screen say about broader socio-cultural issues related to age and to disability. I use a humanities framework to reflect on how we think we know about aging, with an eye on the contextualization cited by Katz, and I foreground age as a critical lens, as advocated by Gullette. I seek to verify the political possibilities of rethinking late life in relation to what public representations promote broadly, without ignoring what representations of the elderly mean for younger age cohorts.

Feminist Age Studies

Sociologist Elizabeth Markson explains that the synecdochical reductive aging, whereby all the vicissitudes of old age are represented by a wrinkle, is particularly vivid in images of older women: 'Whether portraying the good, the bad, or the ugly, older women are at particular risk of madness, decrepitude, death or murder: visual reminders of the loss of mobility, loss of mind, loss of functional capacity, and possibility of lingering or sudden death associated with aging.'[25]

In early Hollywood, women earned *less* as they acquired experience (especially if that experience showed on their faces), rather than being rewarded with higher salaries for their experience. And that's if they could get work at all.[26] Beugnet makes the similar, more direct point that actresses not only lose worth as they age, they lose jobs altogether.[27] As the Ford–Griffith example in the introduction demonstrates (wherein Harrison Ford boldly faces the camera but Melanie Griffith must hide from its ungenerous gaze), women have more reasons than men have to conceal the visible signs of aging.

Much attention has been paid, particularly within the humanities, to women's aging because of gendered discrimination and because of the demographic factor that women live longer than men, the social factor that women typically take on formal and informal caregiving roles, and the cultural factor that women are perceived to experience what Susan Sontag named the 'double standard of aging' in that they 'lose' not just 'youth' but also 'femininity' as they grow old.[28] The anti-aging industry largely targets women.[29] The need for resistance, then, is particularly strong for women. Indeed, the prejudices I experienced at work and at the bridal show are likely attributable in great part to my gender.

Feminist gerontologists working in the humanities, many of them critical gerontologists, advocate for a political and interpretive approach to thinking about and interrogating late life. Woodward's influential exploration of male poets' late-life creativity sets the stage for thinking

about how old age is a valid category of analysis for aesthetic productions.[30] Her *Aging and Its Discontents* pushes the theoretical bounds of
gerontology into a rethinking of the limits of psychoanalysis.[31] Most importantly, her collection *Figuring Age: Women, Bodies, Generations* gathers
the work of feminists working across disciplines in order to demonstrate
the momentum of critical gerontological thought.[32] Barbara Frey
Waxman's explorations of literature and aging in *From the Hearth to the
Open Road: A Feminist Study of Aging in Contemporary Literature* and *To Live
in the Center of the Moment: Literary Autobiographies of Aging* show the importance of genre to conceptualizing late life.[33] Anne Wyatt-Brown and
Janice Rossen's *Aging and Gender in Literature: Studies in Creativity* begins
to fill a gap left by the neglect of age as a category of literary analysis.[34]
Gullette's interdisciplinary interventions move the field forward into
thorough understandings of what it means to age in culture.[35] In my *From
Old Woman to Older Women: Contemporary Culture and Women's Narratives* I
draw on the work of all these feminist scholars to analyse portrayals of
old women in contemporary Canadian literature and film. By using age
as a critical lens for the scrutiny of a set of turn-of-the-century films, I
plan again to contribute to this ongoing dialogue about the political and
interpretive valence of aging.

Aside from feminist gerontology, feminism has shied away from senescence and gerontology from gender. As Biggs states, 'most feminists are
women, but few gerontologists are old … It is also striking that few feminists are old! Or at least they are unwilling to admit it or show a professional interest in a subject as off-putting as ageing.'[36] Calasanti and Slevin
make clear that even those feminist works not afraid of the topic of aging
fear old age, choosing instead to focus on more personally relevant life
stages: 'even studies of women "of a certain age" focus on middle age – a
time when physical markers such as menopause, wrinkles, and the like
emerge and care work for old people begins to occupy women's time.'[37]
While my work is explicitly feminist, I do not focus entirely on women
aging on the silvering screen. I consider it a feminist issue to engage with
old age and its cultural meanings for all genders because its political
ramifications ally with women's liberation.

Within age scholarship and anti-aging discourse alike, wrinkles signify
the supposedly inevitable vulnerability to decay in late life. Diana Tietjens
Meyers focuses on the deeper socially imposed significance that wrinkles
accrue, claiming that women fear not just a fading of beauty in seeing
their changed images in the mirror. As she puts it, 'If aging women do
not hide the signs of age, conventional beauty ideals … authorize us to

read their faces as a mark of inner corruption – the Grim Reaper lurking within.'[38] Many humanities age scholars, in a way uncannily similar to the anti-aging industry, focus on the mirror, or what Meyers calls 'meeting a stranger in the mirror.'[39] Such theorists strive for new ways of seeing aging female bodies so that the apparently shocking change from the youthful self can somehow be productive, and therefore recourse to anti-aging methods can seem less of an obligation. For example, Nancy Miller interprets Gloria Steinem's concept of 'looking within' after breast cancer as 'a way of turning away from the mirror (maybe putting your hands over your face), as a resistance to tracking the damage to that face long enough to think about, say, how it is that we came to think we knew what our face – or body – was.'[40] Although I agree that finding epistemological models other than the visual for self-understanding is valuable and necessary, I find this passage devastating in its postulation of wrinkles as 'damage' and its imagery of the covering of one's eyes as if in horror. 'Turning away from the mirror' may attempt to deny the power of anti-aging discourse, but 'putting your hands over your face' means not only blocking your vision of your self (if that's how you read your face) but also hiding your face, and therefore age in this conceptualization, from anybody else. In fact, it could be tantamount to other more drastic forms of hiding signs of age, such as those advised by the anti-aging industry.

In an inspiring call to arms for future critical gerontology by feminists, Ruth Ray advocates a mode she calls 'personal criticism' in which 'scholars interweave self-narration into their research accounts.' She advocates this approach because 'such writing, when done carefully, succeeds in contesting the established systems of power, authority, and knowledge-making in academe.'[41] Feminist gerontologists very often disseminate their findings via criticism of their personal experiences, as I have done in part in this introduction. Within this discourse that uneasily seems to match anti-aging fears about the facial revelation of time passing, there are feminists who write 'carefully' as Ray advises, stirring up the self-reflexive stew. Frida Kerner Furman posits a productive ambivalence as a model for thinking of aging female bodies, saying 'I propose that women's responses to their aging bodies are not always of a piece: shame and inadequacy frequently coexist with resistance to cultural ideals.'[42] Vivian Sobchack tries to revise the impact of signs of age, saying, 'every time I start to fixate on a new line or wrinkle, on a graying hair, I try very hard to remember that, on my side of that face in the mirror, I am not so much aging as always becoming.'[43] Sandra Bartky provocatively proposes a double-edged benefit from this process: 'I suspect that old age is welcomed by some women because the issue, indeed, the burden of appearance has been settled; one is now an unattractive old crow and that's the end of it.'[44] She seems to write this tongue-in-cheek – if old age really were as superficial as the anti-aging industry promises, then rejection of beauty norms may indeed 'settle' it, but as the long-standing imagined and lived relationships among aging, illness, and disability demonstrate, old age cuts deeper than appearances. As a result, critical gerontology to date, even its feminist interventions, offers a promising yet insufficient framework for understanding cultural representations of aging, and particularly their social resonances.

Cripping Age

Disability frequently is part of the experience of aging. That said, due to the ongoing health-care 'crisis' and fears about who will take care of large numbers of infirm adults, the cultural register is in danger of reducing older people to mere symbols of physical decline. This anxiety shows up most prominently in artefacts of the increasingly powerful and lucrative anti-aging industry. A brief survey of related self-help book titles makes very clear the two advisable ways to approach aging, which I've already touched upon in this chapter:

1) as a state of life to be embraced through canny avoidance. Examples of relevant titles include: *Younger Next Year: A Guide to Living Like You're 50 Until You're 80 and Beyond; The Real Age Makeover: Take Years off Your Looks and Add Them to Your Life; My Time: Making the Most of the Bonus Decades after Fifty*

2) as a disease that must be prevented or, failing that, cured. Examples of relevant titles include: *The Better Brain Book: The Best Tools for Improving Memory, Sharpness, and Preventing Aging of the Brain; The Detox Book: How to Detoxify Your Body to Improve Your Health, Stop Disease and Reverse Aging; The Doctors* [sic] *Book of Food Remedies: The Newest Discoveries in the Power of Food to Cure and Prevent Health Problems – From Aging and Diabetes to Ulcers and Yeast Infections* (note the faulty parallelism that equates the universal process of aging to illnesses and relatively minor health problems)

These titles are highly problematic in many ways, but especially because they assume a normative youthful frame. According to them, all human beings are hale, hearty, attractive, and able-bodied when 'young,' and all prefer to stay that way. But, unless one buys these books and undergoes at least minimal plastic surgery, one will – according to the logic of the titles – become feeble, frail, ugly, and disabled (the logic is especially damaging because it equates disability with ugliness and ugliness with frailty). To highlight one of many problems with this thinking: if age always already implies disability, then what happens if someone with a disability grows old? To play on a common defining factor of disability, a person who has not been 'able' to climb stairs for decades may eventually not be expected to be able to climb them. As a result, what was previously stigmatized could be normalized within an already stigmatized arena of feebleness. In other words, struggles specific to aging with a disability may be cancelled in the process of substituting one identity category for the other, or deemed irrelevant or redundant. Does a person with a disability simply become more natural and normative as he ages? Or does he just disappear from the statistical and cultural register?

Disability is not an accepted, welcomed, or desired aspect of late life according to either popular or gerontological discourse. Non-disabled people do not typically dream of growing up to be disabled athletes, nor do they anticipate with excitement learning Braille in their latter years. Like the anti-aging industry, other popular texts and gerontology arguments stridently assert the capacity for older people to remain active, able, and whole (and the texts work on the assumption that they lived their youths as such); Harrison Ford's interview statement – 'My ambition in action is to have the audience look straight in the face of a character and not at the back of a capable stuntman's head. I hope to continue to do that, no matter how old I get'[45] – is a good example. Social gerontology is largely premised on the idea that older people are dependent, decrepit, and in need of support. As social gerontologist and human ecologist Norah Keating puts it, 'For many years our attention has been drawn to the frailties associated with aging as we attempt to alleviate the suffering associated with age-related illness and disability.'[46] Many social gerontologists, especially those promoting the concept of 'healthy aging,' argue that these defaults (dependence, need for support, illness, and disability) ought to be overcome, preferably by commitment to a positive attitude and an exercise routine. As geriatrician John W. Rowe and social psychologist Robert L. Kahn make clear in their originary definition of a concept that is fundamental to social gerontology, criteria that define 'successful aging' are 'the avoidance of disease and disability, the maintenance of high physical and cognitive function, and sustained engagement in social and productive activities.'[47]

As a result, in order to combat the automatic equation of old age with misery, gerontologists continually attempt to separate old age from disability. If disability can be equated with misery, then separating old age from disability implies doing away with the miserable part of growing old. But equating disability with misery results in the denigration of disability (and disabled people) and is a woefully inaccurate understanding of what it can mean to have a disability. In typical social gerontological terms, it becomes acceptable (a sign of success even) to be old, as long as you don't also become disabled. In reality, the chances of an old age entirely free of disability are slim, but that is not the most important reason for reckoning with disability in an understanding of old age. It would be exciting to redefine 'successful aging' to include seemingly inevitable disabilities as a welcome transformation of self and world. And so, rather than make readers fear disability so that they might take aging more seriously, and rather than hold up the likelihood of late-life disability as a bogeyman, I would like to show how thinking from a place of disability can help disentangle knotty problems facing gerontology and offer a new way to think about 'aging well.'

Snyder and Mitchell point out in 'Re-engaging the Body' that disability is often defined as 'that in the body which exceeds deterministic efforts to predict a life trajectory.'[48] The concept of excess, though figured as waste within a capitalist system that values productivity, has the potential to open up new vistas of expression and even production that go beyond the also necessary resistance to oppression.[49] Whereas 'the Marxist or class-based argument bemoaned disability as stripping a capacity from the body by excessive labor demands,' the disability argument celebrates disability as a possible means by which to disrupt the smooth functioning of capitalist society.[50] Old age *is* part of a predictable life trajectory (the axiom of disability studies, 'if you live long enough,' is unquestionably true of old age), and its excess to productive labour is temporally appropriate in that it ideally occurs after years of productivity. The dominant career model of that trajectory limits conceptualizations of late life either to passive retrospect or to continued vigour; for Hollywood screen queens, there is also the option of representing cultural 'refuse' as horror stars. The problem for older people often becomes not how they *exceed* expectations, but the degree to which they seem to *meet* imposed standards of uselessness. That is, it is not that older people defy normativity, as younger people with disabilities do, but that there is a separate and damaging normativity for older people, once they ignore the adages of the anti-aging industry and accept their inevitable 'decline.'

In terms of both access and attitudes, as disability scholar Jenny Morris puts it when speaking to younger people with disabilities, 'If we don't engage in the debates about old age, then as we age we will find that the battles we thought we had won as younger disabled people are of no use to us whatsoever.'[51] Of course, old age does not necessarily entail disability. Rather than merely read old age as disability, or disability as akin to old age, it is crucial to consider how an older person's body read as having a disability is different from a younger person's body read as having a disability. Similarly, it is crucial to consider how an older person's body read as having a disability is different from an older person's body read as *not* having a disability. It is the assumption that late life denotes decrepitude, as it is usually put, that makes the body – especially the body's failure – paramount amidst circulating conceptualizations of what it means to be old.

I seek to analyse disability in combination with old age, but not in order to point out forms of apparent decay encountered in late life. I combine disability with age here because the theory missing from gerontology is prevalent within disability studies. First, I don't perceive disability (mental and/or physical) to be decay or even to upset a normal or desirable course of life. Rather, for me, disability is a fundamental part of normal everyday experience.[52] Second, I don't want to ignore changes that frequently do come with late life. In most cases, as time passes, we walk more slowly, we gain girth, our smiles show for longer on our faces. Rather than reinvent phenomenological understandings of stigmatized physical and social bodies in order to proceed with critical age scholarship, I plan to draw on extant disability studies work in my readings of the silvering screen. There is no need to chart a new way of thinking about aging as experienced in relation to social and cultural environments because disability studies already clearly, cogently, and consistently articulates that way of thinking. Drawing on disability studies to read the silvering screen is especially apt because my film analysis reveals social preoccupations with relationships among old age, disability, and illness.

Linking discourses of disability and old age presents a danger of conflation; that is, in putting these two ideas together, I may seem to be mirroring a pervasive, damaging thought pattern: that old people are necessarily disabled and therefore necessarily in the way. They might even be called upon to move over to cede space on a bus for younger disabled people. Accordingly, a difficult methodological question animates scholarship that links age and disability: how does one talk about old age as disability without vilifying either? Claiming that old age is *not* disability (i.e., refuting the cultural conflation) risks implying that disability is a negative that age theory could do without. But to claim old age *is* disability would be to appropriate key aspects of disability and thereby risk effacing issues related to aging with a disability. To my mind, old age is akin to disability in the *ways* that they are socially constructed – not just *that* social barriers define both but that they are both constructed as bodily, threatening, and signalling failure. In fact, the similarity comes precisely from the continual failed attempt to enforce a clear distinction where one is simply not possible: between a social element (often called 'disability' in disability studies) and a biological element (often called 'impairment' in disability studies).

I hope to turn the danger of inappropriate conflation into an opportunity by highlighting the important distinctions between disability and old age and by pointing out those moments when disability and old age could benefit each other by being connected. For example, not only do a number of elderly people gain disabilities that they did not have previously (in addition to disabilities that they may already have), but also the social positioning of elderly people frequently coincides with that of people with disabilities. I seek here to expound the relationship between age and disability scholarship in order to develop a model of cultural understanding that clarifies the role of old age on the silvering screen and helps us to face age in all its rich and poor connotations. Picking up on the theoretical work of Robert McRuer's *Crip Theory*, in which he explains the merits of thinking from the politicized, critical place of disability, thinking from a place of old age not only reveals youth as the over-visible norm, but, like critically queer and severely disabled positions, it reveals hetero-ability as an invisible norm. That is, an analysis of old age, and especially of its representations, further exposes the trying cultural importance of the hale, hearty, youthful body.

'If you live long enough': Disability Studies and the Cultural Model

As an alternative to feminist gerontology's approach to cultural representations of aging, disability studies also falls short. Disability studies scholars warn/celebrate that 'if you live long enough' disability will be within your lived experience. Usually, this statement implies that disability applies to everyone and that everyone should think about it, even if it might not seem immediately personally relevant. But the warning's overt reference to 'living long enough' reinforces a fear that old age itself generates disability. The implication is that disability is preferable to death, if only marginally. As disability scholar Susan Wendell puts it in *The Rejected Body*, 'Unless we die suddenly, we are all disabled eventually.'[53] Similarly, age studies scholars like to claim that we all will grow old, something I note above; however, as Gullette points out, 'We are often cheerily reminded that "everyone ages," but that pious fact will not by itself enable us to overcome the divisiveness of the new time machines.'[54]

I recognize the power of the catch phrase 'If you live long enough,' but I question using it when addressing the not-yet-converted. To the disability community, it is of course exciting to contemplate a coming to consciousness, especially a disability consciousness. The slogan's rhetorical force aims to encourage the as-yet-uninitiated to think of disability as important because they might become disabled. Toronto lawyer and disability advocate David Lepofsky makes the strategy clear, saying, 'Disability comes with age, so it affects all of us. This [new accessibility act] helps everyone.'[55] I would prefer a call to consciousness that invokes a sense of social justice for all, regardless of personal experience. In my perhaps overly optimistic scenario, disability is simply important, period.

Despite the age-based slogan, the bodies usually considered by disability studies are relatively young, whereas the bodies in social gerontology are overburdened with disabilities and the bodies in feminist gerontology struggle to contain difference. In her essay 'Seeing the Disabled' Rosemarie Garland Thomson is one of few scholars to include old age in a list of categories that fit under the rubric 'disability': 'Disability is a broad term within which cluster ideological categories as varied as sick, deformed, ugly, old, maimed, afflicted, abnormal, or debilitated – all of which disadvantage people by devaluing bodies that do not conform to cultural standards.[56] Alternatively, old age appears in disability studies as a comparative category relevant to disability. For example, in *The Body and Physical Difference*, Mitchell and Snyder claim that 'while categories such as illness and the aging process also come replete with associations of physical debility and social suspicions of diminished productivity, disability bears the onus of permanent biological condition such as race and gender from which the individual cannot extricate him- or herself.'[57] Of course, extrication from aging – when anti-aging fails – means death. But there is also always a retrospect possible – a frequent feature of novels and films starring old characters – that includes a younger body in the conceptualization of an elderly person. These examples demonstrate that age is theoretically useful to defining disability. Beyond that, age is not yet effectively wielded in transforming disability thought.

The potential for drawing on disability to think about old age is apparent in disability studies work. For example, Michael Davidson describes a 'statue of an aged blind man being led by a young boy' as '[reminding] us of the ways that blindness has been used as a sign of weakness and dependency.' Without spelling it out, Davidson points to how appearing aged is also a sign of weakness and dependency, and is directly tied to appearing disabled.[58] In another example, Susan Wendell explains that we expect different things from older bodies than from younger bodies, saying that young and middle-aged people with chronic illnesses 'are not old enough to have finished making [their] contributions of productivity and/or caregiving; old people with chronic illnesses may be seen to be entitled to rest until they die.'[59] That she draws on a cliché to make her point only reinforces the degree to which the elderly are not expected to be 'useful.' As a result, what has been stigmatized in a younger person with a disability may be normalized for an older person. That is, whereas a seemingly fit young person might be criticized for taking the elevator rather than the stairs, that same person when older is *expected* to need the elevator. Still, accepting the limitations associated with old age is often cast as a failure to appear/act young even by disability scholars; when that failure takes the form of succumbing to disability, an extremely negative reading of disability results.

In order to challenge that negative reading, I redirect the provocative, groundbreaking work of disability scholars in the humanities, work that dramatically rethinks and resituates body, culture, and society. This set of challenges has critical consequences for an analysis of the silvering screen. While disability has long been an object of medical, rehabilitation, and sociological studies, more recently it has become a starting place for anti-oppression scholarship. As historian Bonnie G. Smith explains,

> Disability, a term that has heretofore been so clear-cut to the public, is becoming increasingly polymorphous in the light of a new politics and scholarship. It can suggest a set of practices, kinds of embodiment, interactions with the built environment, an almost limitless array of literary types, frames of mind, and forms of relationships. Gone are the days of a simple and dominant physiological and medical definition of disability.[60]

Old age too has long been associated with: 'practices,' such as retirement; 'interaction with the built environment,' such as leaning on a walker; 'literary types,' such as the spiteful reviser of bequests (an elderly figure constantly rewriting his will to include only those who treat him properly); 'frames of mind,' such as nostalgia; and 'forms of relationships,' such as intergenerational interdependence. That is, though old age is imaginatively linked to ill health, another set of associations has made it resistant to a 'simple and dominant physiological and medical definition.' However, as Woodward argues in 'Against Wisdom,' this set of associations requires revision, even resistance.[61] Gerontology has yet to strongly enact or even endorse an anti-oppression framework, despite the existence of known groups such as the Gray Panthers and the Raging Grannies who play on stereotypes of aging to make political statements.

Foundational work by disability scholars in the humanities shows how representation contributes to disability consciousness and counters mainstream views of disability as a deficit. Images of empowered disabled people help audiences to 'see' new ways of being disabled and proud. Rosemarie Garland Thomson's *Extraordinary Bodies* looks at U.S. images of disability from the nineteenth century to the late twentieth century, arguing that they 'are vital to the American project of self-making.'[62] Wendell's *The Rejected Body* recognizes that definitions of disability affect the social world in which we live. She explains how the typical images of disability – of the athletic paraplegic male or the blind woman who seems independent – do not reflect the vast numbers of people who live with chronic illnesses or conditions that are dominant causes of disability. More representative images of lived disability would create a much more fluid positioning of disability than the dominant examples do.[63] In *Recovering Bodies* G. Thomas Couser examines how life-writing can enable disabled people to counter dominant patterns of representation (within limits).[64] In *The Cinema of Isolation*, Martin Norden notices that social practices of segregation of disabled people appear on film as well as in everyday life.[65]

Early scholarship liberates disabled people through various iterations of the social model, which all remove blame from the individual and place responsibility for inclusion firmly on the shoulders of society.[66] The social model of disability is a viable framework for altering standard readings of old age that limit it to the physical, but the social model of disability risks effacing physicality in connection with aging, as it does with disability. Imagining disability as entirely separate from the body is as oppressive as thinking of any one body as only physically different. Social barriers, both concrete and abstract (such as discriminatory home-care policies and ageist jokes), contribute to making late life into the unpleasant experience it can be (and too frequently is).

Invoking the term 'constructed' in relation to old age, particularly when I – looking too young to know – do so, frequently leads to an insistent reply that old age usually *is* physically different from youth, even if the differences do not prove difficult. However, as disability scholar Adrienne Asch argues, 'Saying that disability is socially constructed does not imply that the characteristics are not real or do not have describable effects on physiological or cognitive functions that persist in many environments.'[67] Similarly, saying that old age is socially constructed is not to deny pain, illness, or change. Construction does not mean fabrication but rather the manipulation of existing material in relation to values, and the social model – by making apparent the forms of that manipulation – shows how arbitrary and misguided many apprehensions about late life really are. Still, as the implications of attempting to separate the social from the physical become clear, a more varied model is as necessary for old age as it is for disability.

Recent disability theory holds vast potential for rethinking critical gerontology, especially in relation to representation. Tobin Siebers points out that the social model has put the medical model in its alienating and depoliticizing place. However, he also stresses that social model proponents' scepticism of identity politics and the theoretical framework's imagined plasticity of the body is not entirely appropriate to disabled people who need political force and may not benefit from thinking of bodies as changeable.[68] Further, he points out that the politics of the social model map physical disability onto mental disability; that is, as he reads it, in poststructuralist terms, the failure to generalize physical disability is a failure of the mind. This transference not only complicates the argument that disability exists in the environment rather than in the individual, it also obliterates mental disability from adequate consideration.

While many are quick to assume and accept that physical disability inevitably comes with old age, others fight that connection, preferring to make sunny claims that it is possible to stay active well into the later years. Though both the assumption of inevitable decrepitude and the assumption that eternal youth is desirable cause harm, neither is as damaging as the assumption that mental decline is the worst possible fate. It might be acceptable that grandma is increasingly slower getting around, but when she's 'losing it,' the 'it' automatically means her mental skills – memory, sense, logic. The separation of the physical from the mental, especially in terms of disability, is not at all neat. However, particularly as associated with aging, physical disability is decidedly more socially acceptable than mental disability. Siebers's 'realist' position offers a way to posit a culture of aging based on what he calls 'complex embodiment,' a culture that adequately accounts for the physical and mental disabilities that may or may not accompany later (or earlier) life.

Within disability studies, the social model now takes its place beside cultural models that call more strongly for an accounting for interactions among social, physical, and cultural dimensions of difference. These cultural models are better equipped than the social model to examine the interplay among visible and invisible disabilities. Snyder and Mitchell's *Cultural Locations of Disability* builds on Homi Bhabha's *The Location of Culture* to demonstrate that disability is sited and that its situation determines its politics; for example, a particular disability culture emerges within a rehabilitation centre.[69] Katz pinpoints the significance of cultural locations for aging when he writes,

> It is the task of critical gerontology to rescue from obscurity the productive and transformative potential of the various cultural institutions that are populated by the elderly. Seen as a means to keep old people busy, housed, entertained, and tended, these institutions are not recognized for what they are: vibrant sites of elderhood's agency in the profound social and ethical contexts of our time.[70]

This acknowledgment of culture emerging as the result of institutional structures disallows a simplistic identity politics based on impossible categories, but it does not entirely dismiss the practical importance of identity politics. The cultural model of disability includes insights from social model theory, especially locating disability in social obstacles more than in biological forms. However, the cultural model emphasizes the interaction between social and physical creations of disability. In it, disability becomes about embodiment broadly conceived, and not either a seemingly neutral impairment or an entirely social prejudice. For age studies, the cultural model illuminates spaces dedicated to the elderly, such as nursing homes, and capitalizes on the forms of consciousness fashioned in these spaces. In this book, I see popular film as one site of 'elderhood' that merits scrutiny for its cultural formation of old age. Drawing on disability theory, I begin that examination in this book.

White Age Studies

Neither age studies nor disability studies offers an adequate framework for thinking through race on the silvering screen. To date, most North American and European films that focus on aging feature white actors.

Disability scholar Chris Bell makes a 'modest proposal' about what he adroitly labels 'White Disability Studies,' a rarely acknowledged field that 'while not wholeheartedly excluding people of colour from its critique, by and large focuses on the work of white individuals and is itself largely produced by a corps of white scholars and activists.'[71] Age studies and feminist gerontology are similarly culpable; without explicit exclusion of other age, gender, or race cohorts, white middle-class academics usually worry about what late life will mean for other white middle-class people. Accordingly, not only do the scholars tend to be white and the arguments tend to be from a white perspective, but the arguments tend to be from a middle-class perspective, even when they try to be unbiased. This is not out of the ordinary for identity-based studies.

Gullette advocates a focus on midlife, saying, 'As decline backs down the life course toward children and positive aging raises its volume the middle-aged are more often swept in with "the elderly" even by gerontologists, quite unreflectively.'[72] While the need to distinguish these two stages is vital, to date age scholarship in the humanities is largely a privileged discourse preoccupied with how middle-aged, middle-class bodies might transform over time. A great deal of the age scholarship that does tackle late life seeks to challenge the cultural significance of physical changes principally so that middle-class white bodies will maintain value throughout the life course.

In this book, I talk about a number of middle-aged actors, or sometimes older actors portraying middle-aged characters. I do so reflectively, understanding that Hollywood calculates age differently from gerontology and that these depictions have significance for imagining and understanding the cultural significance of mid and late life, as well as youth to some extent. Whiteness is a crucial vector in this study, especially in the final chapters of this book as I turn to an analysis of aging masculinity, in which the privilege of white patriarchy is shored up not only by expendable female characters but also by expended black characters.

To think through how race becomes sidelined, I conclude my theoretical chapter with a discussion of the 2008 U.S. election that considers the complex relationships among age, race, gender, and class. Class did not enter the popular debate to the same extent as these other topics, but it underpins the entire identity debate that is still taking place.

'The Old Fart versus the Fresh Prince of Hyde Park'

In 2008, as the U.S. Democratic Party presidential primaries seemingly would not end, the popular press (in the United States and further afield) took a rare opportunity to thrash out the relationship between gender and race. Hillary Clinton was held up as the representative for gender, 'woman' being the shorthand for gender in this instance. Barack Obama was held up as the representative for race, 'black' being the shorthand for race in this instance. Voters were urged fiercely, by proponents of feminism and anti-racism, to vote along their own identity positions.[73] The logic went to the extent that choosing to vote against one's gender or against one's race would be the ultimate betrayal.[74] Not surprisingly, such identity politics haunted the entire contest.

Having previously described Bill Clinton as 'blacker than any black person who could ever be elected in our children's lifetime,'[75] Toni Morrison officially endorsed Obama, though she claimed her support was not based on his race. Instead, Morrison took the presidential race to its end point – a battle between young and old even more than between white and black. She wrote (publicly) to Obama,

> In addition to keen intelligence, integrity and a rare authenticity, you exhibit something that has nothing to do with age, experience, race or gender and something I don't see in other candidates. That something is a creative imagination which coupled with brilliance equals wisdom. It is too bad if we associate it only with gray hair and old age.[76]

Once Obama became the democratic candidate for president, the identity debate shifted to precisely the issue that Morrison lays out in an attempt to refute its importance. It is not just that gender was not in such full view (until Sarah Palin entered the race); rather, age triggered the keywords of the election (especially after Sarah Palin entered the race), wherein 'change' meant youth and 'experience' meant old age. Thus change-driven Obama chose experienced Joseph Biden to be his running mate, and, bizarrely, John McCain chose inexperienced Sarah Palin to be his.

Facing headlines such as 'Campaign Fatigue or Old Age?' and 'Is McCain's Age Showing?'[77] along with Democratic Party advertisements focusing on his age, Republican presidential candidate John McCain (old by gerontology's standards) was not at all associated with wisdom in the popular press, despite his 'gray hair and old age,' as Morrison puts it. Placing Palin on the ballot – in a seeming attempt to satisfy the need for Republicans to appear young and women-friendly – backfired, in part because her relative youthfulness illuminated McCain's aged appearance and her relative cluelessness did little to make him appear sensible.

Doing his best to appeal to younger voters, McCain toured the late-night circuit, willingly mocking his age – pretending to fall asleep and referring to great-great-great-grandchildren – which simply endorsed the stereotypes that added to his downfall.

Polls showed that U.S. voters were more uncomfortable with the chance of the oldest president yet than with the chance of the blackest. Pollster Gary Langer prescribed a fix for McCain, with a clear comparison to a famous Alzheimer's patient: 'Ronald Reagan addressed this very well in his campaign his first time when he was 69, 73 for his second term. Not only with a great one liner, but also by simply appearing very vital, very with it, during the campaign, very robust, and that's what McCain needs to do.'[78] This typical form of ageism via ableism – that there is only one way to age properly and that is to appear to be not only young but also extraordinarily fit – attached itself to the Republican candidate to the extent that McCain felt compelled to release his medical records to prove that he would live through his term if elected president.

Obama faced ageism as well, particularly with his credentials questioned at every juncture, even through the overcompensation of his supporters. But it was ageism without social force. His relative youth signified perhaps naivety but mostly potential. Where McCain had to offer his medical records, Obama had to refer frequently to his résumé. The tension between their age identities is summed up in a phrase from a *National Review* article: 'the Old Fart versus the Fresh Prince of Hyde Park.' This headline implies that McCain ought not be taken seriously because he is an aging gasbag, and Obama ought not be taken seriously because he's young, black, and disadvantaged and has only been adopted into the (extremely upper) middle class.[79] Neither Obama's promises of universal health care and social security reforms that would benefit seniors nor McCain's proposed privatization of health care coloured these characterizations.

Who's this 'We,' Mr President?

English professor Walter Benn Michaels opens his polemical *New Left Review* article 'Against Diversity' with his analysis of the interplay among race, gender, and age in the U.S. presidential race. He quickly moves on to class. Based on statistics measuring the income of people from the top and bottom quintile in the United States, Michaels argues that 'after half a century of anti-racism and feminism, the US today is a less equal society than was the racist, sexist society of Jim Crow.'[80] In targeting exploitation associated with neo-liberalism as the key author of American inequality, Michaels argues:

> Americans still love to talk about the American Dream – as, in fact, do Europeans. But the Dream has never been less of a reality than it is today. Not just because inequality is so high, but also because social mobility is so low; indeed, lower than in both France and Germany. Anyone born poor in Chicago has a better chance of achieving the American Dream by learning German and moving to Berlin than by staying at home.[81]

In drawing attention to the American Dream, Michaels reveals that his preoccupation is with economic inequality, a euphemism for poverty; further, he demonstrates that he is primarily concerned with younger members of the U.S. population who have the time to begin at the bottom and end up at the top – though he would like those two endpoints to be closer together.

The fragility of the Americanness of the American Dream calls into question the interpellation and verity of Obama's most-cited campaign slogan, 'Yes, we can,' a phrase very much associated with youth.[82] As Noam Scheiber points out, this was Obama's jingle long before he was a candidate for president:

> In Obama's first advertisement, the telegenic state senator looks at the camera and explains, 'They said an African American had never led the Harvard Law Review – until I changed that.' The commercial concludes, 'Now they say we can't change Washington, D.C. ... I approved this message to say, "Yes we can."'[83]

The slogan is explicitly about race, a tactic that continued into the democratic primaries with Obama claiming in South Carolina:

> At every juncture in our history, there's been somebody that's said we can't. There's been somebody's said you can't overcome slavery. There's been somebody who said you can't overcome Jim Crow ... If I have your support, if I have your energy and involvement and commitment and ideas, then I'm here to tell you, 'Yes we can in '08.'[84]

The first person plural pronoun ('we') gained force and gathered allies as the slogan travelled forward. Later in the campaign, Obama wisely revised the implications of the saying, declaring: 'When folks were saying, *We're going to march for our freedom*, they said, *You can't do that* … When somebody said, *You can't sit at the lunch counter.* … *You can't do that.* We did. And when somebody said, *Women belong in the kitchen, not in the boardroom. You can't do that.* Yes we can!'[85] The effectiveness of this more inclusive strategy was heightened by Obama's oft-quoted acceptance speech, which delighted queer and disability activists by mention of them explicitly, naming 'young and old, rich and poor, Democrat and Republican, Black, White, Hispanic, Asian, Native American, gay, straight, disabled and not disabled' as the actors who spoke together to say 'We are the United States of America.'[86] Oddly, the list excludes a gendered binary pair (i.e., men, women).

While the 2008 U.S. election demonstrated that, at long last, a black man can run successfully for president, the effect of that victory on race relations and especially on the alleviation of severe poverty that is heightened for racialized people in the United States is less clear. The American Dream depends upon much more than the identity politics that dominated the discourse surrounding Obama's victory. Twentieth-century U.S. health-care policy has determined that late life is indeed a privilege of the rich and often the white people in the United States. As Robin Blackburn puts it, 'The onset of ageing in the United States will be slower than in Europe because of … the failure of its costly medical system to deliver for many sections of the population – lower life expectancy among the Black, Hispanic, and poor reduces the ageing effect.'[87] Even as various reforms gradually take place, this distinction will persist for generations. For the many who cannot expect themselves or their family members to live into old age, the silvering screen is irrelevant, but their absence from it is significant.

More than the full potential of aging – the idea that an old person has value that exceeds the value attached to a young appearance – discriminatory life expectancies reveal the oversimplification of aging on the silvering screen. Its glossy plots overexert themselves in an attempt to distract from a harsh social reality that has little to do with new target markets and advantageously inclusive (of aging) advertising campaigns. Indir Thakrun, a secondary character in Satyajit Ray's *Pather Panchali* (India, 1955), is old, disabled, and a burden on her younger sister-in-law's family. The movie's central young characters witness her death as she runs away after being accused of stealing. Her body is left to rot on a public road as a moral lesson. Her body should also be a lesson for the silvering screen, but Indir Thakrun does not play a central role in *Pather Panchali* or on the silvering screen.

Obama's slogan and its implications, McCain's age as more interesting than his wealth, Thakrun's body, and Bell's incisive demographic analysis (and his untimely death)[88] ominously hang over the chapters in this book. Economic equality would not smooth the wrinkles furrowing the brow of the silvering screen, but gross disparity in financial security, and that disparity's relationship to race, provides the impetus to portray wrinkled white characters. Ignoring discrepancies in wealth and privilege, these films portray older characters as though they are little more than a social burden even when rich; the films assume there are lovely institutional settings in which it is always an option to place older characters, and they portray older characters as though their asserted, ongoing virility proves something of global social significance. Like the well-lit, clean, and friendly care settings the films portray, the silvering screen for the most part neatly contains old age – at least of those old people perceived as worthy of portraying. A metaphorical nursing home, the silvering screen holds the less seemly aspects of growing older in the global north, alleviating the burden from the broader population who can drop by during visiting hours without having to fully reckon with the scope of what an aging population means, positively or negatively. There is then no room in it for those people who also cannot gain admission to the glossy private care facilities that many silvering screen films portray. As for the public facilities: they are a fantasy, as much as a publicly owned, equal-access Hollywood would be if anyone dared to dream of it. For now, there is just the potential of sharing the front seat of the bus.

Screening Age

In the chapters to come, rather than offer a survey of old characters featured in a particular national cinema, I have selected representative films from a range of national cinemas and production contexts (but primarily Hollywood) to show the impressive scope of the current fascination with aging onscreen and to explore its significance. Some films I discovered through research and others were suggested to me. Of course, I watched dozens of other films that complement the ones discussed and I deliberately chose characteristic examples rather than aim for comprehensiveness. Each featured film stands in for a set of representations that do similar cultural work through related portrayals of old age. In most cases, I have chosen films that offer the richest opportunity for analysis, though in the chapter on Jack Nicholson the films were chosen to convey the trajectory of his career rather than because they are especially rich depictions of late life. The book begins in mid-century Hollywood. After charting a relationship between the portrayal of disabled characters and the portrayal of aging characters, focusing on caregiving and, in particular, dementia, I conclude by discussing the significance of the relationship between disability and aging for masculinity in Hollywood film.

Although the majority of the book will focus on the silvering screen as a recent phenomenon, in chapter 2 I turn to early Hollywood films to demonstrate the shift from horror to other genres that occurs later for older women featured onscreen. I examine how in two productions featuring stars from a past era the spectacle of aging film stars replicates and dictates the very cultural attitudes that make acting old in public risky, even when the characters are middle-aged (i.e., by no means old). With close attention to the films *Sunset Boulevard* (USA, Billy Wilder, 1950) and *Whatever Happened to Baby Jane?* (USA, Robert Aldrich, 1962), I argue that the conflation of disability with gender and aging in the character of Blanche Hudson (Joan Crawford) encapsulates the impossible standards placed on all non-normative bodies (that is, all bodies) by Hollywood cinema. In *Baby Jane* the collision of Blanche Hudson's physical disability with Jane Hudson's psychiatric illness relies upon an understanding of the obsolescence of the performers. However, as I will argue, the double-edged performances offered by Joan Crawford and Bette Davis undermine that obsolescence.

In chapter 3, I analyse films that distinguish aging with a disability from supposedly normal aging 'decrepitude' by featuring at least one character as obviously disabled in late life. With a central character who has a lifelong cognitive disability, *Pauline and Paulette* (Belgium, Lieven Debrauwer, 2001) argues for an indomitable spirit that shines through the disabled character's idiosyncratic mind, a spirit that will conquer the four walls of the institution. The film depicts a sense of fulfillment on the part of caregivers that disappears when the disabled character is otherwise cared for. In the film, disability figuratively emphasizes the inevitable solitude of old age, suggesting perhaps that disability is an integral part of experiencing fulfillment in the latter years. By contrast to this aging of lifelong disability, Alzheimer's (and other forms of usually late-life dementia) appears on the silvering screen to dramatize social fears of what aging might mean in terms of loss of control and self. While physical disability may infringe upon individualism and an associated assumed independence, mental disability infringes on subjectivity – subjectivity that is key to the sense of self. A prescient mourning begins for the person who used to be 'there' and who seems to have been replaced by mental ramblings, silence, and fear. The chapter concludes with an analysis of the portrayal of care and dementia in *A Song for Martin* (Sweden, Bille August, 2001) in which a wife witnesses the 'decline' of her new husband and *The Savages* (USA, Tamara Jenkins, 2007) in which offspring negotiate care for their negligent father.

Chapter 4 focuses more closely on the relationship between infidelity and care in a set of films whose central characters are moved to live inside institutional space. Specifically, I examine the representation of care decisions made by family members as depicted in *Open Hearts* (Denmark, Suzanne Bier, 2002), *Iris* (UK, Richard Eyre, 2001), *Away from Her* (Canada, Sarah Polley, 2006), and *The Barbarian Invasions* (Canada, Denys Arcand, 2003). As is typical on the silvering screen, these films portray demands faced primarily by one family member who must decide on behalf of another whether – or more frequently how and when – to change from mostly unpaid care to mostly paid care (represented by an institution).

In these films, past infidelities haunt the present devoted relationship, threatening the social fabric that requires a sacrificial loyal spouse to provide the care lacking from health systems. *Open Hearts, Iris,* and *Away from Her* depict life partners unexpectedly having to decide whether and for how long they can care for their newly disabled loved ones. *Barbarian Invasions* shifts the care responsibility onto a cartoonishly neo-liberal son who barely recovers from his disappointment in his erstwhile socialist, still debauched father. Each film focuses on marriage in some form, questioning that institution as it relates to institutional health care. On these screens, threats to sexual monogamy subtly threaten to strain public purse strings because monogamous care structures benefit a society reluctant to offer more expensive care solutions.

Counter to an argument for monogamy, a fleet of Hollywood films shore up masculine virility by claiming ongoing promiscuity (or at least the potential for it); these films buy into stereotypes about requited lust for younger women, asserting a possibility of freedom into curmudgeonliness, and most importantly, celebrating a geriatric 'American Dream.' In chapter 5 I read a set of these films to show what is at stake in revealing the underlying assumptions of the silvering screen. Notably, none of them take senility seriously except that an aging man's lust for a younger woman is occasionally derided as senility (but more often it is merely accepted as unworthy of comment). In contrast to a failing mind, physical faltering dominates a reassertion of masculinity despite the years.

Starting with the Grumpy Old Men films (USA, Donald Petrie, 1993; USA, Howard Deutch, 1995) to show the template for continued male achievement, the chapter moves on to Robert Benton's *Nobody's Fool* (USA, 1994) which features an aging Paul Newman as Sully – an irascible working-class man who wants to keep on working despite his bad knee. Adapted from a Richard Russo novel, the film revises the romantic plot to enhance Sully's seeming heroism. I compare Newman's late film with two of Clint Eastwood's late-career, vigilante films in which his claim to violent heroism becomes increasingly legitimized by his seeming frailty.

Chapter 6 continues this examination of aging Hollywood masculinity, turning to Jack Nicholson's latest films which set him up as old in relation to other more expendable characters who prop up his virility. In *About Schmidt* (USA, Alexander Payne, 2002), *Something's Gotta Give* (USA, Nancy Meyers, 2003), and *The Bucket List* (USA, Rob Reiner, 2007), as varied as their themes, characterizations, and sophistication seem, Jack Nicholson plays a wealthy, misogynistic, aging white man, unaware and unquestioning of the power he strains (only slightly) to maintain in the face of aging. His Hollywood persona is vital to the portrayals of his aging characters.

As macabre as it is to the end the book, and the introduction, focused on the topic of death, it is appropriate since that is the loudest resonance of old age onscreen. In my conclusion, I illuminate moving instances wherein an actor plays a character close to death when the actor himself is also dying.

The conclusion begins with an analysis of *Il Postino* (Italy, Michael Radford, 1995) to demonstrate the fragility of the automatic relationship between age and death. In *Il Postino*, Mario Ruoppolo, killed in a political uprising, is played by forty-one-year-old Massimo Troisi who died of a massive heart attack twelve hours after filming ended, after having postponed treatment in order not to delay the production. The chapter compares this tragedy with an analysis of *The Straight Story* (USA, David Lynch, 1999) which depicts Alvin Straight, seventy-three years old and in need of hip surgery he refuses to have, resolutely pursuing atop a rider mower on a cross-country trip to visit his dying brother. The VHS and DVD versions of *The Straight Story* poignantly close with a dedication to the actor who portrayed Straight, Richard Farnsworth, who shot himself after filming. The book ends with speculation on the future of aging in cinema and the potential demise of the silvering screen.

Chapter two

Baby Jane Grew Up:
The Horror of Aging in
Mid-Twentieth-Century Hollywood

I didn't go in blind, mind you. I knew that Bette had the best scenes, that
she could top me all along the way. I was a cripple, physically, and she was
demented, mentally, and the mental always wins out on the screen.

Joan Crawford[1]

While the 2000s offered mixed opportunities for film actresses 'of a certain age,' in the 1960s the choices for former screen queens were more
limited. Women who had played some of the strongest Hollywood roles
in the 1930s were now relegated to a back room, a bit part, a grand-
motherly role, or, as this chapter demonstrates, a major horror role.
Fears of growing old surely preoccupied individuals, but there was not
yet the mass panic that grips present audiences. Nuclear war seemed a
likelier prospect in the 1960s than surviving it into a dependent and decrepit long life.

This chapter is concerned with two Hollywood icons and one less-
known figure who reached their fifties only to be thought of as defunct
and cast as dysfunctional. As Robert J. Corber says of one of the actresses,
'from the beginning of her career as a contract player at Metro-Goldwyn-
Mayer (MGM), [Joan] Crawford had been promoted as a kind of female
Horatio Alger, a fiercely ambitious, self-made woman who had overcome
enormous obstacles, including a Dickensian childhood, to become one
of Hollywood's most glamorous stars.'[2] Ambition could not really help
Crawford overcome the obstacle of her aging body perceived by
Hollywood. Consequently, she had little choice but to become a horror
queen and then retire from the business. Actresses only as old as fifty-
something were not considered glamorous in the 1960s, which was more

than twenty years before feminist Gloria Steinem's widely quoted, defi-
ant statement in response to someone who told her she didn't look fifty
(i.e., looked too attractive to be fifty): 'This is what fifty looks like.'[3]

Speaking of Bette Davis's career before she too was fifty, Martin
Shingler and Christine Gledhill praise her laudable film presence,
explaining,

> In the mid 1930s Davis acquired the reputation of being one of Hollywood's
> finest actors, her talent showcased by Warner Bros in a series of star vehicles,
> many adapted from successful Broadway plays. These were much praised,
> receiving major awards from the Academy of Motion Picture Arts and
> Sciences. They also attracted huge numbers of moviegoers, making them
> some of the biggest box-office hits of the late 1930s and early-to-mid 1940s.
> By 1939 Davis was widely considered one of the greatest living actresses in
> the USA, lauded as the Sarah Bernhardt of the screen.[4]

Despite this prodigious talent, Davis's acting skills took her back to
Broadway roles once she appeared too old to play the types of roles available in Hollywood, even for an actress of her calibre. Like Crawford, only
when she agreed to play a horror character did her film career revive.
Similarly, for Gloria Swanson (less known now because her main early
successes were in silent film) reaching fifty meant taking on a part rejected by Mary Pickford and Greta Garbo – both of whom knew better
than to display their aging. In accepting the part of Norma Desmond,
Swanson set herself up to play only compromised roles, none of them as
well written as the *Sunset Boulevard* (USA, Billy Wilder, 1950) part she is
now most famous for. In this chapter, I examine how disability coheres
with images of aging for these mid-twentieth-century screen divas to pro-
duce an unnerving sense of their late careers as distortions of their earlier appearances. The cohesion illustrates how Hollywood uses the aging
frame to promote one meaning of aging femininity as horrifyingly disabled and to obscure other interpretations.

In the context of Pickford and Garbo removing themselves from the
unflattering limelight, Crawford and Davis could be described as brave
for agreeing to portray two elderly sisters in Robert Aldrich's risky
Whatever Happened to Baby Jane? (USA, 1962). Certainly, their willingness
to continue to be in the public eye as they aged markedly contrasts the
choices of other stars. The film's resulting investigation of the potential
ephemerality of star power, suggested by the title, and that power's dependence on youthful beauty startles viewers in its candour about the

actresses' career choices. The onscreen drama amplifies the off-screen decisions made by Crawford and Davis. The placement of Crawford's character in a wheelchair and her consequent depicted dependence on an increasingly unstable caregiver dramatizes the possible fate of the starlet, which in turn symbolizes a larger cultural interpretation of aging women – one that has prevailed. Her physical location in a wheelchair quickly signifies the plight of an aging actress, and it is much easier for audiences to accept the aging of Crawford if she is seen as also disabled. That placement, then, threatens to disguise the real cause of the character – and the actress – being in the wheelchair: Hollywood's ageist-ableist standards and limited roles for older women. Sadly, there is no real leeway offered by the film to redeem the wheelchair seat as one of power, though some critics attempt to read the film's 'surprise' ending as though that were so.

The film's title question, 'Whatever happened to Baby Jane?' refers to the car accident that caused Crawford's character's immobility (physically and professionally) and Davis's character's delusions, and it implicitly inquires into the changes perceived to be wrought by time on two female entertainers who relied on genres that emphasize youth and, by extension, beauty. Baby Jane's incapacity to understand her adult, let alone senescent, self results in a twisted form of what critical theorist Mary Russo has called a 'scandal of anachronism.'[5] Jane's repeated refrain 'I've written a letter to Daddy' and her continued identification with the doll of her childhood likeness make unambiguous the forces that allowed her sister's earlier film career to overshadow her own vaudeville one. Moreover, the narrative's transition from vaudeville (Jane) to film (Blanche) to television reruns (Blanche) signifies the redundancy that faces both of these characters. Like their acting, their performance of gender can only be reframed in an increasingly advanced modern world, and that reframing is drastically affected by the appearance of age on their performing bodies and faces. Refusal to accept that age – and the changes that come with aging – comes across as pathology; accepting that age, while not the same pathological denial, would be to accept social pathologization.

The Scandal of Anachronism

In 'Aging and the Scandal of Anachronism,' Mary Russo explores the positive and negative potential of risking what she labels anachronism. Drawing on Walter Benjamin's famous image of the angel of history propelled, facing backwards, into the future by progress, Russo dwells upon how 'developmental models of aging gracefully' stand at odds with that image.[6] That is, they dictate a compliant acceptance of being old (a propulsion forward into the future) including all the social detritus that elderly status accrues. Taking on what she calls the 'high political and cultural stakes which are always involved in changing the experience of time,' Russo embarks on a 'defense of randomness as a way of understanding and assuming the risks of aging.' In choosing randomness as a model for the life course, Russo defies normative models that prescribe aging as a gradual progress towards death, where the past is to be learned from, the present to be survived, and the future (certain death) to be accepted. As she puts it, 'Acting one's age, in a certain sense, can be understood as a caution against risk taking with higher and higher stakes associated with advanced chronological age until finally, acting one's age means to die.'[7] Russo explores the possibilities of acting *against* one's age, that is, of not conforming to normative ideas of age-appropriate behaviour. She cautions that 'not acting one's age ... is not only inappropriate but dangerous, exposing the female subject, especially, to ridicule, contempt, pity, and scorn – the scandal of anachronism.'[8] Nonetheless, Russo encourages hazarding such a scandal since the dangers of not taking that risk are equally, if not more, intimidating – matching cultural expectations of decrepitude and death. Acting one's age means buying into damaging cultural prescriptions for late life and, by Russo's logic, acting against one's age means defying those prescriptions.

This chapter examines how the spectacle of aging U.S. film stars in a mid-twentieth-century context replicates and dictates the very cultural attitudes that make risking the scandal of anachronism 'necessary and inevitable *as a sign of life*,' as Russo puts it, even when age does not signify death (in other words, even when the actresses are only middle-aged).[9] That is, the representations in these films demonstrate that even middle age signifies decline and, in order not to be redundant, actresses in their fifties must crip their aging, thereby revealing the mechanisms by which tacit norms have displaced them.[10]

With close attention to *Sunset Boulevard* and *Whatever Happened to Baby Jane?*, I argue that the conflation of disability with gender and aging in the characters of Norma Desmond (Gloria Swanson), Blanche Hudson (Joan Crawford), and Jane Hudson (Bette Davis) encapsulates the impossible standards placed on all non-normative bodies (that is, all bodies) by mid-twentieth-century Hollywood cinema. As discussed in chapter 1, aging bodies are not necessarily disabled, but older people frequently face treatment as though they are physically and mentally less capable than their younger selves. These actresses had to take on roles that compromised their reputations as desirable stars, playing characters with visible or invisible disabilities. Desmond's mental fragility in *Sunset Boulevard* and even more so Blanche Hudson's physical disability and Jane Hudson's psychiatric illness in *Baby Jane* rely upon an understanding of the actresses' obsolescence as performers; their seemingly failed physicality mirrors their stalled career paths. However, the double-edged performances offered by Swanson, Crawford, and Davis – as aging women risking scandal to remain onscreen – undermine that obsolescence. My analysis clarifies the connection between disability and old age in screen projections of aging characters. The assumption that disability automatically accompanies late life encroaches on those older people who do not experience significant disabilities, those older people who acquire new disabilities, and those older people who have lived with disabilities since long before they were labelled old. Resisting the assumption is vital, and resisting it by inhabiting disability, though seemingly contradictory, is transformational.

Intriguingly, the format of both of these comeback films is the backstage melodrama. Lucy Fischer explains part of the backstage melodrama's appeal: 'When such films are made, a real actress must take the fictional star's role, thus superimposing the career of an actual performer over the dramatic text.'[11] The resonances of the relationship between a living actor and a dramatic character take on new significance when the topic of aging pervades both onscreen and off-screen scenarios. Aging actors are often called upon to portray characters much older than their actual age (as is the case in *Baby Jane*). As Elizabeth Markson explains it, their own relative age haunts their performance:

> The portrayal of the older female body in film is, by definition, a masquerade. Film stars put on 'a look' designed to make known information about the social status and character's personality being played; this 'look' may or may not resemble the real-life appearance of the individual performers … Yet the performer, too, is old and subject to the same fears about her own body going to pieces as does the character she plays.[12]

Middle-aged performances of old age, and youthful attempts to emulate maturity, do not often meet with praise, recognition, or reward. As Margaret Morganroth Gullette notes, speaking of the theatre, 'Surely I am not the only spectator who notices that younger actors often feign older ages badly.'[13] While actors, and particularly actresses such as

Crawford and Davis, may be thought brave for taking on roles that magnify the aging process, it is not considered a skill to look old onscreen because women are often read as precociously old. Instead, skill is more typically acknowledged in the ability of an aging actor to appear young, worthy, and valuable despite the hands of time, though the effort required must never show.

Crawford, Davis, and Swanson all resurrected their careers at an age thought to be too old for starring roles, a seemingly exciting step for female screen queens. However, they all did so in order to take on the roles of has-been stars, sadly mirroring their real-life status. The strange connection of fictional backstage with supposedly real backstage relies on social and cultural understandings of the process of aging and especially how it is marked on bodies once known for their normative youthful beauty. That these actresses had previously been cast partly because of their beauty contributes to the horror evoked by their deviance from the very norm the casting of their own physical forms had set. E. Ann Kaplan claims, 'The well-known crisis of aging female film stars and performers on the screen and in life exemplifies in the extreme the difficulties of aging for many women.'[14] If these previously ideal bodies deviate from their own previous youthful standard, how much further will everyday audience members 'decline'? Because so many members of the audience imagine aging inscribed on their own bodies, a sense of troubling horror emerges from the disjunction between what they had learned to expect from these starlets and the realization of the stars' aging physical forms as per the frightening logic: if even Hollywood stars age, then so too must we (*memento obsolesci*, as it were). This horror then ironically allows the audience members to distance themselves from the process.

Gloria Swanson's Norma Desmond:
Illustrating a Scandal of Anachronism

Gloria Swanson was around fifty years old when she agreed to play fifty-year-old Norma Desmond in Billy Wilder's *Sunset Boulevard*, and she was fifty-one when it was released. Like the character Desmond, Swanson had worked with Cecil DeMille and Eric von Stroheim, and, like Desmond, Swanson's career had suffered from the shift from silent film to talkies. Described as a 'has-been' at thirty-six by Hollywood trade papers, Swanson somewhat reluctantly agreed to take on the role of a has-been. As Fischer puts it, 'It was from … oblivion that she was called in 1950 to do *Sunset Boulevard*, a film about an actress in oblivion.'[15]

Although reportedly offended by the implications of the part, Swanson took on the role of Norma Desmond primarily for financial reasons, and for the rest of her career she received only scripts that allowed her to re-enact her Norma Desmond has-been role. One can only speculate as to whether her choice to take on a role that depicted rather than hid her (advanced by Hollywood standards) age led to a diminished perception of the roles she could pull off.

Sunset Boulevard pivots around Desmond's relationship with the passage of time, which was likely a preoccupation of Swanson's and undoubtedly a preoccupation of her audience's, which witnesses examples of her preoccupation with time within the film. When Joe Gillis (William Holden) is treated to a night at the movies in Desmond's parlour, he is shown Desmond's former screen successes. Wilder chooses to show clips of Swanson's actual earlier silent films. The plot of *Sunset Boulevard* primarily concerns Desmond's hopes of a screen comeback, and these hopes are depicted as unrealizable, presumably because of her age as marked on her body and in her style of acting. Still, the character at the very least acknowledges, however grudgingly, that the technologies of Hollywood have changed, and she tries to write herself into the new genre of the talkie. She insists on playing the leading role (of Salomé), not understanding that Hollywood does not want to project and audiences do not want to gaze upon middle-aged femininity as a trait of seductresses. As such, she risks the scandal of anachronism for career survival. Her attempt fails because she is unaware of the changing opinions around her. In an attempt to stay onscreen, she writes herself a part that only emphasizes her distance from the youthful celluloid norm.

Gloria Swanson's Norma Desmond illustrates a scandal of anachronism, though she does not quite celebrate its possibilities. She certainly 'exposes the female subject ... to ridicule, contempt, pity, and scorn,' but she does not deliberately take the risk that Russo recommends. Desmond resents the transition to sound in Hollywood because of its effect on her career, but unlike Lina Lamont from *Singin' in the Rain* (USA, Stanley Donen, 1952), her voice does not disqualify her from taking spoken parts. It is ambiguous why Desmond can no longer appear on the silver screen, though the film implies that the combination of her age and her overdramatic style makes her redundant. Since Swanson herself had trouble with the transition, she may have been deliberately overplaying the at times ridiculous physical gestures that animate Desmond, or she may have been simply following her earlier training. Still, despite (or even because of) that theatricality, *Sunset Boulevard* succeeds. So, if Swanson can succeed without fully adjusting to the new requirements of the film industry, why can't Desmond? The answer is supposed to be her refusal to act her age, I presume, but her advancing age does not even appear to viewers except when she takes the stage next to twenty-something Betty Schaefer's (Nancy Olson) dewy complexion.

Swanson chose to emphasize her continued youth-like beauty. She insisted that director Wilder make William Holden, at thirty-one, look younger to make their characters' supposed twenty-five-year age difference credible, since, as she informed him, 'women of fifty frequently look quite good.' To convey the physical trauma Desmond faces, which is not immediately visually perceptible, she must *tell* Joe of the line on her neck, the damage to her hands, and the problems with the space around her eyes since none of these are visible to viewers. Still, in place of witnessing her in a grotesque parody of her own aging flesh, viewers witness her submission to a gruesome series of treatments designed to erase all signs of time passing. Desmond's mental condition does not allow her to recognize let alone acknowledge her age, and viewers cannot quite tell whether Desmond would have accepted the harsh beauty regime as part of her stardom at any age or whether it is meant to be age specific. The eerie and famous line, 'I am ready for my close-up, Mr. DeMille,' likely echoes Desmond's youthful self.

The film depicts Desmond as weakened by her incapacity or unwillingness to acknowledge her own middle age. The mental instability weaves in and out of the diva personality that Desmond maintains in keeping with her inability to lose grip on her stardom. The participation of her chauffeur (who is also her ex-husband and former director) suggests that Desmond either has constantly manipulated others or has been constantly manipulated by others. Nonetheless, when Desmond mistakenly addresses DeMille in the final moments of the film, viewers can be doubly horrified by a portrayal of dementia and by a portrayal of a fifty-something character who refuses to acknowledge what her age signifies. Either way they witness what is presumably meant to be grotesque flesh ignoring cultural expectations. Though not a deliberate risk of scandalous anachronism, Desmond's delusion and Swanson's 'choice' to portray it certainly exemplify the stakes that Russo sets out, showing that women, in particular, daringly resist cultural exigencies when they refuse to 'act their age.'

Norma Desmond (Gloria Swanson) ready for her close-up in *Sunset Boulevard.* ©
Bettman/Corbis

Bette Davis's Baby Jane Hudson:
Exaggerating a Scandal of Anachronism

Bette Davis was in her fifties when she agreed to assume the role of Baby
Jane Hudson. She left her role as Maxine Faulk in Tennessee Williams's
Broadway production *The Night of the Iguana* to take on the controversial
characterization of stardom gone wrong. The offer came after she placed
an advertisement in Hollywood trade publications: 'Mother of three –
10, 11 and 15 – divorcee. American. Thirty years experience as an actress
in motion pictures. Mobile still. And more affable than rumor would
have it. Wants steady employment in Hollywood (has had Broadway).
Bette Davis, c/o Martin Baum, GAC. References upon request.'[16] Since

her recent films had not made enough money, Hollywood directors shunned Davis; infuriated, she decided to throw down the gauntlet and expose the underlying ageism of the silver screen. She explained: 'I wanted everybody to know I was back in Hollywood – and back with a vengeance!' And an actress with a vengeance is quite literally what she was called upon by Aldrich to portray: Baby Jane returning to the Hollywood stage in search of revenge.[17]

Bette Davis's Jane Hudson does more than illustrate the scandal of anachronism; she exaggerates it in her angry attempt to revive her vaudeville routine despite Hollywood's new focus on film and television. She could not be described as celebrating its possibilities, though perhaps Bette Davis could in her portrayal of this excessive character. In Baby Jane's defiance of time, she hearkens back to an age so young as to be disturbing. A visibly aging woman attempting a child's stage antics provides a juxtaposition worthy, in Hollywood's terms, only of a horror film. Jane hopes to rekindle a routine as passé as she seems to be, and the film's emphasis on the progression of the entertainment industry exaggerates the fixedness of Jane's (mis)understanding of her fame.

For her portrayal of Jane Hudson, Bette Davis chooses to wear makeup that parodies the appearance of age expected by audience members who likely compare her older face to her past image on the screen. Jane's incongruous age – magnified by her harlequin make-up – renders her ridiculous, but it is not the only factor that makes her attempt to live against time ridiculous. She tries to return to the business not only because she again wants the attention of adoring fans, but mainly because she wants her own income so that Blanche cannot institutionalize her for her combined psychiatric and drinking problems. However, trying to revive her childhood act will never actually bring in the revenue that she needs in order to be free from Blanche's plot – as she sees it – to sell the house they own together. There is no money in vaudeville anymore. Her comeback attempt exaggerates Russo's scandal because she does not risk ridicule in order to keep a person or a career alive. She risks ridicule in order to keep a fantasy of a past life and past age alive.

Though the actress Bette Davis opts to portray Baby Jane as appearing older than the actress's fifty-some years, the character Baby Jane embodies the opposite anachronism and does not seem to accept any passage of time. Her misunderstanding of chronology crystallizes in her attempt to resurrect her vaudeville act. As Jodi Brooks puts it, 'Jane certainly operates as an anachronism, a kind of cinema dinosaur, but at the same time that she is a figure arrested in time, she attempts to arrest time, to arrest the present and charge herself into it.'[18] Not only does Jane ignore that she differs in appearance from the child who performed successfully, she also does not fully comprehend the technological changes to the entertainment industry that have simultaneously made her style extinct. Such refusal of change typifies the mindset of female principals in backstage melodramas that explore the ephemerality of female stardom, usually by exploiting the anguish experienced by aging stars.

Jane's attempt to resurrect her vaudeville routine startles viewers into recognizing the devastation that youthful standards can wreak. In one memorable scene, Jane hears the music of her doll (an ominous replica of her childhood self), takes the doll's bow onto her own head, and begins to sing. When she sees her image in the mirror, viewers witness a rare moment of Jane recognizing her age. The uncomfortable shot of Jane covering her face and screaming in horror at her reflection unsettles viewers who might also have wanted to cover their eyes at the sight of a grotesque Bette Davis, yet who feel sympathy for Jane's terror of her own image. In *Baby Jane*, the moments for sympathy with Jane are few and are always mediated by her sheer cruelty to Blanche, but the raw anguish depicted in her realization startles the audience in its unavoidability. In *Sunset Boulevard*, Norma Desmond, too, stands before the mirror and encounters her reflection before she goes into the bedroom to confront Joe Gillis. In a moment of candour, she grasps the grotesqueness of her beauty treatments and tears the tape from her eyes and mouth before confronting Joe about his escapades. These mirror moments depict Jane and Norma as viewers, so that when they can see themselves from without, they momentarily engage with external norms of age appropriate behavior. Such moments are short-lived however, and for the most part both Desmond and Hudson are depicted as psychotically avoiding the recognition of how age shows on their bodies or how others interpret age as showing on their bodies. As such, they neatly convey how age is pathologized as mental disability in films about aging so that their depiction reveals a social anxiety about the loss of self in late life.

How Old is 'Old'?

Neither Davis nor Swanson at the time of shooting *Baby Jane* and *Sunset Boulevard* respectively was at an age that signified impending death, even if we exaggerate unreasonable expectations of female bodies. Their age merely suggested a change, usually thought of as a decline, from their youthful images. Of course, both actresses had predicated their careers on their youthful images. In their fifties, Swanson and Davis risked acting their age when doing so would most likely mean death to their careers. Literally *acting* the part of someone their age onscreen signifies a distance from the physical figures on which they had previously based their acting careers. That is, acting their age meant acting *against* their age simultaneously, since it is not considered appropriate for older women (if fifty can be considered older) to play a starring role.

Russo explains the relational quality of age identity, saying, 'We know each other in different ages, and we measure ourselves by the aging of everyone – from close relatives to film stars.'[19] Because of exaggerated standards, acting fifty-something means appearing much older than that to audience members. In Hollywood, acting against one's age entails defying cultural understandings of the appropriate vehicle for display. In *Baby Jane*, both Bette Davis and Joan Crawford chose to amplify interpretations of the aging process as marked on their bodies, and the choice led to a horror film in place of the romantic comedies and melodramas that they each famously starred in previously. (The words 'chose' and 'choice' may be misleading terms, however, since the only other option appears to have been not working at all.) Rather than backing away from the camera at a time when their bodies did not meet industry expectations for appropriate spectacle, these actresses confronted the lens, potentially exposing themselves to the 'ridicule, contempt, pity, and scorn' that Russo describes. To do so, they convey disability as an automatic part of aging, to be pitied and yet to be manipulated so that they can keep working.

The Horror of Anachronism

Age signifies decline prematurely in a Hollywood actress. Like Swanson, Crawford, and Davis were, Desmond and the Hudsons are all at a point when acting their respective ages means, and has already meant, death to their careers because of what their bodies signify culturally. Their desire to revive a past career, now completely outmoded and technologically out-of-date, indicates their misinterpretation of the conventions of the passage of time. The scandal of their insistent anachronism does not participate in the risk that Russo argues is necessary to life preservation. Instead, this scandalous juxtaposition of old body in a youthful role preserves the cultural distinctions that make the female characters redundant.

Hollywood has been, still is, and probably always will be criticized and yet lauded (sometimes by the same people) for maintaining ridiculous standards of beauty that are only attained by the kinds of physical changes we see Norma Desmond undergo at the hands of beauticians. It is perhaps ironic that the older characters' attempts to revise themselves to reassert the value of their faded genres actually mimic the attempts made by 'young' actors to fulfill the supposed desires of the presumed-to-be-young audience. In *Sunset Boulevard*, Betty Schaefer's description of the nose job for which she paid US$300 in order to get rid of the offending shadow cast on her face demonstrates the pressure even sixteen-year-old actresses faced and face to meet Hollywood criteria for beauty. At all ages, aspiring actors manipulate their physical form in desperate attempts to match an elusive yet always youthful norm. Thus, by attempting to maintain a youthful appearance, neither Jane nor Norma rebels against Hollywood expectations. And yet, when middle-aged characters attempt the same transformation as younger actors, their inability to recognize its ridiculousness is literalized as psychosis. Whereas young Betty Schaefer's attempted restructuring of her appearance is at worst portrayed as silly, Norma Desmond's submission to what resemble instruments of torture, in a similar attempt to change her looks, comes off as pathetic, and even demented.

Perhaps the psychoses disallow the possibilities nestled within the risk of Russo's scandal. By characterizing Jane and Norma as deranged, the films ensure that neither can make the logical choice Russo posits of acting against age. Viewers thereby do not have to confront Davis and Swanson's nor Jane and Norma's need to defy time because doing so would also be to confront the impossible aging standards Hollywood imposes. Instead, audience members can think of them as pathological oddities, examples of the extremes to which only few go. Jodi Brooks refers to the mental state of both Desmond and Hudson as 'a breakdown, a crisis which is not the "result" of aging, but of occupying the position of cultural refuse.'[20] The instability of age does not arise directly and necessarily from the process of aging; rather social constructions and understandings of female bodies determine the instability depicted in each case. Portrayed outside the genre of horror, each narrative would tackle not only the difficulty of living into old age, but also the inevitability of growing old, barring tragic events.[21] But within these films, the aging female bodies play into gothic challenges to containment in a neat, youthful body. Somehow, at a certain point, women are no longer expected to be able to transform themselves to match circulating notions of contained beauty and have a different physical choice to make. Davis, however reluctantly, embraces the shift and chooses to intensify the appearance of age that will make her a grotesque parody of her past self. Neither Norma nor Jane recognizes the supposed futility of seeming young, and a highly stylized, sombre drama materializes in each case.

The character Joe Gillis says it best when he tells Desmond: 'Norma, you're a woman of fifty. Now grow up! There's nothing tragic about being fifty. Not unless you try to be twenty-five!' The refusal to act one's age on film translates into tragedy. And the reason Swanson succeeds where Desmond fails is generic. Swanson takes on the role of a middle-aged, deluded has-been to participate in the horror that characterization is presumed to evoke in youthful audiences. She, like Davis, acts someone her age not acting her age, so she adopts horror roles and succeeds only in portraying the tragedy of failed aging as a horror device. The monster, in these cases, is not just a female body challenging circulating notions of beauty, but a female who refuses to acknowledge doing so.

Joan Crawford's Blanche Hudson and the Paradox of Female Disability

Crawford's character Blanche Hudson occupies an even more troubled space (quite literally trapped on the top floor); depicted as paralysed and, thanks to Hollywood's shorthand, terrifyingly passive in the face of Davis's character Jane Hudson's demented refusal to recognize the passage of time. While Crawford is placed in a wheelchair for *Baby Jane*, her characterization does not require bodily transformation to appear disabled – being in a wheelchair simply renders her more obsolete/old in Hollywood's terms. The manipulative depiction of wheelchair life plays into and around cultural stereotypes of disability as complete helplessness and dependency. The film portrays Blanche Hudson as both what Tom Shakespeare has called 'the tragic but brave invalid' and 'the sinister cripple.' The film needs her disability in order to shore up its moralistic narrative and to achieve its most renowned shot (which depicts from above Blanche wheeling herself in a futile circle).[22] But her depiction is, of course, more than two-fold, particularly because of her life-long rivalry with the younger Baby Jane. Whereas ridiculous harlequinesque make-up and wild greying hair exaggerate Davis's age, Crawford's age foregrounds another perceived infirmity that simultaneously trumps and magnifies the physical changes that supposedly come with growing old. Her depiction of Blanche exemplifies the intense connection between the pathologization of disability and the pathologization of age.

Blanche Hudson (Joan Crawford), trapped in *Whatever Happened to Baby Jane?*
© Bettman/Corbis

Though she certainly challenges constructed notions of beauty both in terms of age and ability, Crawford's Blanche Hudson does not misunderstand the passage of time in the same way as Davis's Jane Hudson does. Blanche still clings to the attention from her past stardom, sitting transfixed before the television rerun of her movie and poring over continued fan mail resulting from the broadcast. *Baby Jane* does not reveal Crawford as desiring a comeback; she plays someone her age acting her age. But, in acting her age, she emanates another even more disturbing cultural understanding of what time does to bodies. Blanche's partial physical paralysis, following Hollywood's logic, symbolizes the complete passivity required of a fifty-something actress. Not only does Blanche sit in a wheelchair, she appears increasingly weak physically, in part because Jane, upon whom she wholly relies for nourishment and company, starves her. Her submission exaggerates cultural stereotypes of physical disability to intensify the horror of the film. The film does not need to amplify the horror of her situation through a refusal to act her age because her physical state already defies, and yet paradoxically matches, cultural norms of aging femininity. It is not so much the injuries that land her in the chair but the resulting dependency that creates horror in this production. In this way, Blanche illuminates a social fear that an aging person will require care, especially if that person is physically disabled.

Rosemarie Garland Thomson has written about the double bind that a disabled female body presents culturally: 'Both the female and the disabled body are cast within cultural discourse as deviant and inferior; both are excluded from full participation in public as well as economic life; both are defined in opposition to a valued norm which is assumed to possess natural corporeal superiority.'[23] The aging body also fits Thomson's description, and Blanche Hudson is triply marked as inferior. However, Thomson notes a distinction between the exclusion that accompanies femininity and the exclusion that accompanies disability: 'Within the visual economy in which appearance has come to be the primary index of value for women, feminizing practices normalize the female body, while disabilities abnormalize it. Feminization prompts the gaze, while disability prompts the stare.'[24] To a degree, Blanche's supposed helplessness – portrayed by her location in a wheelchair – magnifies her femininity. Ultimately though, Blanche's disability diminishes the cultural value that Blanche's femininity without disability – literalized through her film career – previously brought. Whereas before she was appropriate fodder for what Laura Mulvey has called the male gaze, now she more appropriately matches what Cheryl Wade has called 'a sock in the eye with gnarled fist,' particularly when her age, in light of Hollywood standards, is taken into account.[25] By this logic, as film audiences stare at Crawford as Blanche, pity replaces desire.

Until its conclusion, *Baby Jane* leads the audience to understand that Jane drunkenly caused the fateful car crash that resulted in Blanche's infirmity. In the final scene, Blanche tells Jane that, counter to what Jane had believed all along, Jane had been too drunk to drive and that Blanche herself had been behind the wheel and accelerated in a failed attempt to injure Jane. Most critics read Blanche's final words as a straight confession and blame Blanche for her own disability. In this reading, the character and the audience believed passive, Blanche, engineered what happened to Baby Jane (and herself). That is, Jane is (literally) driven to insanity through guilt over an act she may not have committed. Disability scholar Martin Norden situates such a reading within a tradition of disabled avengers:

> The film reveals much later that the circumstances surrounding Blanche's disabling accident were far different from the generally believed version of them; it was Blanche, humiliated by her sister at a party only moments before, who tried to run down Baby Jane but missed her target and struck a stone gate instead, the force of which snapped her spine. She was still able to gain revenge on her sister by keeping her awash in endless waves of guilt.[26]

This reading, invited by Blanche's 'confession,' depends upon her having crawled into injured position after her spine has snapped, but the campy flavour of the film does make this seem possible, if unlikely. Blaming Blanche instead of Jane does little to alleviate the automatic connection of age to disability for both characters in this portrayal of their later life, but it does change political valences of disability readings of the film.

The consistent characterization of Blanche's passive dependence and Jane's spiteful care makes possible a more skeptical reading of the bizarre twist presented by this film's final confession. It is entirely possible that Blanche's confession is not genuine, but rather a ploy to win over Jane to save her own life. The exchange matches previous desperate lies that Blanche has told Jane in an attempt to end Jane's cruelty, and there seems little reason to believe Blanche's words now that she is faced with death by starvation or dehydration. Given Jane's immediate quest for food upon hearing Blanche's 'confession,' I read the scene as yet another capitulation to victim rhetoric. If Blanche makes up the confession in order to obtain food, she continues to play the victim role. In this reading, she is her sister's victim (in the car accident), and now she further 'victimizes' herself by placing blame on herself thus releasing her sister from murderous blame.

The most trite, objectionable disability rhetoric precedes Blanche's confession: 'You didn't do it Jane. I did it to myself. Don't you understand? I crippled myself.' The blame she tries to place onto herself, and the blame the film places onto her, buy into the insidious notion of disability as a personal deficit or moral failing. Believing this confession means believing Blanche's last able-bodied action was an attempted murder. Blanche's confession at the end of the film associates Blanche's paralysis with immoral action, which encourages audience members to believe that her physicality embodies her moral shortcomings and not just the fading into the background supposedly appropriate to her age. However, critical audience members can interpret the confession as an extension of her contrived passivity, accepting blame in order to keep the peace and stay alive. If one believes the confession, Blanche is a 'sinister cripple,' and if one does not, she is 'the tragic but brave invalid.' The film holds both readings in a tension it refuses to relieve, however, so that it is possible that audience members will invest in both interpretations to some extent, which leaves disability, and readings of disabled bodies, resistant to neat categorization. Portraying these two aging stars as disabled, then, refuses a simple homogenization of late life in the film but supports a general tendency to reduce aging to becoming disabled.

Through its twist ending, though perhaps ludicrous in its exaggeration, *Baby Jane* injects the preceding odious depiction of disability with a complexity that is difficult to resolve. Blame rhetoric conveniently distances each character's disability from a presumed-to-be-able audience. Audience members might easily experience intense fear witnessing Jane's treatment and abuse of Blanche, especially when they believe that what has happened to Blanche could happen to any 'innocent' person. If Blanche's confession is believed, the revelatory ending enables audience members to exonerate their own bodies from the possibility of sharing Blanche Hudson's fate. Rather than an innocent victim, perhaps she herself is to blame for the accident that changed her mobility and her sister's sanity (and that facilitated Jane's retreat into eternal childishness).

Joan Crawford and Bette Davis in the ambiguous final scene of *Whatever Happened to Baby Jane?* © Keystone/Hudson Archive/Getty Images

Conclusion: Babies Grow Up

Baby Jane presents overlapping ambivalences towards aging and towards disability. The film both celebrates and condemns Jane's refusal to acknowledge time, and it both pities and scorns Blanche's infirmity. The film relies narratively and cinematographically on both age and disability. The two most famous shots, the bird's-eye view of Blanche spinning in her chair and the close-up of Jane's recognition of her age in the mirror, derive their aesthetic power from a horrific depiction of age and disability. The horror appeal frightens audiences through images of changed, supposedly monstrous bodies, undermining the very age and disability upon which the film relies. Similarly, Joan Crawford and Bette Davis stage their appeal to a continued audience by depicting aging bodies, also relying on and exploiting the age and disability of the characters they portray. The metaphoric parallels to their own careers, troubling as they are, resonate with audience members who remember both women as screen queens. *Sunset Boulevard* presents Gloria Swanson in a role she did not exactly choose. In taking on the part of Norma Desmond, she capitulates to Hollywood standards of youthful beauty, but not taking the part would amount to the same thing since it would keep older women off the screen. Swanson relies on the very aging that keeps her out of Hollywood to regain entrance.

Together, these self-reflexive films expose the crux of Russo's scandal of anachronism when applied to screen actresses and their careers. To risk acting against one's age is to risk 'ridicule, contempt, pity, and scorn' in order to remain defiantly alive. But when those audience reactions accompany a choice to act onscreen past a supposedly suitable age, a career dramatically changes or even ends. No longer the objects of stylized romantic appeal, no longer appropriate vehicles for the 'male gaze,' these actresses, in risking the scandal of anachronism, move into differently embodied roles that dramatize the women's helplessness before industry expectations, but at least keep them working. It is for this very reason that Russo's risk becomes 'necessary and inevitable *as a sign of life.*'

These films are set shortly after the beginning of the baby boom and before the panic about what aging baby boomers would mean socially, politically, and economically. Collectively they try to make aging femininity out to be so frightening that it is almost not to be feared. That is, by exaggerating the characters' self-delusions the films encourage audience members to think that just as they could never be quite as beautiful as the young Crawford, Davis, or Swanson, so too their old age could never be quite so horrifying. By reducing the actresses' and their characters' aging to different forms of disability, the films reveal a tension that is exacerbated by the public personas of the actresses. Aldrich and Wilder count on audience members to understand grey hair and wrinkles as obvious decay and decline and to experience a concomitant anxiety about identity, self, and meaning. In these representations, the pathologization of disability – wherein Norma Desmond is patronized, Jane Hudson threatened with institutionalization, and Blanche Hudson incarcerated in her own home – is commensurate with a pathologization of the aging star. Thus, analysing the films from a disability perspective illuminates the triple bind (female, disabled, old) facing the actresses (both fictional and actual). These films collectively reveal the public fixation on the association of aging with disability that preoccupies the silvering screen.

Chapter three

Grey Matters: Dementia, Cognitive Difference, and The 'Guilty Demographic' on Screen

I think there's an inherent drama in the family story because people are stuck together.

Tamara Jenkins[1]

The spectacle of aging femininity onscreen continues to intrigue audiences. A large number of old actors now insist on central cinematic roles, and the automatic association of their age with decline, signified as disability, remains. As discussed in the previous chapter, disability helped to magnify the helplessness of actresses past their prime and whose acting styles were also passé in the mid-twentieth century. However, the actresses were at most middle-aged, and their main anxieties were about the ability to maintain theatrical careers. In more recent cinema, disability on the part of the elderly signifies a broader social spectrum: the burden that aging boomers threaten to become.

Whereas in the last chapter I focused on the conflation of age with disability in earlier Hollywood films, in this chapter I look at three more recent films (two of them made outside the United States) that endeavour to separate out aging *with* a disability from aging *without* a disability, thereby to some extent distinguishing the aging figure onscreen from the disabled aging figure onscreen. In the following analysis of three early twenty-first-century films that single out aging with a disability from aging, I show how contemporary cinema articulates the worst and best case prospects for an aging population given current social attitudes, neither of which prospect is particularly rosy.

The Belgian film *Pauline and Paulette* (Lieven Debrauwer, 2001) depicts a character with a disability who is growing old, the Danish film *En*

Sång för Martin (hereafter *A Song for Martin,* Bille August, 2001) depicts a character who acquires a disability as he ages, and the U.S. film *The Savages* (Tamara Jenkins, 2007) depicts a character who is already old and recently has become disabled. In each case, the disability makes the process of aging extreme and separate from what presumed-to-be-able audience members expect their late lives to be. The first two films offer the audience a touchstone aging character easing into retirement with few worries but the care of a disabled relative. The third briefly touches on a normative old age, but focuses more closely on two almost middle-aged, deeply troubled characters with trite worries that overwhelm them to the extent that care decisions about their father appear to present an unreasonable and unmanageable extra burden.

While these films offer a glimpse of a free and retired life tinged with loneliness, the cognitive disabilities portrayed in these films amplify the normative ravages of age, especially on the mind. Pauline ends up in the most brightly lit, friendly, and nurturing institution imaginable, reassuring audiences who interpret the film as an accurate representation of lived reality that placing a family member in such a setting is in fact the best possible 'solution' to late-life care problems. The institutions that house Martin and Lenny (in *The Savages*) are portrayed as viable and the only rational option for the non-disabled characters who must be free to live their own lives.

The representation of Pauline is relatively unique among those on the silvering screen. Very few films focus on a character already disabled at the point of growing old, and even fewer look at a character who has always lived with a cognitive disability. As such, her portrayal is of keen interest in charting the relationship between disability and old age on film. More typically, the placeholder for cognitive disability in late life is Alzheimer's or, less often, other forms of dementia (as highlighted in *A Song for Martin* and *The Savages*). Etymologically derived from 'going away' and 'the mind,' dementia symbolizes loss not only of memory for the individual but also of the role the family patriarch or matriarch supposedly ought to play for others.[2] Alzheimer's is a form of geriatric dementia that has extreme popular currency to the extent that it has become a polite way to be rude about older people. That is, while it is largely considered insulting to explain an aging parent's behaviour by stating, 'well, he's eighty you know,' it invites sympathy (for the speaker if not necessarily for the 'patient') to explain that same behaviour by saying 'well, he has Alzheimer's.' Similarly, it is the highest praise to exclaim, 'he's eighty, but he's still *with it*.' Everyone is expected to know what this entails and that this is good (and everyone is expected to understand that, unlike Pauline, he has always previously been 'with it').

In mass media, literature, and film, Alzheimer's disease offers a cunning demotic for late life because it magnifies what people fear most about how age could manifest itself – that is, in an apparent loss of sense and self. The erosion of memory feeds well into stories of both loss and regret – especially when what one begins to forget is what one sought to ignore in the past. Alzheimer's thereby becomes a quick way to symbolize not just other forms of dementia but also old age more generally. As playwright and age scholar Anne Davis Basting puts it, Alzheimer's 'has swollen into a fear that permeates the cultural consciousness.'[3] Aging in itself can seem less disquieting when there is a worse way to grow old. When Alzheimer's becomes synonymous with growing old, those not living with the disease can define themselves as not yet old.

This is not to deny the incredible life-changing devastation this disabling illness can wreak on patients, their family, friends, and care workers. Witnessing a relative become demented has its physical horrors, but also equals witnessing a loss of cultural memory, of family history, and ultimately of a past as well as of a future. The general public – with or without personal experience – frequently connects Alzheimer's with the most horrifying possible loss of self. This deeply embedded assumption persists despite the ongoing lack of 'cultural understanding' referenced by Basting. As a result, a character that is becoming demented appears on the silvering screen to neatly signify a set of simple losses rather than to convey the complex transformations that cognitive decline invites and entails.

For cultural scholars, in addition to the most popular notion that dementia eradicates the self, Alzheimer's and related conditions come to signify a fear of lack of memories that translates similarly into a fear of the loss of story. Scholarship on Alzheimer's narratives focuses largely on selfhood, and so there is a strong tendency to think about Alzheimer's narrative role in terms of autobiography.[4] Autobiography theorist Paul John Eakin features a specific man with Alzheimer's as an example of the 'narrative identity system' when it 'breaks down altogether.'[5] For Eakin, the most troubling dimension of this abandoned Alzheimer's patient is not the risk to his life but his lack of stories. The ailing figure symbolizes, for Eakin, 'the fate that might await us all if our social identities should become unmoored from their narrative anchor in autobiographical memory.'[6] As Basting makes clear in another context, this is a limited understanding of identity. As she puts it, 'The history and context of the traditional autobiography, in which a consistent "I" tells a chronological tale of selfhood, make it inhospitable to representations of relational identity.'[7] At stake for Eakin is what he calls 'de-storied individuals' – a potential future for all Americans.[8] Basting imagines a possibility for a re-storied or story-free individual who creates selfhood collaboratively from within a new creative cognitive state.[9]

Eakin's prized narrative of neo-liberal individualism makes the erosion of the self and the dependence that accompanies Alzheimer's disease so powerful. As Basting puts it, 'In a country [the United States] that declared its "independence" and that prides itself on its bootstrap success stories and its rugged individualism, Alzheimer's disease is the ultimate nightmare.'[10] Just as conventional autobiographies stick hubristically to the idea that an individual ought to be able to write coherently from memory his own story, silvering screen portrayals of dementia impose narrative coherence on a fractured self during a confusing and confused time. [11]

Pauline and Paulette, A Song for Martin, and *The Savages* provide a spectrum of the significance of the failure to achieve such coherence. As such, they differ in their gauges of normalcy. In *Pauline and Paulette*, the character Pauline is depicted as always having been extraordinary and, to extend Rosemary Garland Thomson's description of the physically othered body to cognitive difference, always having had a disability and always having required care.[12] In this sense, Pauline's disability does not introduce anything new into the dynamic of the family who cares for her. Instead, it is her caregiver sister's death and her other sisters' advancing ages that call into question what normal will become. In *A Song for Martin*, the character Martin is depicted as having long been extraordinary, but not in Thomson's sense of the word.[13] His prodigious talent and admirable mind set up his decline as a stark contrast from the lives he and his new wife had only recently established as their normal. In *The Savages*, Lenny is depicted as having been an impressively inadequate father who now fits Thomson's description of extraordinary (i.e., disabled), and so merits more attention than he would have otherwise from his disgruntled offspring. A comparison of the films and the care situations they portray brings into question the attempt to impose a distinction between 'normal' old age and 'extraordinary' old age.

As Thomson explains,

The meanings attributed to extraordinary bodies reside not in inherent physical flaws, but in social relationships in which one group is legitimated by possessing valued physical characteristics and maintains its ascendancy and its self-identity by systematically imposing the role of cultural or corporeal inferiority on others. Representation thus simultaneously buttresses an embodied version of normative identity and shapes a narrative of corporeal difference that excludes those whose bodies or behaviors do not conform.[14]

Again, when her explanation is extended to the cognitive realm, this described process of attributing meaning to extraordinary older people works differently for Pauline than it does for Martin or Lenny. Pauline's surviving sisters certainly gain from their comparison to her, though ultimately they are responsible for her care. Martin and his wife are intimately intertwined so that his decline momentarily weakens her. Lenny's children seem youthful in comparison to him, though their life narratives imply that they are still seeking the opportunities that should have been their 'right' in their earlier years (such as career satisfaction and romantic happiness). All three films set up a normative aging – of peaceful but lonely retirement – in relation to the messiness of Pauline, Martin, and Lenny's latter years. More importantly, these filmic constructions picture a world in which there is a clear normative age identity and a clear exclusion of those who simply cannot conform.

Pauline and Paulette interrogates potential caregiver Paulette's retirement as much as it does disabled Pauline's late-life care needs. The two films about dementia (*The Savages* and *A Song for Martin*) focus on time as knowable and retrievable for other characters at a point in the life course when time diminishes in significance for the patient. While such films usually contain at least a veiled lament for the 'patient's' selfhood, they usually are more preoccupied with the selfhood of the figures surrounding the character with dementia. Rather than mourn the fractured subjectivity of the 'de-storied individual,' I examine here how the silvering screen over-stories the cognitively disabled characters, revealing that the apparently automatic significance of Alzheimer's as a simple and horrifying loss of self is in fact strangely forced in order to illuminate a broader range of late-life experiences. Ironically, optimism about potentially liberating later lives (retirement, career pinnacles) requires the depiction of the opposite trajectory. Characters must push dementia away from themselves and onto other bodies to appear to succeed.

'A rock in it': *Pauline and Paulette*

Pauline and Paulette is charmingly stylized; each of the three non-disabled sisters is associated with a colour scheme that includes her dress and home. The intellectually disabled sister takes on the colour scheme of the sister who hosts her. This technique illuminates the ways in which she is dependent on her family members for care, as well as the ways in which her own desires are not valued. At the opening of the film, a very drab and dour Martha (Julienne De Bruyn) in brown helps Pauline (Dora van der Groen) through her daily routine of eating toast with jam, watering flowers, tying her shoelaces, updating her scrapbook, and sneaking off to see her favourite sister, the decadent Paulette (Ann Petersen), who dresses entirely in shades of red and pink. Martha dies suddenly shortly after the opening of the film, launching opulent Paulette and cool, all-white Cecile (Rosemarie Bergmans) into a crisis about what to do with their embarrassing, sixty-six-year-old sister Pauline. The potential care-giver sisters Cecile and Paulette fantasize about how they will spend Martha's sizeable legacy; they argue about the merits of institutionaliza-tion for Pauline, who appears confused about Martha's whereabouts but extremely happy at the prospect of living in her favourite sister Paulette's dress shop. Cecile is against institutionalization but she is not willing to host Pauline. She knows very well that the task would fall to Pauline's fa-vourite sister, Paulette.

A scene in which Martha's will is read out by a solicitor reveals the competing interests among the three remaining sisters. Primary care-giver Martha has anticipated her sisters' antipathy towards actually car-ing for Pauline, having no doubt dealt with it for years previous. The solicitor announces that Martha's will divides her estate evenly among the three remaining sisters provided that either Cecile or Paulette take care of Pauline in one of their homes. The will is explicit that if Paulette and Cecile choose to institutionalize Pauline, all the money will go to Pauline (presumably to pay for her care). The camera focuses on the dismay of the two non-disabled sisters as they imagine their worlds turn-ing the drab brown of Martha's past. The camera then cuts to a close up of Paulette who gives a satisfied and seemingly oblivious sigh.

The provisions of Martha's will initially seem designed to keep Pauline out of institutional care in their articulation that either Cecile or Paulette takes Pauline into one of their own homes. Martha plays on her sisters' greed. However, her will also conveys to her sisters, and to the audience, that the work Martha has done, specifically the care she has given to Pauline, is valuable. If Paulette and Cecile are not willing to pay the price (that is, take on that work), then the monetary cost will be very high and will likely require Martha's entire estate.

Although Pauline's speech is not always clear and her memory seems fragile, she is always absolutely clear on where she would like to be and is unswerving in her desire to spend time with Paulette whom she adores, apparently without reciprocation. Even before Martha's death, she takes every opportunity to run to Paulette's dress shop. After Martha dies, Pauline plainly repeats that she would like to live with Paulette. Viewers may be encouraged to identify with Paulette's desire for an independent life and need to make a living without interruption from her burdensome sister, but they also are compelled to understand Pauline's desire not to move into an institution. The film shows few scenes of Pauline's comprehension, with the exception of repeatedly conveying her intuitive sense that institution talk is bad for her and her dogged persistence in desiring her favourite sister's company.

While Paulette displays only embarrassment and annoyance at Pauline's affections, she implausibly turns out to be able to accomplish feats her dour predecessor never imagined possible simply by trying. Saddled with Pauline temporarily, Paulette cannot possibly imagine the mundane task of preparing Pauline's breakfast each day, and the film implies that it is quite simple for Pauline to change her daily patterns. The camera shows Paulette simply holding Pauline's hands to demonstrate how she can cut her own toast. Further, Paulette is not willing to bend her aging and no longer supple body to tie Pauline's shoelaces, as Martha had struggled to do on a daily basis, and so she improvises by having Pauline place her foot on a step-stool to make the task easier on the two of them. Paulette and Martha's physical limitations are tied to their aging, but they do not qualify as disability in the way that Pauline's differences do. The stiffness of Paulette's body is depicted as a natural part of the aging process and is thereby invisible as disability despite its visibility as impairment.

Despite overcoming these obstacles with relative ease, Paulette argues that she requires – and the film implies that she deserves – an independent retirement by the sea. The burden of caring for and being publicly embarrassed by Pauline is so great that Paulette forfeits her (and Cecile's) inheritance in order to be alone again. The institution in which she proposes to place Pauline is depicted as a haven for disabled adults. The inmates have seemingly unlimited access to individuated assistance with arts and crafts projects, and also seem free to roam the building, visit one another's rooms, and fill their spaces with their own possessions. Once the institution makes room for her, Pauline is finally among equals and she quickly makes friends, but never relinquishes her yearning for Paulette.

While the film reassures audience members about the comfort of the institutional setting, Paulette (free of Pauline) realizes that her solitary life leaves her lonely, and her attempts to converse with strangers who surround her only irritate them. From a potential caregiver taking on a valuable (or at least expensive) social role, she transforms into a redundant old person, who saps others' energy, time, and resources. The value of Pauline's company dawns on her as she also comes to recognize that she had appreciated the quirky details of everyday life through Pauline's eyes. The film had previously depicted Pauline's endearing surprise to find ice in her drinking glass, upon which she always exclaims, 'There's a rock in it!'[15] As Paulette sits alone in a seaside restaurant and fails to engage other customers or the waiter in conversation, she glances across to a neighbouring table and sees an abandoned glass with ice still in it. She begins to laugh; then she cries as she appreciates Pauline's role and her unusual perspective on what to other people might seem mundane.

In the following scene, the two sisters briefly reunite near Paulette's new seaside home, and the breeze catches hold of stamps that Pauline's new friend from the nursing home has given her. They disperse around the sisters like confetti, signalling a potential freedom from institutionalized care if the two sisters – one old and disabled and one merely old and a bit stiff – work together. The scene shows the joy that Paulette has learned to gain from Pauline's company, and it reinforces the film's argument against a solitary old age. Critics and scholars alike read this film as primarily about disability (and are often eager to pinpoint the 'mental age' of Pauline, which they place somewhere between two and six years old, as though such normative measures are meaningful). Indeed, Pauline's disability drives the plot, and the crisis of the film – the need to care for Pauline at a moment when her caregiver's health has failed and her potential other caregiver 'deserves' a peaceful retirement – is unbreakably tied to that disability.[16]

Pauline represents another side of Paulette, as suggested by their similar names. Paulette's old age separate from Pauline's disability is desolate. She requires her disabled sister for a fulfilling late life. People with cognitive disabilities growing older fare much better than those without, and not because those with cognitive disabilities have some putatively youthful 'mental age;' all the inmates of the institution that Pauline stays at, young and old, have the company and care they need. It's Paulette, outside of that setting, who languishes. Her old age requires disability for narrative richness and for normative strength.

'The disaster is a fact': A Song for Martin

Bille August's A Song for Martin poses questions about the responsibility of a new but older wife for a husband who begins to experience symptoms of Alzheimer's. *A Song for Martin* interrogates the ways in which Alzheimer's upheaves romance by portraying a number of clichés about loss of self, physical disgust, and dissonant time. Most importantly, as *Pauline and Paulette* relieves Paulette and Cecile from the need to care for their dependent sister, *A Song for Martin* alleviates Martin's new lover Barbara from her responsibility for the person who is portrayed as no longer the man she recently married, freeing her to return to a 'normal,' that is productive, life. Unlike Paulette, Barbara revels in her regained freedom. Because Martin's and her devoted love is new, unlike the long devotion of so many other films discussed in this book (the focus of the next chapter), viewers need not be taken backwards in time (with the flashbacks so popular on the silvering screen) to understand what is lost. The absence of retrospect emphasizes the need for the maintenance of normalcy in the face of present calamity.

In the opening scene, after diegetic orchestral music foreshadows dramatic calamity, the title character Martin Fischer's (Sven Wollter) lover-to-be Barbara Hartman (Viveka Seldahl) corrects him in a composition error, further foreshadowing the roles they will play for each other. They hastily begin an affair that leads to an equally hasty wedding. Though their ages do not initially hinder them, they receive ageist judgment from very early on in the film; for example, Barbara's son Philip, on learning of her intention to leave his father for Martin, calls her 'pathetic' because she's 'too old for this.' Immediately after the honeymoon montage, signs of Martin's dementia begin to appear in that he forgets actions he has just completed. Not jumping to the obvious conclusion, the couple researches cerebral hemorrhages based on Martin's description of the feeling 'as if something fell' in his head, 'Fell and fell and disappeared.' This figure of loss preoccupies the remainder of the film.

The first of many medical scenes (typical of Alzheimer's movies) shows the local general practitioner informing the couple that Martin must be careful of overexertion and then articulating the cliché 'we're not getting any younger.' With the idea of Martin and Barbara's advanced age well set up, the film treats Alzheimer's as old age writ large. After a CAT scan, a neurologist notably younger than the general practitioner diagnoses Martin with very early stage Alzheimer's, explaining, 'The impairment of memory is a typical symptom of Alzheimer's. Nerve cells in the cerebral cortex have been destroyed – and the blood flow has been reduced.' She then describes Alzheimer's in terms commonly associated with old age itself, saying, 'There's no cure. Not to give you false hope but there have been cases where the disease has progressed very slowly.

But it can also go the other way.' While of course this medical specialist is referring to particular biological processes, which she has illustrated to be quantifiable via the CAT scan images, similar statements are made metaphorically within the film about the progress of age. There is no cure for old age, and it can progress slowly or very quickly.

Following this diagnostic scene, the next image of Barbara shows her stripped of the glamour associated with her role as a first violinist, entirely without the appearance of make-up, her bare face appearing more marked by time than her previously adorned face had seemed. Indeed, she appears to have aged very rapidly. Martin's Alzheimer's and accordingly his old age both progress very quickly, seeming to prove, indeed, Philip's ominous words that the couple is too old for 'this,' that is, heady romance. At their late age, the limits to their health limit their antics.

The title *A Song for Martin* does not refer to any of Martin's compositions, but rather to the traditional birthday song, which his family sings for him shortly before he is moved to an institution where Barbara chooses to make her final visit on their wedding anniversary. Birthdays and anniversaries are ritualized markers for the passage of time. Since Martin doesn't understand why they're singing to him, the family performance amplifies the normative passage of time as incomprehensible to the Alzheimer's patient. As reviewer Stephen Holden puts it, 'Martin's ability to finish the opera he has been working on becomes a losing race against time.'[17] Martin's confusion becomes apparent in a repeated shot of him looking at the clock and checking it against his watch after Barbara has chided him for repeating composition work from the previous day that he has forgotten about.

Shortly after his first lapses, Martin advises his daughter not to give up her career in music because 'you can't separate your self from your creative spirit. They're one.' According to the same logic, after his opera manuscript turns out to contain many blank pages, fellow characters begin pre-mortem to lament his passing. Barbara explains to Martin's friend and agent Biederman (Reine Brynolfsson), 'Martin is in no fit state to finish the opera. What we all feared has happened. The disaster is a fact. I'll send you the blank score, just for the record.' Rather than the horrifying violent and angry scenes that follow, Barbara seems to label disaster as the loss of the 'real' Martin, evidenced by the failure of his previously understandable, conventional creations in the form of classical orchestral compositions. As reviewer Mark Jenkins puts it, 'Martin's illness may be within his brain, but it's an intruder, not part of his personality.'[18]

While she attempts to care for Martin at home despite her growing resentment, time stops for Barbara. In one of her most vicious moments, she snaps at Martin, 'That's why I've given up my job. So I can stay here and look after you night and day. See? I'm washing off your shit. I hate doing it, but I do it all the same because you're a poor helpless soul who's dependent on me. Do you realize that?' This interruption to Barbara's life is emphasized immediately after she is forced to leave Martin at the hospital because he becomes unmanageable. Upon returning home, Barbara goes to the very clock he has constantly checked and stops the pendulum. She explains to Biederman that when Martin stopped composing, music outside her home also stopped for her. Some time after having adamantly insisted that she will not return to work, she accepts the interpretation that her husband effectively no longer exists and tacitly changes her mind. The film ends after she visits Martin in the hospital on their wedding anniversary (a marker of time) to say what appears to be her final goodbye. She goes home and restarts the clock's pendulum before going to Biederman to ask for her job back. In this scene, her face is shown fully re-adorned and her visage does not show the age that appeared in the close-up shot immediately following Martin's initial Alzheimer's diagnosis.

This return to her life as though uninterrupted crystallizes the ways in which normalcy raises its ugly head in relation to the effect of Alzheimer's on Martin and Barbara's lives. The neurologist prescribes normalcy, saying, 'The best advice I can give you is to try to live normally.' In describing Martin's state to her son Philip, Barbara sets up a very clear sense of normalcy impinged upon by the changes to his cognitive state, 'His memory lapses affect our lives. It hurts his pride especially now – when he's writing his opera. So much is at stake. And he's aware of it, which doesn't help. Then suddenly his memory is fine and things are back to normal.' After a predictable scene wherein Martin fails to conduct himself as an ordinary audience member at a performance of *The Magic Flute* – an opera he had earlier shown his great expertise in – Barbara chastises him, saying 'We can't go out for one night and act like normal people.' By acknowledging Martin as lost, never again having the potential for a 'normal' working or romantic life, Barbara frees herself to pursue normalcy, returning to 'act like a normal person' in regaining her career.

After witnessing the opera audience debacle, Biederman explains to Barbara his cowardly avoidance of his former friend and client, saying 'I can't stand to see Martin like this. The man that I admired, worshipped even, is no more. I don't know how to relate to him, what to do or say. It hurts me to see him like this.' Though these words initially appal Barbara, she later adopts the same perspective on her husband once the neurologist advises her, 'It would be best for you to accept that he's no longer your husband. Not the man you married.' She cannot contain her disgust, exploding repeatedly at Martin and thereby seeming to cause confusion for him as well as more stress than his Alzheimer's inflicts. In the end, the film tries to make acceptable her choice to pursue a normal life, wherein she can politely not just attend but perform in the opera. Martin foils normalcy only for the amount of time it takes Barbara to explore the limits of acceptable daily life, to witness the degradation of the body – both defecation and urination humiliate the couple – and to rewrite Martin as lost because his compositions make no sense to her or his former audiences. Alzheimer's creates an old person who can responsibly be abandoned in order for a previous caregiver to make room for a socially endorsed, youth-emulating late life, an approach embraced by Barbara in the final scenes.

During the honeymoon montage, Barbara and Martin are pictured solemnly pledging to stay true to each other, and especially not to hide anything or lie to each other. Alzheimer's challenges this vow. As Barbara tells Martin shortly after the initial diagnosis, 'You can't just disappear into yourself. You promised never to shut me out.' Ultimately, however, the film depicts Martin not disappearing *into* himself but disappearing *as* himself. The loss of normalcy is also interpreted throughout the film as the loss of Martin's self not so much for Martin, who is perfectly content when repeatedly composing the same passages of music, but for those who expect a certain performance from him.

'You are the guilty demographic': *The Savages*

In Tamara Jenkins's *The Savages*, estranged siblings are called upon to care for an objectionable father who is sliding into dementia, but who is only slightly more repulsive in his ill state than he seems to have been previously. In the absence of a normalcy to return to, *The Savages* offers a gritty comedy about having to care for, or find care for, a relative who is despised for good reason. The early middle-aged characters in *The Savages* try to fit themselves into popular ideas about responsible offspring despite their apparently radical leanings. The film opens with a surreal image of Arizona's retirement perfection to which Lenny Savage (Philip Bosco) has retired, away from his estranged children Jon and Wendy Savage (Philip Seymour Hoffman and Laura Linney); this opening scene highlights the drudgery of late-life care that appears later in the film. A montage of clean, sunny, symmetrical retirement images – including palm trees, synchronized water aerobics, and lawn bowling – is accompanied by the Peggy Lee version of H.W. Petrie's 'I don't want to play in your yard,' signalling that this eerie symmetry is not viable.[19]

Even with this opening suburban idyll, viewers are quickly met with the horrors contained within the simulacrum. As reviewer Ella Taylor neatly summarizes it, 'An instinctive provocateur, Jenkins gleefully rubs the more graphic symptoms of dementia in our faces – as well she should, given the emotional fallout of dealing with a man who covers a bathroom wall with his own feces.'[20] Lenny's act – rather than flushing the toilet as requested, he paints the walls with its contents – is depicted as 'savage' (a reference to the film's troubled title) as well as premeditated, though it seems to baffle him. When his wife dies suddenly during a manicure, her children call upon Jon and Wendy to leave Never Never Land and take responsibility for feces-friendly Lenny who appears to be re-entering the childhood they are reluctant to relinquish.

In *The Savages*, the white-coated doctor's authority makes little difference to the altered subjectivity of the patient or the positioning of his newly involved family members, but a seemingly obligatory appeal to empiricism helps clarify the bizarre new situation of this dysfunctional family unit. In the prototypical medical scene explaining Lenny's condition, a doctor goes into minute detail in his explanation to Jon and Wendy. To Wendy's question, which points to a cultural benchmark of unsuccessful aging, 'Is it like Alzheimer's?' the doctor offers the maladjusted siblings (and the viewing audience) a patient lecture in reply, 'There are a lot of illnesses that can cause dementia. I'm not prepared to make a diagnosis yet, but I think his symptoms are much more characteristic of Parkinson's disease.' The distinction is irrelevant to the silvering screen, but the film takes pains to make it seem pivotal in order to set up a comparative figure (Alzheimer's) that the audience understands as devastating and symbolic of a worst-case scenario in late life.

While the siblings gaze at images of Lenny's failing brain, the doctor spells out the prognosis with the only source for optimism being the potential for an early death, saying, 'Well, he's not a young man, so cardiac or respiratory failure may spare him from the worst of it.' The doctor explains that there are plenty of physical symptoms likely to accompany the cognitive lapses: 'tremors when the limbs are at rest, a shuffling walk, freezing up, unable to initiate movement, more and more loss of motor coordination in general.' From the eerily orderly shrubs in the Arizona suburb and the similarly sterile atmosphere of the hospital, the siblings enter the disarray of a symptomatic lack of physical and mental control.

Some reviewers claim it makes perfect sense for *The Savages* to avoid Lenny's perspective in favour of his children's because, as John C. Williams puts it, 'This is a film about life – by virtue of his disease, Lenny can't be a part of it.'[21] In fact, the loss of that 'life' could very well have guided the film, and the avoidance of that narrative is telling.[22] The film focuses more on Jon and Wendy as immobilized by their father's past treatment of them and by his present need for care from them than it focuses on his mental immobilization and his decline from his past self. Rather than witness Lenny's fear at a loss of faculties and concomitant sense of self, viewers see only glimmers of his reactions as he glowers and turns off his hearing aid so as to not hear his arguing offspring. In fact, Lenny is more or less characterized as always an obstacle to happiness for his children, but Wendy at least tries to perform compassion due to his condition. His past treatment of her provides material for her budding authorial career, and his current condition provides material upon which she can build a transformed sense of self, based on altruism and significant action.

Lenny's dementia offers an agile symbol for the plight of the baby boomers, with healthier (for now) boomers quickly paraded through his for-sale Arizona home as an example of the proliferation of the retirement set. Jon and Wendy's generalized malaise (neither has a satisfying career or a fulfilling love life) more clumsily symbolizes the boomers' effect on Xers. Worried about seeming too 'self-important and bourgeois,' these lost souls struggle with what care situation they can best afford, apparently never having had access to the career opportunities open to Lenny's age cohort.

As a cynical Brecht scholar focused more on argument than on emotion, Jon skeptically rejects Wendy's susceptibility to the discourse of what one brochure calls 'distinctive innovative stimulating senior living,' choosing instead Valleyview, which, as he describes it, 'has an empty bed, they take Medicaid and it's right near my home.' Audiences witness Wendy captivated by a different facility's promotional video's claims: 'We know this is one of the toughest decisions of your life. What to do with the parent who took care of you when they can no longer take care of themselves?' As Jon points out, Lenny was not the parent 'who took care of' Wendy, and Jon tells her, 'We're taking better care of the old man than he ever did of us.' Wendy's increasing desire to place him in Greenhill Manor reveals her desire to be interpellated into an idealized family narrative. While the film articulates almost too clearly the mechanisms behind this process in a dialogue between the siblings, it likely touches on the competing perspectives among audience members facing similar limited choices and desiring to feel better about the available options, especially those changes that least impose upon 'normal' life while appearing to be 'best' for the patient. Jon tells Wendy, 'you are the consumer they want to target. You are the guilty demographic. The landscaping, the neighborhoods of care – they're not for the residents, they're for the relatives, people like you and me who don't want to admit to what's really going on here.' The following scene shows Wendy's capitulation which takes the form of her furnishing Lenny's Valleyview room with decorative objects more to her taste than to her father's, attempting to alleviate the guilt.

'What's really going on here,' as Jon puts it, is that the siblings are witnessing their father decay towards death. The worry for them seems to be arranging a care situation, but Lenny is characterized as deteriorating at a rapid rate. Though his actual death is paid little heed in the film, predictably the Generation X characters find new life after the boomer character dies and especially when they are freed from the responsibility of having chosen what care he would receive. Wendy rehabilitates a dog that had been doomed to euthanasia, and sees her semi-autobiographical play produced. Despite his career-long commitment to argument, Jon dissolves into emotion, crying at a dress rehearsal of Wendy's play before leaving for Poland to attempt to salvage a relationship that was not significant enough to him prior to his father's death. *The Savages* is an obvious moral tale of what Generation X will gain when freed from the burdensome demographic of the boomers: namely, work and family stability. However, it exceeds a predictable oedipal pattern. In order to teach that lesson, the boomer representative must succumb to an Alzheimer's-like affliction, losing self, story, and control.

Conclusion

While neither of the characters who are becoming demented in *A Song for Martin* and *The Savages* has properly fit the role of patriarch, each still stands in for the loss of such a figure. Each of these films attempts to confer a role that is lost in the malaise of modernity onto a senile character. In *A Song for Martin*, marriage has dissolved into fractured 'blended' families; in *The Savages*, abuse has torn apart a family. In these films, other characters try to understand the senile characters in order to shore up their own sense of self and justify their ways of moving forward in the world. Martin's wife Barbara needs him to be competent enough to finish his opera or to step aside so that she can play in the orchestra again; Lenny's children need to find him adequate care without it impinging on their inadequate work lives. The horrifying loss of self much mourned in Alzheimer's discourse is such a given in these films that it serves mainly to magnify the self-explorations it enables in surrounding characters.

Other characters' senses of the patients' past selves dominate narratives about the erosion of self in extreme representations of old age. Collectively the films show that whether read literally or figuratively, dementia on the silvering screen stands in for larger cultural interpretations of what it means to grow old; not only does this mean a terrifying loss of control, but also a loss of self. The films focus on the responsible family members who must take on care of their relative who is becoming demented and that person's legacy. The films each convey an unsettling mix of guilt and liberation on the part of those 'left behind,' in the face of a loss of self that can translate into a loss of story.

The epigraph to this chapter cites an interview with *Savages* director Tamara Jenkins explaining that family evokes drama because it consists of people 'stuck together.' Paulette and Cecile are stuck with Pauline who transforms their latter years but not their earlier ones because of the mediation of their sister Martha. Barbara has stuck herself to Martin, marrying him hastily in late life only to find that he, or she, is not up to the commitment. Because they are not really 'family' in the sense that Jenkins implies, the drama can resolve itself by Barbara resuming a normal life, free of Martin and of his Alzheimer's. Jon and Wendy Savage are stuck with Lenny only through the accident of their births, and the film subtly reinforces an unexpected theme of family values in that these supposedly unconventional Xers buy into the compulsion to care for their father through a sense of familial duty that they want to, but cannot seem to, reject.

In each film, cognitive disability symbolizes the overall horror that is assumed to be part of the aging process. With Pauline, this is a milder fear of dependence or of having a loved one who is dependent. The loss of creative ability and physical control, evident in Martin through the fading from what little presence he had with his children and evident in Lenny, are more potent signs of what people most fear age to automatically mean. However, in these films, each of these signs of aging more significantly resonates onto those surrounding the patients, the 'guilty demographic.' The films actively contain deeds that threaten the perception of the human frame as contained and neat – particularly Martin and Lenny's defecation. These threats ooze through the simplistic narrative frames that attempt to control dementia in an effort to soothe social worries about an aging population. By contrast, *Pauline and Paulette* argues for an indomitable spirit that shines through the disabled characters' idiosyncratic minds, a spirit that – have no fear – will conquer the four walls of the institution, lovely though that place seems to be.

Chapters 2 and 3 have focused on the imbrication of disability with old age in both early and silvering screen films. Tied to the careers of the actors portraying them, disabled characters' late life is prime dramatic material. Beyond a metaphor for social decay, though, these bodies represent an imagined burden – particularly an economic one – when the matter of care comes into the picture. The next chapter picks up explicitly on the thread of caregiving and illuminates how the silvering screen worries about the increasing responsibilities falling to spouses in an aging world.

Chapter four

'Sounds Like a Regular Marriage': Monogamy and the Fidelity of Care

While romantic comedies and most screen dramas preoccupy themselves with mating, the societal function of the couple dominates the silvering screen. The eroticism may be toned down – though any hint of sex will result in repeated comments from reviewers because of its seeming incongruity – but the importance of heteronormative, monogamous units is heightened. This attention results in part from the connection between disability and aging that I have charted in the two previous chapters. While growing old seems to automatically imply disability, the type of disability that the films usually imagine is one that requires care. For example, the films do not imagine an elderly person going blind and then learning to walk with a white cane, but instead they imagine cognitive failures or terminal illnesses that require another person's attentions for the safe or comfortable existence of the disabled person. In this chapter, I examine how the spouse is deemed responsible for those attentions.

Particularly when faced with a lover's physical and/or cognitive 'decline,' a devoted spouse conveys the poignancy of elderly illness, which signifies impending death. To build on the work of Robert McRuer (especially in *Crip Theory*), while compulsory able-bodiedness can perhaps be relegated to the past for an older, ill body, compulsory heterosexuality persists. McRuer explains, 'Compulsory heterosexuality is intertwined with compulsory able-bodiedness; both systems work to (re)produce the able body and heterosexuality. But precisely because these systems depend on a queer/disabled existence that can never quite be contained, able-bodied heterosexuality's hegemony is always in danger of collapse.'[1] On the silvering screen, threats to able-bodiedness heighten heterosexual frameworks, resulting in unconvincing attempts to contain both.

queerness and disability. Projected relationships tend to be long term, which allows the films to meander through the past from the perspective of the lover who knew the patient when she was 'whole' and when either lover was less loyal.

This chapter shows how the silvering screen is deeply committed to spousal monogamy, particularly at a point when physical care is required, and yet its films tend to alight upon couples whose monogamous commitment has been challenged. Accordingly, I look at a set of love stories shadowed by infidelity. Each story involves a newly disabled or ill patient in need of care that must come either from within the 'family' or from the medical system in the form of a physical institution. The structure of family (i.e., childless couples) in three of the films discussed in this chapter especially demands monogamy and absolute commitment on the part of spouses who have not always conformed: *Elsker Dig for Evigt* (hereafter *Open Hearts*, Denmark, Suzanne Bier, 2002) depicts a young fiancée facing a future with a newly disabled potential spouse and a potential lifetime of his dependency; *Iris* (UK, Richard Eyre, 2001) depicts an older couple struggling to maintain their life independent from institutional care; and *Away from Her* (Canada, Sarah Polley, 2006) depicts spouses unexpectedly finding themselves amidst a challenging transition to institutional support. In all of the films, past infidelities haunt the present devoted relationship, threatening the social fabric that requires a sacrificial, loyal spouse to provide the care. As a respite, that care is depicted as equally available from institutions which appear in each film as shiny, efficient, desirable habitats.

The final film, *Les invasions barbares* (hereafter *Barbarian Invasions*, Canada, Denys Arcand, 2003), depicts a divorced couple with offspring and accordingly shifts the care responsibility onto a capital-obsessed son who barely recovers from disappointment in his erstwhile socialist, still debauched father, whom he ultimately helps to commit assisted suicide. While the dying character's former wife is present at his deathbed, so are two of his past mistresses, illustrating that even after the disintegration of the marriage, the infidelity that sank the couple pervades the care situation. The ex-wife still feels responsible for her dying ex-husband – a responsibility she is able to pass on to the son, who expertly negotiates the sub-par medical institution. The past marriage becomes little more than a bawdy joke that spawned a caricature of the contemporary market (as embodied by the son).

The institution in *Barbarian Invasions* is dirty, inept, and repulsive, and its corruption is forgivable only because the system is overburdened. The son's ability to buy off the hospital union and set his father up in alternate quarters emphasizes his father's present willingness to compromise on (betray) his socialist beliefs. By portraying formerly radical characters giving up on socialized medicine, and portraying the failure of the social safety net, the film conveys fiscal and social conservatism as obligatory but ultimately leading only to a comfortable rather than a disgraceful death. The patient cannot pretend at monogamy, even if he can undermine (Canadian) Medicare, and so he chooses not to submit to ongoing care (that is, he opts for illegal euthanasia).

On the silvering screen, ongoing care requires heterosexual monogamy even if that is only proven through infidelity. A focus on caregiving reveals a deep social anxiety about the institution of marriage and the role of the declining family in supporting boomers as they age. While care itself may not be sexy, need for care brings sexuality to the fore. In this chapter, I examine this process in *Open Hearts*, *Iris*, *Away from Her*, and *Barbarian Invasions*.

Open Hearts

In Suzanne Bier's Dogme 95 *Open Hearts* a young, nearly wed couple's bliss is cut short by an accident that leaves Joachim (Nikolaj Lie Kaas) paralysed and in a hospital bed. This film is not about old age, and though contemporaneous with the other productions, it is not a silvering screen film. However, age works as a fundamentally revealing category of analysis, and reading *Open Hearts* through its portrayal of age helps to clarify the work accomplished by similar films that do participate in silvering screen conventions. Joachim is an exaggeratedly active young man who is hit by a car as he sets off for a pre-marital climbing expedition. Age is pivotal to reading the film – not just because he is cut down before his 'prime,' but even more so because his potential caregiver (his fiancée, Cecilie [Sonja Richter]) has her 'whole life ahead of her.' She is not depicted as an aging spouse who has already lived the life she ought to and who owes him a debt of loyalty. Rather, she is a potentially fertile, aggressively sexual, yet naive young woman who only really knows how to express her love for Joachim through erotic attempts to physically arouse him despite his quadriplegia.

Writer Anders Thomas Jensen sets up a narratively convenient scenario wherein Cecilie has no living parents and Joachim's parents live in the United States so that the pressure of Joachim's newfound dependence falls on Cecilie. Stereotypically taking on the role of the bitter cripple, Joachim begins his convalescence sacrificially conveying spite towards Cecilie in order to free her from the burden of caring for him. That is, he treats her with cruelty not for his own relief but to drive her away. Joachim remains in critical care for the duration of the plot, and so the film never depicts a day-to-day caregiving routine. Rather, it highlights the drama of transitions: from a virile, risk-taking, young man to a 'boiled-spaghetti-armed' patient, and from a nubile wife-to-be to a promiscuous potential servant.

The only role for Joachim's future wife, once he is immobilized by the accident, is caregiver. Joachim says to her with vicious sarcasm, 'Let's get married tonight, and you can spend our wedding night wiping my ass.' While he appears to simply be taking his frustrations out on his fiancée, viewers witness, via the wise medical worker who knows better (and who also receives his spite), that Joachim sees that the only escape for Cecilie lies in his arousing hatred for him in her. Through the transition to awareness of a new lived reality for Joachim, the film focuses on the help that Joachim needs and who should best give it. Cecilie understands her moral obligation to be a sacrificial wife, saying to a very resistant Joachim, 'You're going to have to let me in on this. You're going to have to let me help you.' But hospital workers support his position, taking the time to tell her, 'The only way you can help him is by getting on with your life.'

Throughout the film, viewers witness Cecilie 'getting on with her life.' She begins an affair with Niels (Mads Mikkelsen), the doctor husband of Marie (Paprika Steen), the woman who mowed Joachim down. Joachim relents into a loving, non-sexual encounter with Cecilie. Reviewer Stephen Holden notes, '*Open Hearts* makes the point that an accident like Joachim's has an inevitable ripple effect, as crosscurrents of guilt, sympathy and the urge to fix what's broken collide.'[2] Extravagant need on the part of a spouse threatens the fabric of monogamy at the same time as it exposes a social need for it. *Open Hearts* exaggerates this strain further by portraying not only the dissolution of Cecilie and Joachim's fidelity, but also the sudden suspension of Niels and Marie's mutual devotion. Somehow the stereotype of a father leaving his children's middle-aged mother for a younger woman gains purpose in this setting. Disability disintegrates new and longstanding family units, in this case because it reinforces the ever-looming threat of sudden, externally motivated change and because it enhances corporeal being. In *Open Hearts*, the hospital picks up the social slack so that viewers can imagine that devotion, and not care work, is at stake in both Cecilie and Niels's actions.

Cecilie (Sonja Richter) 'getting on with her life' in *Open Hearts*. © Sundance/ Handout/WireImage/Getty Images

When Joachim allows Cecilie to 'help' him for an evening, the hopelessness of their new situation weighs on both of them, prompting him to (politely) set her free from obligation. He thus places himself in the capable hands of an institutional care-worker to whom he has been similarly cruel by bitterly attacking her grief over her dead son. Ultimately, rather than depicting renewed betrothal, the scene of recognition shows Cecilie being freed morally, emotionally, and actually from the bondage (as the film depicts it) of a life-long caregiving role. The bondage of the care-worker is portrayed as irrelevant as she only functions narratively to reassure the couple and the audience that Joachim will receive the care he requires. As Joachim tells Cecilie, as though he is moving towards solitude rather than institutional care,

All I ask is for you to come to see me from time to time and to help me a little especially at first. As time goes by more and more time will pass between visits. But by then I'll be much better at coping. There's no reason for *you* to suffer.

The accompanying scene begins with a stock feature of disability-themed, mainstream cinema: a dream shot (usually read as Cecilie's fantasy) wherein Joachim is still able to move his arms, if only in order to wave goodbye. Following this fuzzy fantasy that reassures audience members the virile young actor is distant from the patient he performs for their pleasure, the scene progresses to a more brightly lit, realistic shot of the institutionalized care setting he has chosen. The last view is of the reflection of the medical worker in the glass that separates her from her patient.

Iris

Richard Eyre's biopic *Iris* continually reminds viewers of the youthful vigour from which the title character Iris Murdoch's decline occurs, so the film does not as easily reassure audience members of their separation from the disabled character in the way that *Open Hearts* does. The *New Republic*'s Stanley Kauffmann offers an apocalyptic understanding of the film when he states,

> The people who made the film about Iris Murdoch began with several handicaps. Obviously no film could deal adequately with her ideas in philosophy, a subject that she taught and wrote about through most of her life; nor could it convey the texture of her novels. These limits would apply to any film about an intellectual and artist; but the handicap increases in *Iris* (Miramax) for the very reason that Murdoch was chosen as the subject. The mature Murdoch sickens with Alzheimer's, declines, and dies. This is not drama, it is certainly not tragedy; it is calamity.[3]

Iris is devastating in its repeated appeals to pathos, but the progression from vivacious philosopher to person with dementia to corpse is not quite as calamitous within the film's depiction as Kauffmann claims. Rather, as it does in *Pauline and Paulette* (see chapter 3) and *Open Hearts*, a residential institution appears, albeit implausibly, in the penultimate scenes as a clear example of the care that Iris needs in order to die happy, which she does moments after entering the institution.

Whereas *Open Hearts* depicts the choice on the part of a newly disabled person to get out of the way of his former lover and to succumb to high-quality institutional care, *Iris* depicts the imposition of an external will on a longstanding couple when the title character lands in an institutional space that has equally impressive facilities. An exaggeratedly sunny institutional solution relieves the silvering screen of responsibility for working out the mundane day-to-day care solutions that threaten to accompany an aging demographic. The older John Bayley (Jim Broadbent) is depicted as the selfless yet inadequate life partner and sole caregiver to the aging Iris Murdoch (Judi Dench), who increasingly experiences symptoms of Alzheimer's. Similar to in *Open Hearts*, the spectre of a shiny, efficient institutional care solution in *Iris* haunts John Bayley's attempts to keep his lover at home with him. While Cecilie and John may feel obligations to their afflicted spouses, there is another (possibly more desirable) solution evident (i.e., institutional care) that allows the issue of care to appear to be about sexual fidelity rather than about material means, physical realities, and social policies.

In *Iris*, the caregiving dilemma takes place between husband and wife. Iris's emerging need for care tests and proves the endurance of the corny love portrayed throughout the film. For Iris the issue is her aging as well as that of her caregiver. Judi Dench is marvellous in her depiction of Iris through the stages of her illness, but the role of older Iris is hardly exciting. Elaine Showalter explains,

> Totally without physical vanity, Dench is willing to look old, crazy, shabby, and fat – a heroic act of self-abnegation in Hollywood terms. But frankly, Dench could play this role with her eyes closed and both hands tied behind her back; parts for crazy old ladies are not scarce in the English theater, and she has already played most of them.[4]

Indeed, *Iris* is more about 'stuttering paramour' John Bayley's (Hugh Bonneville as the young John) struggle with Iris Murdoch's (Kate Winslet as the young Iris) irascible sexuality in youth and her unruly illness in late life than about her own reckoning with acquired disability. The fluidity of her sexuality morphs into a fluid sense of self, disrupted by Alzheimer's. Iris has to die the moment she enters the institution because John's heroic efforts end there, as does her unpredictability. The film *is* a tragedy, but it is John's tragedy.

At the climax of the film, John has long been plagued by Iris's profligate worldliness; her hatred of convention bumps up against his apparent desire for a monogamous, long love relationship despite his attempts to be as iconoclastic as she is. It is only in their twilight years that she appears to turn solely to him, at a time when she increasingly requires care to the point at which even his devotion cannot offer him the means to provide it.

The depiction of older Iris may be devastating, but the depiction of younger Iris by Kate Winslet is largely irritating. Critics praise the interweaving of the 1950s plot, when Murdoch is finishing her first novel, with the 1990s plot, when she is completing her last. For example, C. Joanne Grabinski claims of *Iris*,

> This is an especially rich film because of its use, intentional or not, of a life *course* perspective that weaves scenes from across Iris and John's 44-year relationship into the story of their final journey together through their experience with her Alzheimer's disease. Life-*stage* and chronological approaches that start at the beginning and work their way through the life story from beginning to end would not have made it possible to see the present immediately played against the past.[5]

While her point that a chronological approach would not be appropriate is well taken, I would argue that this film does take a life-stage approach. It does not 'weave scenes from across' Iris's life offering a life-course perspective; rather, it merely juxtaposes one brief stage of her youth (her university days) with her old age, which is especially intensified by the presence of Alzheimer's. As is typical of retrospective gerontological plots, the film makes no attempt to portray the middle years. The depiction of Iris's youth helps to convey the depth of the relationship ravaged by her late-life illness, but mostly amplifies the loss implied by the portrayal of her dementia.

Ironically, in the late-life plot, when John no longer worries that Iris will leave him, she flees from their home, and is unaware of her own whereabouts in a stereotypical scene of Alzheimer's movies. The wandering off frequently serves as the motivation to institutionalize a character with dementia as it serves as 'proof' not only that she is truly seriously ill, but also that her caregiver cannot adequately cope. The issue of safety serves as an unavoidable justification for a move into a professional care situation. When Iris runs away, John resorts to phoning the police and, in doing so, sacrifices the couple's apparent autonomy. A police officer arrives, and the camera follows her gaze to focus on an apple rotting beside the kitchen sink, a sight which interests her far more than John's words. As the camera pulls back and follows the police officer on a tour of the home, it nudges the viewer for the first time to notice the mess, squalor even, of the dwelling. Previously, viewers have been held within the captivating (if frustrating) romantic world of John and Iris juxtaposed as young adults and as older adults, without being called to notice

Judi Dench at home in *Iris*. © AFP/Stringer/AFP/Getty Images

the deteriorating condition of the house. The new focus on the distressing state of the couple's home allows audience members to gently shift from wanting Iris to stay at home with John to seeing the apparent need for her to enter an institution.

Iris's powerful effect comes from the portrayal of the deterioration of a great mind, 'a very clear mind,' as John Bayley explains to Iris's doctor. The film opens with her speech about the importance of education and the freedom of the mind, which emphasizes the progression of the disease later in the film when she does not understand why Tony Blair emphasizes 'education, education, education' in a televised speech and her mind evaporates (as shown in medical scans replicated onscreen). It is possible to read against the grain and argue that Iris has always had a free mind, incomprehensible to others, and that Alzheimer's merely intensifies that freedom to 'be in her own world.' However, her liberty bumps up against the pragmatics of her husband's incapacity to simultaneously take care of the house and his wife. Signs of squalor, Iris's incontinence, and dishevelled clothing emphasize the material effects of the lack of a 'woman's touch' in the home space. Audience members feel horror that even someone as brilliant as Iris Murdoch suffers the extreme ravages of old age, and yet are reassured that her old age is as unique as her intelligence, affected by a disease that, although growing in prevalence, still affects only a minority of the elderly population.

While in *Open Hearts* Cecilie is depicted as too young to be saddled with the burden of caring for Joachim, John is depicted as too old to competently care for Iris. In each scenario the moral obligation of care falls to a spouse, but each film ultimately frees the spouse from that obligation on the basis of age, though the characters' ages are vastly disparate. Each film values autonomy and so-called independence, so the ideal would be that Joachim would still be able to climb mountains and Iris would still be able to pursue her sexual freedom. However, when those active freedoms are no longer possible, the wounded parties must retreat to institutional care to leave the former spouses bereft but apparently autonomous.

Iris features an eerily parallel scene to that of Pauline's stamps caught in a sea breeze (discussed in chapter 3). Iris, deeply affected by Alzheimer's, reacts to her friend's (Penelope Wilton) request to sign her latest book by lifting stones from a row of notebook paper sheets that she has carefully placed beside her on the beach in an act that takes the place of writing. As the papers float away on the wind and into the ocean, her husband's desperate hopes that Iris will write again dissipate. While perhaps the liberated sheets symbolize the new freedom of Iris's mind, the film focuses more on John's perspective. Overall, the blowing paper in this film symbolizes the freedom that John will gain when the couple accepts that Iris needs professional care. When John concedes that Iris must go into care, she travels to a place with incredibly attentive caregivers who understand John's desire to stay nearby. Iris dances in a brightly lit hallway, showing herself to be utterly free, and then she dies. Like the papers, Iris floats away to death, leaving John yearning as he did in youth to have what she has.

While the film leaves a devoted John grieving Iris's death, the life story on which the film is based continues differently. In 'real life,' John Bayley went on to marry again within two years of Iris's death. He declared publicly that Iris benevolently haunts his new marriage, reinforcing through his declaration the structure of that institution through its apparent perversion. As described in an *Observer* interview, for Bayley 'marriage seemed once more the best defence against unwanted fuss.' To protect himself, as Iris's presence had, from an outside world, John proposed to

Judi Dench on the beach in *Iris*. © Clive Coote/Stringer/AFP/Getty Images

Audi Villers, a woman with whom he and Iris had long been friends. The new couple jokes about John's strange honeymoon quip: 'You know, I don't think I've ever missed Iris quite as much as I do right now.' Even in an article about his new marriage, his devotion to Iris persists. John and Audi's attempts to collectively hold off external pressures simply result in a new public union as John partakes in what is popularly named 'serial monogamy.'[6] After all, he has taken care of Iris, but who will take care of him?

Away from Her

Sarah Polley's directorial debut, *Away from Her*, adapts literary icon Alice Munro's short story 'The Bear Came over the Mountain' into a feature-length film that, like *Iris*, interrogates relationships among autonomy, monogamy, and institutional care. In her foreword to a revised (re-ordered and retitled) edition of Munro's story collection, Polley explains,

'I first read the story on a plane on my way home from Iceland, where I had just finished acting in a film with Julie Christie. My grandmother was gradually losing her grip on her independence and her memory.'[7] The film developed while Polley thought about her grandmother's situation through the words of Alice Munro's story. Polley writes, 'As my grandmother's health deteriorated, it became necessary to look for a retirement home for her to live in. It was a complicated process, and as we toured many institutions, I constantly heard the descriptions of Fiona's retirement home, Meadowlake, ringing in my ears.'[8] In the foreword, Polley lays out a clear conception of the relationship between fiction and experience, explaining that Munro's work functioned as a critical lens that helped her to understand her grandmother's ultimate relocation, writing, 'this story reshaped my idea of love, gave me a keener eye into the experience of my grandmother as she moved out of her home and into her final years.'[9]

Both the story and the film focus on Grant (Gordon Pinsent) and Fiona's (Julie Christie) forty-four-year marriage as affected by Fiona's increasing affliction with Alzheimer's and her choice to enter institutional care so as not to require Grant's aid. The story and the film meander through Grant and Fiona's romantic past, demonstrating its effects on their current living and loving situation. Polley captures these transitions with opening images of Fiona and Grant cross-country skiing, first on parallel tracks and then on diverging ones.

Casting Gordon Pinsent and Julie Christie in the lead roles, and Olympia Dukakis in a supporting role, allows Polley to tap into her audiences' familiarity with past roles in order to create a sense of aging and what it means for the characters. While critics mildly praise Pinsent, and acknowledge him as the focus of the camera, they rave about Julie Christie and comment on her role in relation to her past onscreen personas.[10] The film, then, is likely to resonate differently with different age cohorts. For example, while younger viewers may revel in the continuing onscreen grace, skill, and beauty of Christie, they are less likely to be familiar with her past appearances.[11] In addition to adoring Christie, critics praise Polley's film for focusing more on romance than on Alzheimer's. Almost all reviewers mention that the film would risk becoming a movie of the week if not for delving into the complexities of the flawed yet enduring love relationship between Grant and Fiona. Sean Axmaker writes, '*Away From Her* ... is less a drama about Alzheimer's disease than a cinematic poem of love and loss.'[12] Sean Burns claims in his subtitle, 'Sarah Polley's debut is a heartfelt look at marriage and Alzheimer's disease.'[13]

Fiona (Julie Christie) and Grant (Gordon Pinsent) at home in *Away from Her*. Image courtesy of Capri Releasing and Mongrel Media

Geoff Pevere summarizes the film by describing the marriage as primary to the secondary plot about Alzheimer's, saying, 'The actor-filmmaker's feature film debut is a quietly wrenching account of a marriage bond slowly being severed by the memory-erasing intrusion of Alzheimer's.'[14] These critics' comments about the dominance of the love story over the illness narrative are significant because they highlight one aspect of Munro's story that Polley changes most when she films it: the portrayal of the love relationship between the central characters; but they downplay another important change: Polley adds narration from biomedical and self-help books about Alzheimer's.

In Munro's story, Grant has been a perpetually unfaithful husband, continually tempted sexually by his university students, and rarely able to resist. However, he 'did not go overboard, at least in comparison with some people around him.'[15] His chief virtue seems to lie in having been a kind lover to his many conquests while still not leaving his wife; his luck lies in having indulged in what is now treated as sexual misconduct before sexual harassment policies permeated the academic setting.[16] He is cast as unique in this devotion in that his colleagues were mostly 'husbands and fathers who had been among the first to throw away their neckties and leave home to spend every night on a floor mattress with a bewitching young mistress, coming to their offices, their classes, bedraggled and smelling of dope and incense.'[17] Munro's Gordon and Fiona tacitly strike a deal wherein he retires early and gets away from the never explicitly confessed temptations to where there are 'no more hectic flirtations. No bare female toes creeping up under a man's pants leg at a dinner party. No more loose wives.'[18] They leave behind Grant's colleagues who eventually turn their backs on profligacy to replicate the marriages they had betrayed in new alliances with their former 'bewitching young mistress[es],' and subsequently offer Grant the cold shoulder for his misdemeanours.

Polley's film transforms Grant's betrayal by placing many of Grant's words from the story into Fiona's voice. In this way, she expands the potential of the silvering screen to an unparalleled sense of female agency, demonstrating that the films I discuss in this book vary in their representations of gender and of the possibilities of old age in spite of some telling similarities with relation to disability. The differences set Polley's work apart from the more mainstream images of aging I discuss elsewhere in this book and especially in the following two chapters (which both focus on Hollywood masculinity). Polley's film still dwells upon infidelity, incorporating Michael Ondaatje's poem 'The Cinnamon Peeler'[19] into the script as a text Grant reads to Fiona and naming a Czech student Veronica, with whom the film is more preoccupied than with his 'mature' mistress Jacqui Adams. Maintaining some sympathy for a male philanderer who invites praise for his seeming dedication to his once-scorned wife, the film nonetheless creates a vision of his self-sacrifice, sacrifice that may even involve further infidelity in order to incite an event that will create happiness for his wife. Polley transforms Grant's infidelity from the tired cliché of a licentious professor into a vague, unspoken memory that haunts the audience insofar as the concept of memory plagues the plot – that is, Fiona's capricious memory is what brings the past into the fore in the film narrative. In this way, the notably young director redirects sexual power into Fiona's hands even more so than Munro does in the written story.

At the fourteenth annual Screen Actors' Guild awards, Christie caused a stir by tacking on to the end of her speech a glib comment about Fiona's memory lapses, which are portrayed as humorous in the film.

Christie said, 'And if I've forgotten anybody, well, it's just that I'm still in character.' Peter Braun, chief executive officer of the California Southland Alzheimer's Association, does not assign blame for these thoughtless comments to Christie but rather to a broader set of misunderstandings about dementia. As he puts it, 'I don't think it's so much Julie Christie. I just think it's part of society's response to an issue that makes people nervous.' [20] The aspect of her character Christie jokes about, Fiona's forgetfulness, lands Fiona in Meadowlake, and the role of memory haunts the narrative, which is based largely on Grant's reminiscences. As Polley puts it, 'the things you remember, not in words but in the very molecules that make up your being, can be more painful than the things that are forgotten.'[21]

To Grant, the first signs of Fiona's dementia appear to enhance her 'direct and vague' personality, functioning on 'eccentric whims.'[22] He tries, in the story, to explain to the doctor that it seemed as though Fiona was 'playing a game that she hoped he would catch on to.'[23] In the film, Fiona is perplexed by what eludes her, as she tells guests at a dinner party before she moves to Meadowlake, 'The thing is, half the time I wander around, looking for something I know is very pertinent, and I can't remember what it is. Once the idea is gone, everything is gone, and I just wander around trying to figure out what it was that was so important earlier. I think I may be beginning to disappear.' As Grant drives her to Meadowlake, she miraculously picks up on a sight cue to remember a past outing, and Grant asks himself, 'If she could remember that, so vividly and correctly, could there really be so much the matter with her?'[24] In the film (but not the story), Grant takes her on a home visit, past the same spot, and she is unaffected.

Polley situates an explicit conversation between Grant and Fiona about their past on the drive to Meadowlake. To prove the power of her memory, Fiona speaks, as mentioned above, what are Grant's words in Munro's story. She expresses empathy for the temptations (the bare toes of students) he could not have been expected to resist, especially when his colleagues hadn't. She is grateful both that he didn't leave her, not even for a night, and, astonishingly, that he still made love to her 'despite disturbing demands elsewhere.' She is annoyed with other more exacting wives who would not put up with their husband's own submission to temptation, saying, 'I think people are too demanding. Aren't they? People want to be in love every single day. What a liability.'

Fiona's transition to Meadowlake becomes more about sexual fidelity than about Alzheimer's, which functions narratively to trigger the move and to call into question notions of monogamy. Polley intensifies this focus in that she writes in a last conversation between the couple that occurs before their separation and that is about infidelity, specifically Grant's prior choice not to forsake Fiona (despite his philandering). Polley also adds a sex scene: Fiona begins the Meadowlake stay initiating sex with Grant, after which Fiona instructs Grant to leave. Institutional policy dictates that he will not be able to visit her for 30 days, during which time her intermittent memory seems to dramatically shift. In both the story and film versions, during this month, Fiona develops an uxorious attachment to fellow resident, Aubrey, a man who has 'suffered some unusual kind of damage' and who is in Meadowlake temporarily to provide his wife respite.[25] In this union, Fiona seems to, or pretends to, forget her actual husband Grant. Grant himself cannot decide which it is, telling himself,

> She could have been playing a joke. It would not be unlike her. She had given herself away by that little pretense at the end, talking to him as if she thought perhaps he was a new resident.
>
> If that was what she was pretending. If it was a pretense.
>
> But would she not have run after him and laughed at him then, once the joke was over? She would not have just gone back to the game, surely, and pretended to forget about him. That would have been too cruel.[26]

Whether she deviously and vengefully plays on her newly acquired unreliability, or whether she genuinely forgets him, does not lessen Grant's suffering. This portrayal allows the film to offer up Grant as the sacrificial spouse willing to endure any fantasy that provides care to his ailing wife and, eventually, to cheat again in order to try to get Fiona what she needs.

Viewers must assess Fiona's memory to judge her actions or fathom her intentions. If she has forgotten Grant, then her attention to Aubrey acquires the innocence often attributed to Alzheimer's patients entering what can be thought of as a second, yet tragic, infancy. However, if she knows very well who Grant is (and what he has done to her), her attachment to Aubrey becomes a coy yet manipulative way to make Grant reassess, regret, or at least suffer for his own past treachery. Whereas most of the film offers Grant's perspective, in a rare glimpse Polley offers a shot from Fiona's window of her viewpoint on Grant speaking to the nurse Kristy (Kristen Thomson) in whom he confides and who implausibly provides him with plentiful support during his attempts to understand Fiona's actions. As Fiona watches her husband flirt – yet again – with a younger woman, his wife's motivations and potential for subversion are palpable. However, from Grant's dominant perspective, Fiona's repudiation is endearing, yet painful.

In both the film and the short story, Grant visits Fiona regularly with flowers 'like a hopeless lover or a guilty husband in a cartoon,' insists she ought to be dressed in her own clothes, and manipulates Aubrey's wife Marian (Olympia Dukakis) in order to convince Marian to return Aubrey to Fiona's side.[27] Though his attentions are apparently invisible to Fiona, they are hypervisible to the audience as his renewed devotion contributes to an irony: Grant cares too much now that Fiona no longer desires his attentions and now that he has, in a sense, left her. Grant considers a plan to break Marian down by requiting her attraction; he views it as 'a challenge and a creditable feat. Also a joke that could never be confided to anybody – to think that by his bad behavior he'd be doing good for Fiona.'[28] The extent of this manipulation remains vague in the written version but results in another sex scene added to the film; Marian's advances towards Grant are consummated, implying that Marian also has some sexual agency. The consummation dissolves her determination not to sell her house so that in the end she can afford moving Aubrey permanently into Meadowlake.

Early in the film, after Fiona attends an assessment during which the word 'mailbox' eludes her, she reads aloud to Grant – not poetry as he has read to her, but popular information about her condition. The passage is rife with language about monogamy, especially about one person being most loved in another's life:

> Should the person afflicted with the disease remain at home, the caregiver will very often be the spouse. The caregiver must preside over the degeneration of someone he or she loves very much. Must do this for years and years with the news always getting worse not better. Must put up sometimes with deranged but at the same time very personal insults and must somehow learn to smile through it all. Caregivers must be able to diagnose a wide variety of ordinary ailments under extraordinary circumstances. Imagine the person you love the most suddenly upset about something but completely unable to communicate the problem or even to understand it himself.

Fiona's following quip, '… sounds like a regular marriage,' overlays the entire narrative, in that the marriage bond often includes infidelity. Spousal care relies on betrayals of, and tests to, that relationship.

Significantly, while her voice speaks the above words, visual footage shows Fiona skiing off alone into the distance, where she gets lost, prompting her to finally make the critical move to Meadowlake.

Much later in the film, as Grant contemplates Fiona's potential treachery during her tryst with Aubrey, he reads medical textbooks as though they were the Ondaatje poetry featured early in the film. He says, 'Throughout much of the thinking brain, gooey plaques now crowd neurons from outside the cell membranes, and knotty tangles mangle microtubule transports from inside the cells.' Meanwhile the camera shows Fiona meeting Aubrey at Meadowlake and Grant skiing solo. Grant's narration continues, 'All told, tens of millions of synapses dissolve away. Because the structures and substructures of the brain are so highly specialized, the precise location of the neuronal loss determines what specific abilities will become impaired. It is like a series of circuit breakers in a large house flipping off one by one.' From this description, Fiona is – as she fears early in the film – 'beginning to disappear.' The film inhabits medical language to express the loss experienced within Grant and Fiona's marriage and to illustrate the anguish of losing an already elusive loved one.

While indeed Grant and Fiona's 'marriage' bond is deteriorating under the pressure of her illness, it also continues to be assaulted by infidelity, this time on the part of both spouses. Diminishing Grant's past treachery and intensifying his present sexual actions, Polley highlights how Alzheimer's is so often viewed in the public sphere. The devastation to the brain is mostly of interest because it changes who family members understand the patient to be (or to have been). Grant and Fiona's marriage is depicted as always having been compromised and based on compromise – as Fiona strays into her altered memories, Grant seems to want to keep her as healthy as possible, and keep her living on the first floor of her new (institutional) home rather than relegated to the ominous second floor (where she is at the end of the film). Film reviewer Peter Bradshaw explains, 'Grant wonders if he has ever really known his wife, in all their decades together, and Alzheimer's has made explicit to him the fear that his wife has always had a secret, secluded identity which will be forever unknown.'[29] In his attempts to alleviate this fear, Grant is willing to indulge Fiona's relationship with Aubrey – vengeful or not. To bring that about he returns to his own carnal conduct. As Fiona changes more and becomes less reliable, Grant settles into his own unchanging ways, which ironically involve unreliability as a monogamous spouse in order to express his undying devotion.

Polley artfully portrays Fiona's Alzheimer's as a site of commingled power and powerlessness in that she must surrender to Meadowlake before she is surrendered to it. She is free within her unreliable memory to attach herself to Aubrey, and in her dotage she becomes undyingly attractive to Grant yet simultaneously unavailable to him. Accordingly, Polley offers a sophisticated adaptation of old age as always already a disability – Alzheimer's being the quickest way to convey late life to a broader public. Fiona's need for care trumps other institutional structures in her life; that is, she is in institutional care instead of immersed in the institution of marriage. This transfer reveals deep social anxieties about what an aging population means for marriage as an institution and puts matrimony into question only to uphold it as the best way to age and ail.

While replicating a common plot structure of the silvering screen – a retrospect in which only youth and old age are of interest, with a present conflict over where to live when one part of a couple requires care – *Away from Her* poses pressing practical questions. Meadowlake is depicted as an impressively ideal setting with 'lots of natural light,' as the supervisor takes care to point out to everyone who visits. Grant and Fiona never mention money, but, as Marian and Aubrey's situation points out, plenty of it is required to come by that level of care in the current Canadian context.[30] Typically, even in this idyllic institution, there is no room for the aging couple (though Fiona tries to create a couplehood that can fit). Care is treated as entirely individual to the extent that the patient cannot receive visitors until she is fully acclimatized. For a couple less well-heeled than Grant and Fiona, as Fiona's textbook reading conveys, care would come down to the unit of the couple, in that a spouse is the cheapest option for late-life care. But for Polley's Grant and Fiona, as well as characters depicted in *Open Hearts* and *Iris*, there is another available care solution making audience members able to imagine that love and fulfillment in marriage are the primary – even sole – issues at stake.

Barbarian Invasions

In Denys Arcand's *Barbarian Invasions*, care is openly portrayed as an issue of social status and public under funding. The central character, Rémy (Rémy Girard), is depicted as already ailing to the extent that institutional care is required, rather than being at the point of choosing between home and hospital care. Domestic space functions in this film as a place of freedom from monogamy, past habits, and medical ethics. Audience members are introduced not only to actors they have previously had the opportunity to witness, but also to characters who have aged from their past political and social selves as depicted in *Le déclin de l'empire américain* (hereafter *Decline of the American Empire*, Canada, Denys Arcand, 1986). *Decline of the American Empire* opens with two women recording an interview for radio as they walk through a Montreal subway station. The topic of the interview is one woman's recent book in which she argues that the intense societal pursuit of happiness typically precedes social collapse. She uses matrimony as an example: 'Take marriage, for instance, in stable societies, marriage is a mode of economic exchange or a unit of production ... The success of a marriage doesn't depend on the personal happiness of the two individuals. The issue never even comes up.' This statement encapsulates the two concepts that bump up against each other in the films discussed previously in this chapter. That is, the economic facet of social coupling (not in terms of dowries and family alliances but in terms of care work) is set up as though it relies upon personal happiness in terms of sexual fidelity and profligacy.

Haunted by AIDS and the possibility of nuclear war, *Decline of the American Empire* consists mostly of bawdy misogynistic jokes that illustrate the lack of personal happiness elicited by various characters' marital and extramarital unions. *Barbarian Invasions* depicts the same characters and many of the same relationships as *Decline of the American Empire*; the characters are now notably older and still under threat. This later film depicts heroin addiction and puritanical capitalism as the ironically inevitable results of baby boomer attempts at radicalism. As the dying Rémy says, 'My son is a capitalist, ambitious prude when all my life I've been a socialist, hedonist lecher.' The film is as much about the aging of a soft socialism, more committed to sexual than to economic freedom, as it is about bodily aging. Rémy Girard reprises his role as Rémy, yet another lecherous professor who has been forced to relinquish his Lothario role, as well as his pedagogical position, due to terminal cancer.

Tiresome in its references to Rémy's lecherous past, the film captures the trite culmination of past political efforts. The most cited scene in the film involves Rémy and his friends, actors also reprising their prior roles, listing the many 'isms' they have espoused:

> 'Separatists, independantists, sovereigntists, sovereignty-associationists.
> At first we were existentialists.'
> 'We read Sartre and Camus.'

'Then Fanon. We became anti-colonialists.'
'We read Marcuse and became Marxists.'
'Marxist-Leninists.'
'Trotskyists.'
'Maoists.'
'After Solzhenitsyn we changed. We were structuralists.'
'Situationists.'
'Feminists.'
'Deconstructionists.'
'Is there an "ism" we haven't worshipped?'
'Cretinism.'

With this final ableist term, the film encapsulates what has happened to their political ideals, which have been at best stunted, but more accurately forgotten or abandoned.

Opening in a shared hospital room, *Barbarian Invasions* offers an indictment of the Quebec health care system as well as an understanding condemnation of those who buy themselves out of it, especially the hypocrites. For example, Rémy proclaims, 'I voted for socialized health care, and I'm prepared to suffer the consequences!' However, once faced with the prospect of slowly dying in a public shared ward, he is more than willing to benefit from his son's investment-banking income that buys him his own hospital floor and heroin to ease his pain. The cluttered scenes of the other hospital hallways, echoing shots near the end of *Jésus de Montréal* (hereafter *Jesus of Montreal*, Canada, Denys Arcand, 1989), express the failure to sustain socialized medicine, representing an overall social decline. Rémy berates the nurse-nun (Johanne-Marie Tremblay) throughout the film, which indicates that Catholicism is not going to be the final 'ism' for Rémy, as it offers him no respite and makes no sense to him. When Rémy's estranged son, Sébastien, arrives he is both mocked for and powerful because of his possession of capital and his ability to wield it. As Rémy and his friends point out in their ongoing playful banter, this neo-liberal invasion is as two-edged a sword as past invasions by all those labelled barbarians.

Though he may wish it otherwise, Rémy is above all known for his promiscuity, and his past exploits with women continue to interest him even more than socialism. He even cuts short the list of 'isms' cited above with a misogynistic digression about stupid comments he made about the Cultural Revolution to a Chinese scholar who had lived through it, illustrating that, in fact, perhaps 'cretinism' has been his focus all along. He describes himself predictably as weak before the scholar's charms, and her as 'an archaeologist with a skirt slit to the crotch.' Needless to say, after his comments about the Cultural Revolution, his visions of 'doing the Pekinese lotus' fade faster than his charms and beliefs have. Though he realizes the absurdity of having believed that he understood material socialism based on Godard films and Sollers treatises, he now entertains his friends with a story about the scholar's sexual appeal and not about her political experiences. That is, even faced with the failure of Canadian socialism, Rémy is more rueful of past failed sexual forays, and it is their fading that marks his old age. As he says, after listing many of his past conquests, 'All my life I went to bed with the world's most gorgeous women. Then one morning I awoke realizing I'd fallen asleep dreaming of the Caribbean. I'd grown old. Women had deserted my dreams.'

Arcand draws on Rémy's experience of aging to convey a world in which inversions overwhelm invasions. That is, while Rémy compromises his political beliefs to accept care otherwise unavailable, Sébastien – conservative keeper of order – is the one who breaks rules: hospital rules, union roles, drug laws, and assisted suicide laws. As Roberta Imboden puts it, 'Arcand's film depicts bribery, the purchase of illegal drugs, and euthanasia, all actions that violate the law, to depict the manner in which a hostile, indifferent son is transformed into a loving son.'[31] Mark Kermode explains how Rémy condemns 'his own fantastically successful son as the true Prince of the Barbarians – the puritanical capitalists whose materialism has superseded the sensual socialism of their collective past,' and Kermode goes on to claim, 'Ironically, it is within this relationship between estranged father and son that the film's best hope of redemption lies.'[32] Such readings of the film as rescued by the father-son plot miss the commentary provided by the film about the aging of the Quebec (frequently read as Canadian) health-care system tied to the aging of socialism, which is tied to the aging of Canadian baby boomers who now, more than ever, need the social safety net, the loss of which is represented by the new generation.

Coupling overwhelms *Barbarian Invasions*. Rémy's ex-wife, Louise (whom he still introduces as his wife), immediately points out, for those viewers not familiar with the characters from *Decline of the American Empire*, that she had thrown him out due to his sexual exploits. He describes the witnesses of his illness as 'my exquisite daughter-in-law, my heroic wife, and two most charming mistresses.' As his friends come to join him in his final days, they each appear in the midst of their domestic and sexual lives. Like Grant's former colleagues in *Away from Her*, his friend Pierre (Pierre Curzi), formerly involved with his masseuse/student, has now settled down with another student; Pierre is reduced, from all his 'isms,' to consumerism in the form of buying diapers at Costco. While Pierre's partner is cast as a nag, Pierre praises her large breasts and youth as an antidote to his dwindling sex drive. Claude (Yves Jacques) has settled into a simulacrum of heterosexual domesticity with his partner Gilles Levac (Roy Dupuis). The two ex-mistresses have not found the same domestic stability but are presented as being in satisfying, if slightly compromised, sexual relationships.

Overwhelmingly, however, the film is about the effect of the older generation's disregard for marital values on the younger generation. Sébastien and his childhood friend Nathalie (Marie-Josée Croze) collectively represent the double-edged nefarious effects (capitalism and drug addiction, respectively) they have suffered. Sébastien resents his father's past absences from him to be with women hardly worth the time, and has found a form of aggressive stability that rejects all that his father valued – books, lust, and socialist articulations if not actions – choosing instead to make money and marry Gaëlle. Sébastien is introduced cosily sleeping next to his fiancée rather than hungrily in the throes of passion. Though tempted by a connection to Nathalie after he misguidedly kisses his childhood friend, he remains Gaëlle's faithful partner – never even so much as objectifying her verbally – thereby righting more than just his father's past socialist wrongs. Nathalie's heroin addiction is the vicious flipside of Sébastien's overly responsible rebellion. Harmed by her mother's promiscuity, knowing marriage only to the extent that married men 'never stayed until morning,' Nathalie's reckless approach to her addiction combined with Sébastien's monetary strength collectively buy Rémy the death of his choice.

Conclusion

The silvering screen is fascinated by the heteronormative couple and struggles to uphold a fantasy of devotion by repeatedly representing its past failure and present reincarnation. When the able body can no longer be convincingly believed as possible (McRuer stresses its ultimate impossibility), heterosexual monogamy compensates narratively. In *Open Hearts*, while Cecilie begins an affair with Niels, she expresses her ongoing devotion to Joachim and her willingness to accept her role as eternal caregiver. In fact, his rejection of her in that role promotes her reception of the sexual encounters with Niels. John Bayley's devotion to Iris, driving frantically down dizzying streets looking for her as she runs away, at least momentarily keeps at bay the pressures that push her into the nursing home. In *Away from Her*, Grant's dogged attempts at romance, always schlepping flowers, have the aim of improving Fiona's situation within the institution. In *Barbarian Invasions*, it is Sébastien who embodies monogamy, despite his momentary embrace with Nathalie that only underlines his commitment to Gaëlle. In that film, the decay of both care (in terms of the social welfare state) and marriage (in particular, Rémy's union as previously portrayed in *Decline of the American Empire*) leads to Rémy's transgressive death (an illegal assisted suicide), which above all undermines the system in which he had so endeavoured to invest.

In an article about his experience of Alzheimer's in his long-time wife, Emery Castle addresses what he calls 'the many faces of intimacy.' As in the films discussed in this chapter, the issue of devotion on the part of a long-time spouse arises. Emery attempts to care for his wife Merab at home until a fall renders her in need of greater care than he can provide. After she enters an impressive institutional space, the local 'Mennonite Nursing Home,' Emery becomes more aware of the physical and emotional strain her care has placed on him. His candour is impressive, particularly in the section of the essay he titles 'Betty.' He describes a new romantic relationship that he begins with Betty while Merab is still alive and in care. Rather than perceived as treachery, even by those around him, this relationship is portrayed as part of a fluid domesticity that is possible without betraying a commitment Emery has made and kept to Merab, who Betty insists he 'never neglect.'[33]

This example points out a great threat to the heterosexual hegemony that the silvering screen seeks to uphold and simultaneously reveal. Emery, Betty, and Merab's family structure suggests that the threat is ultimately not one to decent care. Disability strains heteronormative social structures, even when heterosexual unions persist. Family and care can involve more than a dyadic couple. Rather than allowing even for the simple deviation that Emery and Betty's relationship with Merab represents, the silvering screen struggles to uphold a fantasy of uxorious devotion by repeatedly representing its past failure and present incarnation. While the films discussed in this chapter reveal glimpses of Emery's reality – Cecilie seeks to accommodate both Joachim and Niels in her changing reality; the 'real life' John Bayley moves on to another marriage that does not exclude Iris; Grant begins a sexual affair with Marian in order to convince her to help Fiona – they all return to the idea of heterosexual monogamy as fundamental to successful care situations.

Chapter five

Yes, We Still Can: Paul Newman, Clint Eastwood, Aging Masculinity, and the American Dream

> The old dad or granddad in American movies is always a respected figure seated in the corner clutching a glass of whiskey and making sometimes comic but also determinedly wise judgments on life. The foolish behaviour of the young is usually his material, along with informed speculation on the Super Bowl.
>
> John Mortimer[1]

In this chapter and the next, I shift the focus from connections of old age to disability through visions of wheelchairs, diagnosis narratives, and caregiving scenarios to an even more figurative relationship between old age and disability. This chapter begins my overt analysis of the perception of late-life masculinity as revealed by Hollywood depictions of the aging male. Though illness and infirmity poke up their heads in each of the films discussed, they mostly make the main plots dramatic or comedic. Looking primarily at roles taken on by Paul Newman, Clint Eastwood, and (in the next chapter) Jack Nicholson, I set up the invisibility of privilege against the visibility of physical aging. Morgan Freeman plays a supporting role in each chapter, as he does in countless films, demonstrating the apparent expendability – but actual necessity – of the racialized body to the silvering screen and to ongoing investments in social power. The visibility of his race obscures the visibility of his physical aging, so that his black body props up the aging white male bodies around him and then disappears.

In this chapter, I argue that films about late life transform the older male figure from a man whose masculinity is perceived to be fading to a man whose masculinity is exaggerated and compensatory. This process magnifies a larger social fear that masculinity diminishes when physical aging shows. Stories that feature larger-than-life heterosexual mating attempts reveal that a male sense of romantic entitlement extends into the latter years, even when actual entitlement might diminish. Further, the masculinity in these films is very clearly tied to a certain – racist – understanding of Americanness.

This chapter explores the aging of the onscreen bad boy; that is, it is about the figures that do not age gracefully into the 'old dads and granddads' of the epigraph, a description that applies to typical minor figures of the aging male in Hollywood film. In general (as the short lives of James Dean, River Phoenix, and Heath Ledger attest), the bad boy does not age well – and often doesn't age at all – because what transforms an upstanding young man into a bad-boy figure will also kill him (for example, smoking, drinking, doing drugs, and driving too fast). That said, the upstanding young man does not age into an interesting Hollywood dramatic figure either, since Hollywood is obsessed with infidelity and tragedy. The actors Paul Newman and Clint Eastwood appear in this chapter as test cases of what happens to the silvering screen when the rebellious male, known for his anti-hero roles, matures into senescence in the public eye. Whether demurely (Newman) or violently (Eastwood), the white patriarch confidently sets and sometimes follows his own rules, superior to those of the system in which he finds himself, especially as the system disintegrates around him. He draws on his venerable status to signify both rebellion and order, and in doing so, demonstrates that he has aged with his masculinity fully intact, if more on display than ever.

Yes, We *Still* Can

Quintessential representations of the funny old man, the *Grumpy Old Men* (USA, Donald Petrie, 1993) and *Grumpier Old Men* (USA, Howard Deutch, 1995) movies remake *The Odd Couple* (USA, Gene Sacks, 1968) into, as reviewer Stephen Holden puts it, 'The Old Couple.'[2] At odds for reasons they don't even remember, Max Goldman (Walter Matthau) and John Gustafson (Jack Lemmon) live an American Dream gone slightly stale; both are retired and extremely bored. When Ariel Truax (Ann-Margret) in the first film and Maria Ragetti (Sophia Loren) in the sequel roll into town, the humour takes off in that the old men dust off their romantic skills and awkwardly, yet successfully, go courting. The *Globe and Mail*'s Geoff Pevere sums it up well in his review of the first film: 'To wit, they're cute and they talk dirty. They're the Golden Geezers.'[3] Playing thus into Hollywood clichés, the talented actors ask for and offer little in their late careers. Roger Ebert, always generous to aging male actors, describes them as 'a couple of old shoes, broken in and comfortable, but still able to take a shine.'[4] Other reviewers are less generous, such as the *Ottawa Citizen*'s Noel Taylor who writes that *Grumpier Old Men* 'doesn't balk at any implausibility as long as it raises a titter about senility.'[5]

The laughs about senility are directed most towards Gustafson's father, the ninety-four-year-old (ninety-six in the second movie) Grandpa Gustafson (Burgess Meredith), who remains ribald and randy. Grandpa is portrayed as disgustingly sexual and humorously old in order to make less pressing the sense of aging experienced by the younger Goldman and Gustafson. Goldman and the younger Gustafson struggle to some extent in their later years – they face new health problems and run from the taxman. But they are portrayed as still very much able to take what they want and live as they please. Their main concern is their access to bait for ice fishing, and they suffer no lack of access to romantic love. As Holden notes, the 'vision of old age is giddily reassuring.'[6] The films gently play on the stereotype of the grumpy old man, offering little but a set of jokes that are only really funny as long as each male character remains sexually active.

Tom Shakespeare argues 'masculine ideology rests on a negation of vulnerability, weakness, and ultimately even of the body itself.'[7] I pick up in this chapter's title on Barack Obama's 2008 campaign slogan (discussed in chapter 1) to note that a 'Yes, we can' set of films featuring aging male characters reveals an insistence that older men needn't relinquish any of their power or dominance, despite the apparently humorous manifestations of their physical aging. Unlike Obama, these men have not previously had to defend their qualifications. The aging – usually white – man is frantically depicted as still able to indulge in all the benefits of his past privilege. This frenetic contention reveals a deep anxiety not just that particular white men may lose their power as they age, but also that white men in general may have to cede their spots to other identity groups. Hence, the films adamantly avow on the part of their central male aging characters 'Yes, we *still* can,' where they needn't have even declared 'Yes, we can' on behalf of the characters' younger selves. This previously redundant statement reveals the fragility of the aging characters; that is, the need to declare their fitness demonstrates the change in the aging men's status.

To further demonstrate the reassurance of the silvering screen's vision of late-life masculinity, along with its precarious assertions, I focus on the careers of male screen icons who, unlike Bette Davis and Joan Crawford, remained in roles similar to their youthful parts even as they aged. Though age is a dominant theme in their later films, other themes from their prior careers persist. In the following section, I examine the performance of Paul Newman in an adaptation of Richard Russo's novel *Nobody's Fool* (USA, Robert Benton, 1995), exposing the transformation of a sex symbol into a sex symbol with a sore knee. Subsequently, I turn to the performances of Clint Eastwood in *Unforgiven* (USA, Clint Eastwood, 1992) and *Gran Torino* (USA, Clint Eastwood, 2009) in which he continues to play violent vigilantes reinstituting order, even when his characters begin to creak and crave a quieter life. Enormous effort is made to shore up each male star's increasingly fragile sense of virility at the expense of others, usually women dismissively treated as potential or rejected sexual objects and racialized men easily killed off. While I am far from arguing that white patriarchy is losing its grasp on hegemony, these films reveal a social concern about that possibility and worry that the aging of society will clinch its demise.

Grumpy Old Man or Just a Fool?

Contemporaneous with the Grumpy Old Man films, Robert Benton (of *Kramer vs. Kramer* fame) adapted Richard Russo's novel *Nobody's Fool* into a film of the same title. Both the novel and film portray Donald Sullivan (Paul Newman), also known as Sully, as a hard-working, barely employed sixty-year-old man with a newly acquired bad knee and longstanding bad judgment. In contrast to Matthau and Lemmon's past as comic actors, casting seventy-something Newman in the role of Sully allows Benton to convey the ongoing elegance of an aging ruffian. Rather than a parody, Newman's Sully is the portrait of the aging of white working-class Americans – representing the fading of sympathy for poor white men, an elegy for pre-box-store small town culture, a new era for the aging actor, and the durability of patriarchy.

Unlike Bette Davis, Joan Crawford, and Gloria Swanson, Newman was not really courageous for continuing to act in his later life, and the opportunity to maintain his star status was available in part due to his gender and in part due to his generation. Whereas when Davis and Crawford appeared aged at fifty and had to portray characters much older than themselves as horrifying, Newman in his seventies manages to appear as a sixty-something in a Don Juan role similar to his past characters. After he won an Oscar for his role in *The Color of Money* (USA, Martin

Paul Newman with his Oscar. © Fotos International/Contributor/Hulton Archive/ Getty Images

Scorsese, 1986), Newman indulged in his relative freedom from the age-ist judgment that plagued the earlier starlets, telling reporters,

> [Winning the Oscar] was nice, but it did destroy an image that I had, that had always been floating around in my head, where the auditorium goes berserk, my name is mentioned, a stretcher is brought up on the stage, with this grungy, knotted, gnarled hand that comes out from underneath the sheet, grabs hold of this thing [the Oscar], and pulls it back underneath the sheet ... And then, they take the stretcher out, see. So, they have deprived me of that particular dream, and I don't know whether I am happy with that.[8]

Rather than feeling he needs to hide his aging, either by retreating or undergoing cosmetic surgery, Newman gleefully puts forth a grotesque image of his imagined late-life infirmity in order to signal how long he has been made to wait for recognition from the Academy of Motion Picture Arts and Sciences. Different from Davis's campy oldness in *Whatever Happened to Baby Jane?* (USA, Robert Aldrich, 1962), Newman's image of his own campy oldness is merely tossed into an interview; he does not have to play the part of refuse onscreen. As a film star, he remains the figure he always was. Newman decided to retire from acting – though not from public life – in his eighties, and he attributed that decision to changes that were happening to him as the result of age, saying, 'You start to lose your memory, you start to lose your confidence, you start to lose your invention ... So I think that's pretty much a closed book for me.'[9] If he is to be believed, his retirement came as the result of a fear about his ongoing acting abilities, rather than as an attempt to maintain a particular physical image in public view.

Newman receives praise for his quiet performance of Sully, a character who, on the surface, goes against the actor's public persona as a committed, loving family man. Many reviews directly compare this performance to Newman's youthful forays. Rick Groen spells out these past attempts in the opening of his review of *Nobody's Fool*: 'Time and again – in *The Hustler, Hombre, Cool Hand Luke, Paris Blues, The Left-Handed Gun, Slap Shot, The Verdict* – you see Newman serving up a variation on the same ambivalent theme, the man divided against himself, the guy who is neither as good as he could have become or as bad as he might have been.'[10] Caryn James makes the comparison to Newman's past roles just as directly, saying, 'Though the character's humor carries traces of earlier Newman heroes, the effect is as natural as if Sully had watched Butch Cassidy or Cool Hand Luke and decided on a strategy: take life as it comes and face it down with a wisecrack.'[11] Edward Guthmann, though not convinced Newman pulls off the transformation, offers begrudging praise for the actor's efforts: 'All the dirt in the world never transforms him into a working stiff. He remains the glamorous leading man.'[12] Though framing it in ageist rhetoric, reviewer Rita Kempley expresses her admiration for how Newman adapts to the role: 'Earlier in his career, he tended to play the anti-hero from back to front – shiningly exalted on the outside and awfully troubled within. Age has reversed the direction of the process but not the basic ingredients – these days, the exterior is wasted and weak, while the inside is heroically pure.'[13] Critics agree that Newman's transformation into an aging, working stiff is effective theatrically and builds on his past image.

Sully is no Butch Cassidy, but he's not exactly clean-cut inside or out. Granted Sully would like to be more pure, and his actions in the film as compared with the novel make him heroic on an extremely small scale, but in both he's still a selfish, sexist senior who needs a snow blower to do work he used to do by hand. As a working man who can't find work in a dying town, Sully reveals the limits of the bad-boy character. It is difficult to work against the system when you need the system to prop you up. In that sense, the anti-hero doesn't age particularly well.

Sully's hometown, North Bath, is populated by stock figures – the wise fool, the young entrepreneur, the motherly landlady, the sexy neglected wife, and the senile old woman. In order to illustrate Sully's role in the town, the film shows him in relation to three female characters. The oldest woman Hattie's role (though her appearance in the film is incredibly brief) is vital to establishing the fitting response to aging poorly as well as establishing the wrong way to age. As she yet again wanders onto the snowy street wearing a bathrobe and slippers, Sully limps out to help her find her way, guiding her back to the restaurant she used to run that has become her reluctant daughter's responsibility. Simply put, Sully might be aging, but he's doing so more gradually and more gracefully than Hattie. As long as he can help her, he can maintain an aura of strength.

Similarly, Miss Beryl Peoples as portrayed by Jessica Tandy (who had been playing the role of graceful aging for years prior to the filming of *Nobody's Fool*) illustrates Sully's relative youth. Viewing fallen tree branches as a signal of her impending demise, Miss Beryl fears that old age will bring her to the end of her road, as it indeed does to Jessica Tandy soon after the filming of *Nobody's Fool*.[14] By looking in on Miss Beryl every morning, and by doing essential work such as shovelling her walk and fixing her porch railing, Sully manages to remain apparently robust as well as still youthful, slipping at times back into the role of student to Miss Beryl as he had been in eighth grade. As Kempley notes, 'In its elegiac final scene, Ms. Tandy walks toward her kitchen to make tea, still lively and clear-headed. Sully is asleep in her chair, physically back where he started but emotionally several leaps ahead.'[15] The film leans on Tandy to show that older people can remain sprightly and mentally agile, and that Sully – despite the encroaching passing of time – is resistant to all visible change. Miss Beryl's dialogue is often dedicated to highlighting Sully's resistance, to the extent that her last line is 'other people change; I keep hoping you might.'

As a sign that he is mildly capable of change, even if those changes only land him in the same place, the film version of Sully makes a significant decision in relation to his boss Carl Roebuck's (Bruce Willis) wife, Toby, played by Melanie Griffith whom one reviewer describes as 'a woman whose beauty is almost ready to fade' (the actress was thirty-seven years old when the film was released).[16] Sully's dealings with Toby are flirtatious, playing into the needs created by her husband's neglect. Because of his age, this courting makes him the butt of jokes, even on the part of Carl who scoffs, 'Sixty years old and still getting crushes on other men's wives. I would hope by the time I'm your age, I'm a little smarter than that.' Toby also repeatedly seems to be jeering Sully, making suggestive remarks about 'breaking and entering' along with gestures such as flashing her naked breasts at Sully before teasingly calling him grandpa. Sully cajoles Toby by talking of running away together to Hawaii in the unlikely event that his daily trifecta bet comes in. Paul Newman remains a sex symbol, and Toby does come to Sully at the end of the film, having taken him seriously and bought the tickets so that the not-yet-couple could run away together to Hawaii.

This action brings Sully to a minutely heroic penultimate scene – in many ways the climax and turning point of the film. Importantly, this scene does not occur in the novel from which the film is adapted. Accordingly, it plays heavily on tropes of the silvering screen, which typically offers more simplistic constructions of late life than novels do. In the film, Sully stands up to Carl Roebuck, who is present when Toby makes the proposition concrete. The older man rises to protectively embrace Toby in front of Carl's topless mistress, and escorts her outside asking his semi-competent friend to keep a gun trained on Carl who nonetheless mocks Sully's impotence and inability to commit. Sure enough, once outside, Toby begins to weep sooner than Carl had predicted, and Sully compassionately backs out of the deal. Ironically, however, it is the responsibilities Sully has belatedly accepted – as a grandfather and father – rather than his usual irresponsibility that give him a way out of a commitment to Toby Roebuck.

Sully's inveterate inability to commit is not as visible in the film as it would have been in the novel had the scenario of Toby's proposition materialized in the book. In Russo's novel, Sully makes no headway with Toby except that she mockingly supplies sexual innuendo, making his age more incongruous. Rather than languish without her husband's attentions or seriously proposition Sully, the novel's Toby has a fling with Sully's son as well as an ongoing affair with an unnamed woman from the next town. The film entirely leaves out Sully's love interest in the novel, a married woman closer to his own age who magnifies Sully's aging. He will not enter into a full committed relationship with her, so they repeatedly take breaks from each other, one of which lasts most of the time period of the novel. Reviewer Caryn James uses disability rhetoric to claim that 'Ruth's absence plagues the film like a phantom limb, making Sully more isolated, stranding him without a sex life and perhaps making him more acceptable to mainstream movie audiences.'[17] Removing Ruth from the film leaves Sully as a sympathetic character who seems to be doing right – having taken himself out of the romance game because he's no good at it leaves him to flirt harmlessly until action is required. Without Ruth as evidence of Sully's failings, the film can feature his decision to forego romance with Toby as courageous and even sacrificial. While audiences would likely accept Paul Newman as a sexual being at any age, they are even more delighted to see him being fatherly to Toby as well as to his own son, and his heroic decision not to run away with her signifies his overdue emotional development. Above all, whereas the novel depicts Sully's lust for Toby as only a joke, the film makes it requitable – Paul Newman still gets the girl, and his aging does not mean a loss of virility, even as it signifies an acceptance of responsibility.

Whereas earlier in the film Sully is unable to play by the rules, viewers learn that Sully has a legitimate inheritance – his family home – that he has refused to accept because it comes from his physically abusive father. At a time when real estate in fading North Bath seems extremely promising, Sully still would rather fight with Carl Roebuck for his rightful back pay and odd jobs than accept his family legacy. As a result, when a North Bath development scheme goes south, Sully does not lose as much as others who invested based on promises from a Texan corporation. Not only has Sully let the house fall into shocking disrepair, he has also refused to pay its taxes, so that he believes his stake in it is reduced to zero.

Through one of many convenient coincidences, Sully learns that Miss Beryl has paid the taxes on his behalf, legitimating him as a citizen and a landholder.

Nobody's Fool is a film about social security. Hollywood audiences cannot bear to see a white man – though slightly hobbled – suffering without redemption. Rather than leaving the cinema having to imagine Sully destitute after Miss Beryl's seemingly imminent death, audience members can assure themselves that his eighth-grade teacher-cum-landlady has secured his future financial security. He may not be able to perform the kind of physical labour he's gotten by on, and he may never come into the money he is owed due to his injury, but he is self-sufficient and free to continue to flirt in the face of jokes about his virility.

There are repeated jokes in both the film and novel about Sully's 'one-legged' lawyer Wirf, Sully's long-time friend who is himself figured as aging, but primarily as disabled. Mysteriously, he has a prosthetic leg, which he loses to Sully in a poker game. In a poignant, almost final, seemingly throwaway scene, Sully goads his timid grandson into swallowing his fear and carrying the limb across the bar to return it to Wirf who waits standing on crutches. On the one hand, this is just Sully's way. Rather than help people directly, or in the way they need, he waits until it is almost too late (as when he fixes Miss Beryl's railing) or teases them mercilessly so that they almost do not notice the aid (as when he rehires his 'best friend' Rub). But, Sully does change slightly through the narrative and, as Groen points out, that change is 'presented not as an 11th-hour redemption but simply as a logical revelation: Sully is just becoming what he always was, the gruff old goat giving way to the decent soul.'[18] So, on the other hand, Sully – while taking new responsibility for his relationship to his son and grandson – is passing the mantle to the little boy, enabling and yet forcing him to bring a prosthetic leg to Sully's aging friend. To build on the Obama slogan ('Yes, we can'), the film Sully still 'can' (for example, run away with Toby), but he doesn't necessarily want to anymore. The power – and the choice – remains resolutely his.

Most reviewers describe *Nobody's Fool* with clichés often reserved for descriptions of old age itself. Guthmann says, as though speaking condescendingly of an aging aunt, '[*Nobody's Fool* is] more graceful than [folksy and sentimental], more surprising, more essentially true than simple sentimentality allows for. It's a gem.'[19] Groen describes the film as though it were Scully's aging body, saying, 'Twisting lazily and meandering anecdotally and ending quietly, this is a feel-good flick that doesn't look like one – it's smart enough to hide its smooth polish beneath a scuffed-up veneer.'[20] James emulates descriptions of old age as wistful but emotionally rich and graceful when she explains that 'if *Nobody's Fool* is often heartbreaking in its sense of loss, it is also hopeful in the strength of its emotions and the sheer beauty of its performances.'[21] These comments collectively compensate for what viewers are most edgy about: what will Paul Newman's changing physical frame mean for Hollywood cinema? If this exquisite man ages, please let it be beautifully.

Nobody's Fool is a narrative of a muted American Dream with the central character, Sully, ending up considerably wealthier than he had been at the beginning of the film to the extent that he has a small amount of money to offer to his son to support a grandson in a way that he did not support his own son. Typically, the American Dream focuses on opportunities for more youthful characters, but Newman's ongoing screen presence makes Sully's achievement plausible and desirable. This story plays out in a markedly white middle-American town in which the only character more downtrodden than a working, poor, white man is the dog he harms during a botched break and enter attempt.[22] Most importantly, Paul Newman maintains his status as sex symbol and as everlasting in his claims to masculinity – manifest in property ownership, crude jokes, and physical prowess.

Make Him Go Away

Ever an advocate for the working white man, Clint Eastwood's career has similarly been dedicated to offering nuanced depictions of the American Dream, taking care not to transform it much from its most mythical bootstrap structure. His characters very often protect the downtrodden, even though his characters are in similarly downtrodden positions; his characters' downtrodden positions – because of the entitlement offered to a fighting white American man – are marginally stronger than the positions of those whom they protect. An actor who loves to play a white man not afraid to stand up for himself, as well as represent the 'system' as corrupt, Eastwood increasingly plays characters who reinstitute order through unsanctioned but apparently justified violence, waving the (U.S.) flag for white male heroism. His visible aging has only made him more qualified for the part.

Generally reviled by the disability community, Eastwood was not afraid to stand up for himself when he felt oppressed by the Americans with Disabilities Act, which compelled him to make his Mission Ranch hotel physically accessible at his own expense. As disability rights activist Mary

Clint Eastwood's aging face. © Gabriel Bouys/AFP/Getty Images

Johnson sarcastically puts it in her book *Make Them Go Away: Clint Eastwood, Christopher Reeve and the Case against Disability Rights*, 'The seasoned Hollywood actor had his script and he stuck to it: He wasn't against disabled people. He wanted to help disabled people, who were being preyed on by moneygrubbing lawyers. The law was the problem; had been all along. The law needed to be fixed.'[23] Like the heroes he typically portrays, Eastwood was determined to fight the law rather than 'back down ... because of all these people ... who can't defend themselves.'[24] He goes so far as to ask: 'Who in America gives these lawyers the right to be the self-appointed vigilantes to enforce the law?'[25] In the face of such injustice, Eastwood characteristically holds his ground, boldly proclaiming, 'If you're right, you've got to hold your ground ... I also fought for the businessmen and businesswomen who own small businesses who are trying to get by and they get worked over by those people.'[26] That is, someone in America (in Hollywood specifically) gives *him* the right that wasn't granted to the lawyers to 'be the self-appointed vigilante to enforce the law.' He extends here the position forwarded in many of his films, ever the cowboy knowing right from wrong and not afraid to show it.

As he ages, Eastwood's masculinity comes into question largely because of its intense suspect fortification. Dennis Bingham argues that

> Eastwood's own debatable evolution shows, if nothing else, that masculine domination represents not nature but artifice and effort, that it is a burden for men repeatedly to convince themselves and their peers of their indispensability. Arguably, then, the patterns of subversion and recuperation cited in film studies have recurred throughout film history, demonstrating the fragility of patriarchal gender constructions, offset by a resilience rooted in power.[27]

Progressively more able to play the vigilante as hard-done-by champion of the underdog, Eastwood increasingly leans on his aging frame to elicit sympathy for his hard-boiled heroes who can then go ahead and do as they please in the name of justice.

'For what you done to Ned': *Unforgiven*

Eastwood's famous flick about an aging cowboy drawn back into violence by his compulsion to protect women with hearts of gold from uncontrolled male brutality, *Unforgiven*, begins as though it is a film about a woman – 'a comely young woman and not without prospects,' as explained by white text scrolling across a country sunset scene – but she turns out to have died before the beginning of the narrative. Eastwood's character, William Munny, is introduced in the same lettering as 'a known thief and murderer, a man of notoriously vicious and intemperate disposition.' This is very much Eastwood's ongoing onscreen role, a bad boy who ultimately uses his bent for violence to restore an order he prefers to that imposed by officialdom. But he goes down fighting for misunderstood right. As Susan Jeffords puts it, '*Unforgiven* may offer the best clues to the kinds of masculine models being set forth for the United States in 1992, both as Hollywood heroes and as models of national identification and foreign policy action.'[28] In his early sixties when *Unforgiven* was filmed, Eastwood brought a cowboy past his prime to life and used that aging frame to full advantage.

To understand Munny as cowboy hero, audiences must adjust expectations as well as develop a new comprehension of what legitimately con-
stitutes male heroism. As Jeffords explains, 'In addition to showing
Eastwood as a mud-covered hog farmer in the film's opening scenes,
Unforgiven constantly reminds viewers of his body's failings, principally
because he is unable to mount his horse, usually a casual act for every
western hero.'[29] Eastwood, it appears, is more willing to offer reasonable
accommodations in his films than in his hotels. As an aging cowboy figure, Munny represents the fading of a sense of justice wherein real men
are free to fight for what is right, even if it is an outdated and paternalis-
tic set of morals. Because he can no longer physically do what he had
been able to do as a younger man (partly because he is apparently no
longer as vicious, having been reformed by his wife, but also because he
is less physically agile), Munny's masculinity has to be established through
astonishing yet apparently justified violence.

Having given up his hating ways on account of his love for his now-
dead wife, Munny is enticed back into a bounty hunt by a young cowboy
awed by his reputation. Not only is Munny motivated by the prize of a
sum of money, but also by his belief that the targets deserve what they
have coming to them. The Schofield Kid (Jaimz Woolvett) tells him that
the targets are wanted 'for cuttin' up a lady. They cut up her face an' cut
her eyes out, cut her ears off an' her tits too.' This is all Munny needs to
be convinced to leave behind his two young children to tend to the ailing
hogs and search out his former partner Ned Logan (Morgan Freeman)
to pick up where they left off. To convince Logan that he too should
leave his newly comfortable life, Munny embellishes the tale of wrongs,
saying that the two marks 'cut up a woman. Cut her eyes out, cut her tits
off, cut her fingers off … done everythin' but cut up her cunny, I guess.'
In contrast to Munny's own awkwardly aging body, still somehow able to
perform physically despite its shortcomings, the cut woman Delilah's
body is figured as past repair, no longer useful to her employer and so
worthy of more compensation than the sheriff's (Gene Hackman) pen-
alty of a fine paid in ponies to Delilah's employer.

Proving his own genitalia intact remains important to Munny in a film
that takes the time to spell out a common connection between the gun
and the penis to the extent that an off-screen character is nicknamed
Two Guns not because he has two weapons but because he has 'a dick so
big it was longer than the barrel on that Walker Colt he carried.'
Explaining to Logan his new morality, Munny says of his sexual options:
'The only woman a man like me could get you'd have to pay for. And that

ain't right, buying flesh.' To Logan's question, 'So, you just use your hand?' Munny responds, 'I don't miss it all that much.' To make the connection to gunfire obvious, this exchange is immediately followed by a botched gunfight in which Munny bleeds not from a heroic gunshot wound but from hurting himself falling off his horse.

Broken down as Munny is – unable to mount his horse, easily catching the flu, turning into 'nothin' but a broken down pig farmer,' as the Schofield Kid scoffs – he is able to help viewers understand the physical hardships faced by younger characters. One reviewer describes him as 'a truly tragic figure, a country-western combination of Lear and Richard III.'[30] As Munny tells Delilah, 'I didn't mean you was ugly like me, hell no ... I just meant how we both had scars.' He turns down her offer of a 'free one,' assuring her that the rejection is because of his love for his wife and not his disgust at her disfigured face. To preserve his masculine integrity, he must convey that it is his *choice* to indulge in neither gunplay nor sex.

In the end, Munny's killing the two cowboys who attacked Delilah is peripheral to the film's climax. Against his will, Munny is drawn by a code of honour to avenge his friend Logan, who is caught on his way home after deciding not to help Munny because he has too much conscience to kill the cowboys. Ned Logan is whipped to death by the sheriff, Little Bill, and then publicly laid out as an example to would-be assassins. A cute subplot of *Unforgiven* reveals a preoccupation with accurate representation, featuring a naive biographer who is continually surprised to find that his subjects exaggerate their stories to benefit their own images. Munny is angry that his friend is dead, but he appears even more furious that there is an inaccurate sign around his friend's neck labelling him an 'assassin.' This becomes even more justifiable of violence than the attack on Delilah had been.

Upholding the level of violence necessary to a successful Western, Munny's vicious slaying of a room full of men becomes necessary in obtaining justice for his friend, and neatly reasserts Munny's masculinity. As reviewer Julie Salamon puts it, 'There's an anti-violence sentiment running through the piece, though it's explicated with so much violence it's hard to take the sentiment very seriously.'[31] Eastwood's Munny proves his ongoing purchase of power by annihilating his enemies through no real choice of his own, having been drawn back into violence in order to make money for his children, fighting on the side of right even if he does so against the law. He manages to appear simultaneously helpless and powerful, but always a 'man.'

Missed in all reviews, besides the odd throwaway reference to integrity, is Freeman's Logan who ultimately appears simply helpless and in need of help from his white hero – who is also circuitously his executioner. He too plays an aging cowboy, one who has truly reformed, regrets his past to the extent that he refuses to relive it, and dies violently as the result of loyalty to his friend. Ultimately, he becomes yet another expended black body with his corpse on display in front of a bar, disturbingly akin to an image of racially motivated lynching. Logan's race is never once raised in reviews or in the film but it is integral to setting up the power of white America just as Morgan Freeman's race is integral to setting up ongoing white virility on the silvering screen. Famously criticizing Black History Month on *60 Minutes*, Freeman angrily confronts host Mike Wallace saying, 'You're gonna relegate my history to a month?' To Freeman, 'black history is American history,' and the way to rid the world of racism is to stop talking about it.[32] Certainly, in his silvering screen appearances, that is precisely what he's done (even in *Invictus* in which Freeman's Mandela sets aside racial differences and political involvements to support the white South African rugby team in their quest to win the World Cup).

'Kill you to buy American?': *Gran Torino*

The importance of a violently dispatched racialized other to the ongoing justification of white male privilege cannot avoid comment in Eastwood's most recent vigilante feature, *Gran Torino*. This vengeful fantasy essentially portrays the racialization and subsequent whitewashing of the American Dream. Eastwood plays Walter Kowalski, an aging Korean War veteran whose racism is overcome only by his gruffly disguised big heart. The bigot with a heart of gold mourns his wife, finding himself abandoned by a family he doesn't much care for. He cherishes his neighbourhood, which from his perspective has been taken over by immigrants, who he also does not much care for; as far as he's concerned, they are all 'chinks,' 'gooks,' or 'nips'; the specifics of their histories are unimportant from his perspective and the epithets are his only available vocabulary to describe them. The nuances of the Asian world mean nothing to this soldier. Having been one of the white European immigrants to settle in the neighbourhood, and taking pride in such Americana as its postage-stamp-sized, well-manicured lawns, always adorned flagpoles, and freshly painted shutters, Kowalski has little patience for anyone with what he sees as un-American values. This includes his Toyota-driving son and all immigrants of colour.

His patriotic pride is overwhelmingly symbolized by his 1972 Ford Gran Torino in pristine condition, which represents the durability of American craftsmanship next to the run-down, imported cars driven by other residents. When the teenaged neighbour Thao (Bee Vang) tries to steal the Gran Torino, in a half-hearted effort forced upon him by Hmong gang members, he attacks all that is dear to Walt – specifically, American values. This allows the old man to demonstrate that his own feet are firmly planted in the soil by bringing out his shotgun and not being afraid to use it. After he subsequently demonstrates again his penchant to bear arms, rescuing the would-be thief's sister Sue Lor (Ahney Her) from neighbourhood ruffians, she informs him (and the audience) that the Hmong are exiles because of their support of the United States in the Vietnam War. Although he never expresses it, this opens the door to the unlikely camaraderie that develops between Kowalski and his neighbours who are drawn by circumstance to again fight on the same side.

In true Hollywood broad strokes, Thao turns out to be a 'good' Hmong, different from the 'bad' Hmong who run around in gangs, and his traditional family forces him to make amends with Kowalski by spending time doing odd jobs for the crotchety neighbour. Perversely, Walt uses the opportunity – and the Hmong body – to re-Americanize 'the old neighbourhood,' having Thao tidy yards, fix loosened shingles, paint siding, and reaffix shutters that the immigrants have neglected. Kowalski can yet again feel comfortable sitting on his porch and gazing across the street, without recognizing that he has capitalized on traditional Hmong values to achieve his idea of order. This transformation is another step towards the affinity that develops between him and his neighbours. The film subtly moves towards its argument that what really links Walt to his neighbours is a deep conservatism; in this view, 'good' Hmong are just like crusty, old Americans.

Kowalski is above all an unreformed racist, but audience members are encouraged to see through this 'crusty' exterior to his good will, especially to his ultimate commitment to American values. He hates that his son not only drives an imported car but also works in sales for Toyota when Walt had built Fords all his life. He doesn't like the easy wealth of his white offspring any more than he likes what he sees as the unclean poverty of the Hmong immigrants who live next door. While the requited hatred of the grandmother figure next door is perhaps meant to temper his distaste for the other immigrants in the neighbourhood, *Gran Torino* indulges in overt intolerance while simultaneously appearing to condemn it. In the process of proving Kowalski wrong in his interpretations of the neighbours as having no concept of civility or culture, the film offers audience members such jokes as Kowalski's doozy: 'A Mexican, a Jew and a colored guy walk into a bar, the bartender looks up at them and says, "get the fuck out of here."' The good Americans (i.e., fellow vets) laugh heartily at the joke that momentarily seems to lack a punch line. Part of Thao's transformation into a true American is his adoption of this racist rhetoric.

Thao internalizes Walt's racism to the extent that he pleasantly accepts the terms of Kowalski's will which predictably and yet ironically bequeaths the behemoth car to Thao, who Kowalski had always called Toad. The text of the will is full of hateful idiom: 'And to my friend, Thao Vang Lor, I leave my 1972 Gran Torino on the condition that you don't chop-top the roof like a damned spick, don't paint any idiotic flames on it like some white-trash hillbilly and don't put a big gay spoiler on the rear-end like you see on all the other zipper heads' cars.' By common logic, Kowalski's narrow-mindedness can be chalked up to his advanced age – he comes from different times – and through that he provides the audience a safe conduit through which to exercise some otherwise condemned reactions.[33] This representation, as well as the representation of Phong, the racist Hmong grandmother (Chee Thao), is, of course, an ageist view of racism that assumes that somehow people know less in late life than they knew previously and so are not accountable for their shortcomings. It is another one of the ways in which the silvering screen alleviates social anxieties while highlighting them. Thao does get the car (and the girl) after all.

Reluctant – if still racist – generosity to his neighbours, even to the extent of a genuine affection for them, is arranged to redeem Kowalski's hidebound persona. As he gives in to ironically becoming the hero of the community he had despised, he becomes an unlikely native informant, showing Thao how to fix houses, stand his ground, and get a job. That is, he teaches Thao to be a man, and that masculinity is of course directly tied to being 'American.' Early in the film, Thao is established as womanly in Walt's eyes because of his willingness to wash dishes, garden, and listen to his sister's advice. Once Walt takes the boy under his wing, he declares the necessity to 'man him up a bit.' The transformation begins by Walt teaching Thao to talk like a man, modelling this with his barber friend in a conversation which includes references to 'a Pollack,' a 'chink,' and a 'dumb Italian prick,' and asking his friend whether he'd 'jewed some blind man.' After learning that the 'nip' with Walt is 'some pussy kid' that Walt has decided to 'man up,' the barber agrees to help. The white men are subsequently surprised that Thao adopts their racist language, and they find it rude when the teenager speaks as they do.

This interchange demonstrates the ways in which Kowalski, and by extension *Gran Torino*, both rescues and abuses the Hmong body. Thao is a gentle soul, never likely to achieve Walt's manliness, and so always in need of the older man's help. Walt's manliness provokes an all-out assault against not just Thao but his entire family by the Hmong gang who had wanted the boy to enlist. Having physically threatened a gang member who had attacked Thao, Walt precipitates a full machine-gun attack on the Lor house as well as a vicious assault on Sue. After staccato bullets have crashed through the house, grazing Thao, the family appears to have escaped unscathed until they realize Sue is missing. When she enters the family living room visibly the victim of a horrendous attack, with blood streaming from several orifices as well as having swollen facial features, Walt realizes that his violent threat to these unruly teenagers is in part to blame, or at least that his actions had not been the appropriate approach to the situation. Grandmother Phong had wisely predicted the attack, saying at Walt's first entrance to their home, 'Why is this white man in our home? A man like him brings nothing, nothing but sorrow and death.' Walt has been able to Americanize Thao, but not the Hmong gang members who don't understand the code of righteous violence that he has tried to impose.

Walt has told no one, although Thao and Sue have witnessed signs of it, that he is very ill. The film only vaguely shows his medical chart and his attempt to phone his bourgeois son about it, but the implication is that he has cancer brought on by his lifetime of smoking. Thus, he is expendable – not only because he is old, but because he is old and sick. The diagnosis narratively enables the final clever act on the part of Walt, in which smoking does indeed appear to cause his death.

After locking Thao in Walt's basement to protect the younger man from learning how to kill, Walt flushes the violent Hmong gang members out of their own homes by intimidating them slowly with his seemingly courageous or foolhardy presence. After watching the gang members tremble behind their hyperbolically extreme weapons, Walt asks them for a light and deliberately reaches for his own prized lighter (a memento of his exploits in Korea), fooling them into thinking that he's reaching for a weapon. Walt's revenge, that the gang members finally have witnesses to their violent actions, appears non-violent. But the close-up of his lighter reminds the audience that he is a war veteran (dubiously a hero, in that he received a medal for killing a defenceless boy) who once callously used dead young male Asian bodies as sandbags.

Despite failing to teach the Hmong rebels the codes of American vengeance, he still forces them into American order, provoking them to neaten their neighbourhood just as he used Thao to tidy up his own.

As reviewer David Denby puts it, 'Clint Eastwood appears as, in effect, the last white man in America, guarding what might be called the last American car.'[34] In a changing country, Kowalski must find new ways to manage the security of his country. Violence has a new place and a new meaning in this new world. Denby explains that 'at least since *Unforgiven*, the act of killing another human being has been depicted as one that leaves a permanent scar on men's psyches. In *Gran Torino*, that strain of investigation reaches its apotheosis in an inversion of *Unforgiven*'s climactic barroom standoff, a scene that brings the curtain down on Eastwood's cycle of urban-crime films as hauntingly as the earlier one did on his Westerns.'[35] While Munny allows the Schofield Kid to kill one man in order to learn that he ought to choose a different approach, Kowalski gets himself killed in order to ensure that Thao never learns what it is like to murder someone. Both younger characters need Eastwood's character as a role model because they cannot themselves take on the violence that marked his America, living as they do in different times.

In *Unforgiven*, Eastwood as Munny is read as the embodiment of powerful white America. As Vincent Canby views it, '[The passing years] have given him the presence of some fierce force of nature, which may be why the landscapes of the mythic, late 19th-century West become him, never more so than in his new *Unforgiven*.'[36] But, as Bingham argues, 'masculine domination represents not nature but artifice and effort'; Eastwood is only a force of nature in so far as 'nature' is constructed to be vitally supportive of the 'wild west,' itself a highly artificial space. Similarly, critics read *Gran Torino*, and especially Clint Eastwood, as quintessentially American in a decidedly positive way. That Americanism is tied directly to both a naturalness and a fierce masculinity. For example, interviewer Bruce Headlam describes encountering the actor as 'something like seeing a California redwood for the first time. The difference is that this redwood, even at the age of 78, reaches out to shake your hand with a firmness that still intimidates.'[37] Reviewer Manohla Dargis agrees, describing Eastwood's face as 'a monumental face now, so puckered and pleated that it no longer looks merely weathered, as it has for decades, but seems closer to petrified wood.[38] But in *Gran Torino*, Eastwood's character occupies a space similar in its artificiality to the old west in a film that is essentially a requiem for the Northern United States Rust Belt.

Eastwood earns praise in the popular press for taking on pressing U.S. issues even when they are complicated. As Dargis puts it, she awaits his productions 'not because every film is great – though, damn, many are – but because even the misfires show an urgent engagement with the tougher, messier, bigger questions of American life.'[39] At last, in *Gran Torino*, he has decided to take on directly the issue of race that haunts his prior efforts, especially *Unforgiven* and *Million Dollar Baby* (USA, Clint Eastwood, 2004), in each of which Morgan Freeman's sideline appearances exemplify the role of the black man in Eastwood's projected America. But Eastwood isn't really out to undo intolerance, as he explains in an interview: 'A lot of people are bored of all the political correctness. You're showing a guy from a different generation. Show the way he talks. The country has come a long way in race relations, but the pendulum swings so far back. Everyone wants to be so sensitive.'[40] This icon of white male Hollywood has long proven – including in his Iwo Jima films and *Invictus* (USA, 2006, 2009) – that he has no such sensitivity.

Eastwood is not sensitive about ageism either, so that he deserves and receives praise for continually portraying characters his own age. In *Million Dollar Baby* he portrays tough-talking, soft-hearted Frank, a character who is the exact age of the actor. As he tells Headlam of a similar choice in *Gran Torino*, 'It's ridiculous when you won't play your own age.'[41] Reviewer Patrick Goldstein puts it simply, 'At 78, when most filmmakers have lost their fastball, been put out to pasture or are racking up posthumous awards, Clint isn't just still making great movies, he's still a big-enough movie star to open them all by himself too. It should be a good lesson for age-obsessed studio executives who'd rather toss their Crackberrys in the ocean than greenlight a picture with a grizzled old actor – or God forbid, a middle-aged actress – in a starring role.'[42]

In *Gran Torino*, Eastwood's willingness to appear old is not limited to references to him as an old man hiking his pants up to his nipples, or to a stereotypical grumpiness. Not only is he willing to have a diagnosis hang over him and to show the physical effects of his exertions, but within the montage of Kowalski preparing for his final battle, the film features a shot of Eastwood in the bathtub so that not only his clearly aged neck but his slightly sunken chest are fully on display. Perhaps this is a hint of the fragility that will allow audience members to accept his sacrifice to come as the only option left to this erstwhile goliath, but at the same time it revels in the pure physicality of Eastwood's own age as written on his body. This physical vulnerability is only visible, however, in relation to the pure bravery of Kowalski's next gesture: to stand in the face of multiple firearms, knowing that he will be executed.

Conclusion

In all of the films discussed in this chapter, the house stands as a potent symbol of the aging male's relationship to the American Dream. In *Nobody's Fool*, Sully has refused to own the house he was given but leaves the film frame offering a secure future to his son by bequeathing him the family estate. In *Unforgiven*, William Munny is pictured failing at domesticity on the pig farm he has to leave in order to keep, and Little Bill, the sheriff, is depicted as an incompetent carpenter who finally builds his dream house. Little Bill feels a violent death is unjust because of his participation in domesticating the frontier, saying, 'I don't deserve to die like this. I was building a house.' In *Gran Torino*, the domestic motif is the dominant marker of Americanness. Walt Kowalski uses his house and his idea of a model American home to transform the neighbourhood and teach his Hmong neighbours how to live appropriately. A house that is falling apart is a sign of a rejection of America – Walt Americanizes the Lor family first by helping to fix their home and then by teaching Thao how to get a job building more houses. He is the purveyor of the American Dream even at a time in his life when he realizes achieving it in small measure has offered him little. All of these characters have humble ambitions. Most of all, they want to remain virile and at peace as they reluctantly accept physical changes that come with age, be they knee problems, susceptibility to infection, or cancer.

As a background character, the aging male offers cinema both grounding and a comparative fragility, indicating the tension that growing old offers to narrative. That is, 'old dad' is both predictable in his ways and frail in his ability to continue in them. Taking this aging male centre stage heightens the tension, resulting in an unconvincing weight on the side of the predictable patterns. As a result, on the Hollywood silvering screen, the central aging male character – typically a character presented in order to prop up normative youthful characters – leans on dubious characterizations of women and racialized men in order to seem to stay in his rightful social place of privilege. The transfer of weight works best in depictions of the seemingly bad guy who actually works on the side of good. The tension between seeming right and actual right distracts from the other, more troubling tensions between predictability and ability illuminated by bringing age to centre stage. To present more than just the jokes offered by the Grumpy Old Men films, Paul Newman, and Clint Eastwood take on parts that claim a form of unlikely heroism, adapted to changing times and changing bodies.

Chapter six

As Old as Jack Gets: Nicholson, Masculinity, and the Hollywood System

By now, after a quarter century of loaning out his swagger to safe projects whose inanity guarantees he'll have pizzazz, Nicholson's gloating roguishness just rots the screen. Yet he may have no choice but to soldier on as 'Jack' into senility, since on the rare occasions when he pursues his former hobby, acting – as in 1992's *Hoffa* – he can't hold an audience's interest.

Tom Carson[1]

This chapter continues the argument about white masculinity on the Hollywood silvering screen. I change my focus to the late career of Jack Nicholson in order to explore the ways in which the privilege of the aging male character (and actor) depends upon the malleable and malicious depiction of those who surround him. A key difference between this chapter and the last is that compared with Donald Sullivan (Sully), William Munny, and Walt Kowalski, Nicholson's characters are comfortably well off, or even filthy rich, and do not seem to have had to labour excessively to be so. That the focus on masculinity is still excessive shows even more the overwhelming commitment of Hollywood to male privilege.

Gender debates within film studies include disputes about whether masculinity or femininity is easier to maintain into late life. On the one hand, Jackie Stacey makes a typical argument that the opportunities that characterize masculinity only deepen with age, so that male actors are always at an advantage: 'There is both a greater variety of masculine ideals at one particular moment, and a greater range across a lifetime. In contrast to ideals of femininity, which construct desirable femininity as "youthful" and thus vulnerable to deterioration with age, ideals of masculinity become increasingly realisable and cumulative with age.'[2] On the other hand, though he agrees that masculinity transforms, Dennis Bingham argues that it too is ephemeral whereas the limits of femininity guarantee its longevity:

> Far from being static and stable, masculinity is in constant danger of slipping away, of losing its coherence; thus it must be repeatedly re-earned … We can see examples of this in male genres such as the Western, in which courage, stamina, and prowess with guns must be proved again and again. While woman, assigned to her passive position, need only stay 'in her place' to keep her gendered identity, man must 'act' in order to keep his.[3]

Both claims and the entire debate depend upon definitions of masculinity. Where Stacey seems to wield masculinity as an effect produced by enacting a set of ideals, Bingham wields masculinity as a set of actions most often attributed to men. While the passivity apparently expected of 'woman' might be simpler to maintain, that passivity requires what feminist film theorist Laura Mulvey calls 'to-be-looked-at-ness' which is arguably harder for older actresses than younger actresses to achieve due to youthful beauty norms. The effect of masculinity becomes arguably harder for older actors to achieve as actions are made more difficult by physical changes brought on by aging. Consequently, in films that feature iconic masculine screen idols, it becomes increasingly necessary for a female character to 'stay "in her place"' (per Bingham) to shore up aging masculinity, regardless of what it does for her own status. This is a marked contrast to the more complex gendered depictions discussed in chapters 2–4 in this book. Through a frustratingly backward logic, recent films portraying old men preoccupied or hobbled by their aging often do so at the expense of decent depictions of women. The depictions of older male characters set them up well to more easily 're-earn' their masculinity through their demonstrations of their courage and stamina, and their prowess with guns (metaphorically and sometimes literally).

In one of the most significant advances in recent disability studies scholarship, Robert McRuer analyses Jack Nicholson's role in *As Good as It Gets* (USA, James L. Brooks, 1997), in relation to which McRuer posits his concept of compulsory able-bodiedness. Importantly, compulsory able-bodiedness – which is inextricably linked with Adrienne Rich's 'compulsory heterosexuality' – covers 'over, with the appearance of choice, a system in which there is actually no choice'.[4] To speak here of compulsory youthfulness would be unnecessarily simplistic and derivative, since the obligation to appear young is more visible and openly discussed than heteronormativity and physical normativity. However, the issue of choice, and the invisibility of obligation, persists in relation to aging in that to age well means having no choice but to appear not to age at all. This dilemma is presented as though remaining active and looking young is a choice that 'successful' old people will make.

McRuer sets up the ways in which normativity is upheld in *As Good as It Gets*, particularly its ties to the casting of Nicholson, saying,

> That Melvin is played by Nicholson, a major star who can be read as portraying one of the outrageous characters he is famous for, makes it possible for the film to pass Melvin's behavior off as individual eccentricity ... This construction of the 'outrageous character' allows the audience – which, supposedly, does not identify with Melvin but nonetheless laughs at the scenes in which he makes bigoted wisecracks – to indulge without avowing its own racist, sexist, homophobic, and ableist fantasies. Melvin's bigotry is more complicated, however, than individual eccentricity, because Melvin himself is established from the start as someone living with a disability of sorts, explicitly identified later in the film as obsessive-compulsive disorder.[5]

As McRuer points out, Melvin is recuperated by the conventions of romantic comedy except that his character requires not just the love of a good woman, but the love of a good woman *and* the ingestion of a shiny new pill. Further, and most important to McRuer's argument, Melvin's recuperation relies on the flexibility of less normative characters in the film – particularly disabled and queer ones. Melvin's able-bodiedness is transformed into near normalcy due to the compliance of another character's queer disabled stance. In this chapter, I examine how similar compliances maintain youthful virility on the part of characters played by Jack Nicholson in his late career.

Having shown considerable skill as an actor in taking on serious acting roles as well as mere caricatures, Nicholson has made his career playing notable misogynists. For example, his performance of Melvin in the acclaimed *As Good As It Gets* was deemed Oscar-worthy even though – or perhaps because – he plays an author who memorably explains how to write a female character: 'I think of a man, and I take away reason and accountability.' While generally seen as a contradictory figure who has espoused anti-establishment roles even at the Oscars, Nicholson nonetheless has managed some consistency even after quite clearly selling out (insisting that he make extra money off the sales of Joker figurines).

Since he hit stardom, Jack Nicholson has always been a little too old for Hollywood. As Bingham explains,

> Nicholson in *Easy Rider* was already thirty-two in an era when the ad for *Wild in the Streets* (1968), a youth-protest fantasy film from Nicholson's home studio, AIP, proclaimed, 'If You're 30, You're Through!' Nicholson's age, his receding hairline, and his characters' sympathy with sixties youth culture dampened by their inability to be an actual part of it, made him a transitional figure.[6]

As he ages past this positioning, and as his age becomes an explicit topic of his films, Jack Nicholson's characters require even more passivity and stasis on the part of female characters to illuminate his multi-faceted, always powerful masculinity.

Though always a little old for his stardom, in recent years Nicholson has turned to making films that showcase his increasing age, trafficking in clichés that fit quite neatly into his past career but with a different focus. The films *About Schmidt* (USA, Alexander Payne, 2002), *Something's Gotta Give* (USA, Nancy Meyers, 2003), and *The Bucket List* (USA, Rob Reiner, 2007) constitute as mixed a bag as his past career in terms of the style and level of acting required. Similarly, the sophistication of the statement about aging varies among them. In each, however, of prime concern is that the character Nicholson plays maintains his virility, Viagra-dependent though it might be. To draw on Bingham and McRuer, this re-earned masculinity relies upon the flexibility of marginalized characters to take on the characteristics shed by the aging male characters Nicholson plays. Though not impressively concerned with right or wrong, but rather with personal happiness and satisfaction, and without proposing any form of heroism, however minute, these films all participate (as do the films discussed in the previous chapter) in unfair portrayals of women and racialized people in order to convince a needy public that white straight men can maintain their status even in an aging world.

About Ndugu

Alexander Payne's *About Schmidt* offers a wistful examination of retirement through the eyes of Warren Schmidt (Jack Nicholson), a man who is meant to represent the average American. As reviewer Peter Bradshaw puts it, this character is a summary of Americanness:

Payne has dynamited the strata of mannerisms and crazy laughing-man tics that have settled and solidified on Nicholson over the years and found something molten underneath. The resulting portrayal of an angry, depressed old man has something of Willy Loman, of Walter Matthau in *Kotch*, a little of Spencer Tracy in *Father of the Bride* and perhaps the old man at the end of Ozu's *Tokyo Story*, enigmatically unmoved by his aged wife's death.[7]

This portrait misleadingly presents Schmidt as a figure deserving pity when in fact the film is terrifyingly revealing of the persistence of male white entitlement. As Bingham argues of his earlier roles, 'Nicholson remains a vivid example of a male star who often displayed the consequences of male privilege and the void that it obscures.'[8] In this way, the role fits well into Nicholson's career despite having him embody submissive conformity rather than edgy rebellion.

Immediately after he retires from a dull and ultimately meaningless job, Schmidt's loathed wife Helen (June Squibb) dies, leaving him to indulge fully in a self-exploration that is as telling in its form as in its content. Intriguingly, the film resurrects a clunky voice-over device uniquely realized through letters that Schmidt pens to Ndugu, a Tanzanian orphan he has 'adopted' for US$22 per month, though he occasionally feels buoyant enough to enclose a small bonus. While audiences are cajoled to pity Schmidt for his banal existence, the comparative framework – accentuated by the one-sided correspondence – redirects the pity from an aging man to a young boy with little future (from the American standpoint unthinkingly espoused in the film). Schmidt and smug moviegoers can feel better about his hollow retiree plight.

The confessional structure with its invented 'third world' narratee pushes Schmidt into a reflective autobiographical mode that allows the 'first world' audience to evaluate the dissonances between screen events and his written version. His first letter is the most revealing. After disclosing his age, Schmidt tells Ndugu that his brother has had a leg amputated, demonstrating that these two characteristics – age and increasing disability – are related in his mind. He launches into an emotional diatribe about his erasure from the workplace, but strikes it out as unimportant, which it quickly becomes to his everyday life. These letters reveal Schmidt's attempts to find value in his life now that his past actuarial calculations prove empty. Schmidt's construction of Ndugu as implied audience is similarly revealing. In referring to his widower habit of missing the odd meal, he flippantly compares that experience to what he

Warren Schmidt (Jack Nicholson) contemplates his barren existence before retirement in *About Schmidt.* © Claudette Barius/AFP/Getty Images

assumes is Ndugu's ongoing battle against starvation. Nonetheless, he makes a series of assumptions that reveal his frame of reference to be unshakeable. For example, he tells Ndugu, 'I highly recommend that you pledge a fraternity when you go to college.'

Besides the counterpoint of young Ndugu, who compliantly absorbs pity often reserved for the old, leaving Schmidt powerfully beneficent if disingenuously bereft, the film also sets up disposable female characters from whom Schmidt must shake free in order to maintain his threatened masculinity. He depicts and imagines his wife as thoroughly physically disgusting. Though we see her very thoughtfully cooking his first post-retirement breakfast in their Winnebago as a symbol of the adventures to come, he tells Ndugu that he wakes up wondering, 'who is this old woman in our bed?' Shots of her feature Schmidt's revolted perspective on the butchering of chicken pieces, her flabby upperarms, and the invasive presence of the vacuum. In what is seemingly not meant to be an ironic scene, Schmidt tells Ndugu how much he hates her interrupting, though the accompanying example shows *him* trying to interrupt her (and failing). Even as he mourns Helen's passing once he has to make his own sandwiches and has only Hummel figurines as company, more than her absence he laments her past inadequacies. His deepest concern in relation to her is that she might think badly of him, the very thought of which impedes his journey of self-discovery and search for value in his new life. Even in death, she gets in his way.

Similarly, the film offers a licentious mother (Roberta, played by Kathy Bates) of his daughter's groom to illuminate further that the horrors of growing old are far more apparent in female flesh. Though she is naked in a very brief shot in a much discussed hot-tub scene, the vision was so large a part of the promotional materials (including the trailer) that Roberta's nudity frequently overtakes conversations about the film.[9] Indeed, the film sets her up as repellent, and her raunchy moves on Schmidt highlight his unreliable body. The hot-tub scene occurs because Schmidt has woken from an uncomfortable night on a waterbed with an extraordinarily stiff neck. After hand-feeding him, emptying his bed pan, and giving him drugs she has on hand because of her recent hysterectomy, Roberta offers to see to what she perceives to be his other physical needs. Her sexual advance provides Schmidt the opportunity to reassert his vigorousness in his ability to leave the hot tub quickly.

In his uninterruptible epistolary narrative, Schmidt whines to Ndugu that Helen used to force him to urinate sitting down. As such, the symbol of his liberation prior to his escape from Roberta's clutches is a scene in which he dares to stand to relieve himself, refusing even to use his hand to guide the stream, which ultimately goes all over his bathroom floor before he sets out on his journey of self-discovery. Picking up on the can-do American-way rhetoric discussed in the previous chapter, Schmidt overcomes apparent adversity after communing with Helen via newly appreciated Hummel figurines. He bizarrely declares, 'I know what I want, I know what I need to do, and nothing's going to stop me ever again,' leading viewers to query what has stopped him in the past, besides his resentment of the villainized but obviously innocent Helen. In a deleted scene, Schmidt reads this declaration out from a letter that he is writing in a café in which he attempts to order an omelette with tomatoes rather than potatoes. As the preamble to the scene points out, this deleted scene is a direct homage to a famous scene of Nicholson's from *Five Easy Pieces* (USA, Bob Rafelson, 1970) about breaking rules – however mundane – to get what you want. In the earlier film, Nicholson plays privileged Robert Dupea who rebels against his wealth and antagonizes a waitress who insists on a 'no substitutions' rule at the diner. Dupea revels in a youthful, misogynistic rebellion against conformity at the expense of a waitress. In the *About Schmidt* deleted scene, upon learning of the same 'no substitutions' rule, the aging and bereft Schmidt simply adjusts his order to fit the menu. As the preamble stresses, Schmidt is oppressed by his conformist culture, and as the original context of the scene shows, his resolve to do whatever he likes quickly fades.

The film features two empty rituals meant to highlight life achievements that instead mark the meaninglessness of Schmidt's conformist existence. Near the beginning, we witness his retirement party at which his young replacement disingenuously claims that he will require Schmidt's sage advice and a colleague of Schmidt's age makes a speech that frames Schmidt's search for meaning:

> What really means something, Warren, is the knowledge that you devoted your life to something meaningful. To being productive. And working for a fine company; hell, one of the top rated insurance carriers in the nation. To raising a fine family. To building a fine home. To being respected by your community. To having wonderful lasting friendships. At the end of his career the man can look back and say, 'I did it. I did my job.' Then he can retire in glory and enjoy riches far beyond the monetary kind. All of you young people here, take a good look at a very rich man.

Compared to Ndugu, of course, Schmidt is extraordinarily rich, but by the speech-maker's terms he is destitute. His 'fine company' has thrown his files out immediately upon his retirement, and he has been seamlessly replaced. He has no community, his longstanding friend turns out to have been his wife's lover, and his daughter is impressively average. The convention of the retirement dinner is a mere ritual to mark the passing of time.

Towards the end of the film, at what could be labelled the anti-climax, Schmidt is called upon to give the father-of-the-bride speech at the wedding he has tried to talk his daughter out of. Critics rave about this scene, which portrays an unremarkable man half-heartedly going through the motions not so much for his daughter's sake but out of a deep sense of resignation. Viewers seem excited to see randy Jack take on this role – perhaps because if even he has to submit to such a dull role, then they all can feel a bit better about their mundane worlds.

Refusing yet again to step outside the bounds, despite his new resolve to pee standing up and to not let anything stop him ever again, Schmidt puts on a pathetic replica of fatherhood in this conventional ritual. His performance almost invites pity for his powerlessness within the family that, according to the equally empty retirement speech, is supposed to be the basis of his wealth.

The film stops short of really pitying a patriarch, inadequate though he may be. Instead, the final scenes of the film conjure up a clearer image of Ndugu as the appropriate source for sympathy. Upon his return to Omaha from the Denver wedding, Schmidt receives a reply from Ndugu. Not yet literate, Ndugu has a nun write a formulaic note on his behalf to thank Schmidt for his generosity. After noting a recent malady, the letter conveys Ndugu's wish for Schmidt's happiness, allowing for a self-indulgent realization that this little boy is the only person who desires this for him. Enclosed is a childish painting portraying large white stick person holding a smaller white stick person's hand under a blazing sun, writing large the deep human connection that Schmidt lacks.

Though he and the audience know that his letters have been impressively deceitful, not only in painting a rosy picture, but in portraying choices he has not made and actions he has not taken, Schmidt witnesses in Ndugu's pictorial reply the response a better lived life – the life he has described – would have invited. Ndugu, with his eye infection, has not seen through the epistolary conventions to the meaninglessness that Schmidt and the audience grapple with. Schmidt's entitlement to shape his own story, accompanying his magnanimous gesture of tossing pennies at the problem of massive global fiscal inequality, obscures for the young boy the meaninglessness of middle-American life. Similar to how Simon in *As Good as It Gets* embodies disability and queerness so that both can exit neatly, Ndugu embodies off-screen the frailty and poverty that threaten old age, leaving Schmidt onscreen, pathetic but apparently whole and affluent. This is the fantasy future for the aging average American, and casting Jack Nicholson, better known for his offbeat characters, as this mundane rule-follower only enhances the fantasy's potential veracity.

A Woman to Leave

In contrast to the enormous praise he earned for stepping outside his usual casting in *About Schmidt*, Nicholson receives comment for playing a character too much like his own public persona in *Something's Gotta Give*.

As critic A.O. Scott puts it, 'Mr. Nicholson may not, strictly speaking, be playing himself, but he seems to have prepared for the role by studying a few decades' worth of interviews and magazine profiles celebrating his unapologetic libertinism.'[10] Roger Ebert makes a similar point, saying, 'After playing an older man entirely unlike himself in *About Schmidt*, Nicholson here quite frankly and cheerfully plays a version of the public Jack, the guy who always seems to be grinning like he got away with something.'[11] Though Nicholson is remarkably older than his *As Good as It Gets* co-star Helen Hunt, the decades that separate them are not an explicit theme in the film, nor is Melvin's aging. In *Something's Gotta Give*, that age difference becomes the entire point of inquiry into what to make of an aging playboy.

Accordingly, *Something's Gotta Give* takes the tiresome Hollywood commonplace of men cozying up to much younger women without inviting mention and refreshingly comments upon that age difference. The film is premised on the impossibility for Harry (Jack Nicholson) to resist younger women (all of whom are beautiful, white, and slim),[12] as well as his reluctance to ignore signs of aging – kept at bay by Viagra. Harry arrives at his much younger girlfriend Marin's (Amanda Peet) Hamptons beach house only to discover that her (beautiful, white, and slim) mother Erica (Diane Keaton) is considerably more suited to him, a revelation that takes some time to set in. While Nicholson's character goes through the expectable, yet unconvincing, transformation from childish man to responsible spouse-type, Keaton's character oppositely goes from composed and cynical to an embarrassing replica of her Annie Hall neuroses without the excuse of being young and clueless.

Erica's sister Zoe (Frances McDormand) spells out the scenario explicitly in an early awkward dinner scene during which she draws attention to the unevenly ageist world which the characters inhabit. A Columbia women's studies professor, Zoe opines,

> The over-50 dating scene is geared towards men leaving older women out. And as a result, the women become more and more productive and therefore, more and more interesting. Which, in turn, makes them even less desirable because as we know, men, especially older men, are threatened and afraid of productive, interesting women. It is just so clear: Single older women as a demographic are as fucked a group as can exist.[13]

As the film progresses, over-sixty Harry is more intimidated by over-fifty Erica's accomplishments, once he learns of them, than is her other romantic partner, Harry's doctor Julian (Keanu Reeves), who is twenty years her junior. Nonetheless, Harry has no problem attracting and desiring much younger women (with the help of Viagra), and he never doubts his own charm, whereas Erica is depicted as having thought she would never have another chance at sex despite not relying on Viagra for her libido and despite having instantly attracted hunky Julian. Early in the film, she asserts that she desires a quiet life without the intrusion of masculine attention, but she stops mentioning that wish once she attracts Harry. The transition from desire for daughter Marin to attachment to mother Erica is triggered by Harry's infirmity. Harry's body fails him in a stereotypical scene in which his attempt to have sex with his much younger girlfriend is interrupted by an unexpected heart attack. This weakness transforms him from paramour into a passive patient and Erica – not Marin – reluctantly takes on the role of nurse.

Harry's libido is constantly a threat and under threat throughout the film. Upon arriving at the hospital, medical personnel must determine whether or not Harry has recently taken Viagra. In an apparently humorous, almost slapstick scene, they ask Harry about this prescription just as Marin, Zoe, and Erica pop their heads around the curtain to check on him. Of course, in their presence, he must assert his sexual prowess and deny the need for pharmaceutical enhancement. However, once he learns that the nitroglycerine in his intravenous drip will fatally combine with any Viagra, he has to confess. After he is sunk low by publicly revealing his need for external libidinal support, Harry's convalescence must focus upon regaining his (hetero)sexuality which symbolizes youth in that it demonstrates the eradication of ill health.[14]

Thrown together by his health catastrophe, Erica and 'Old Hare,' as Harry calls himself, find that they have much in common, reminiscing together about how quickly their 'full' lives have passed. Once Erica establishes that Harry had never consummated his relationship with Marin, interrupted as he was by cardiac arrest, she and he fall into bed together. The protracted scene crystallizes the gendered and sexual dimensions of the mainstream silvering screen. Harry releases Erica from her concealing turtleneck by cutting her free with scissors she has handed him, symbolically freeing her from her previously demonstrated shame in her aging body. Meanwhile, she frets about his blood pressure. Rather than a heart attack interrupting, Erica interrupts their sex act, taking a break to strap blood pressure cuffs onto Old Hare. This action establishes her appropriateness as a safe sex partner, unlike her daughter. Once his safe blood pressure levels are verified, the cuff flies through

the air like cast off lingerie and the scene concludes rather stereotypically with each of them in tears – both seemingly because they thought
they would never (be able to) have sex again (but thinking so for very
different reasons).

Despite his years of experience, Harry does not become emotionally
mature, and his tears are literally diagnosed as the normal aftermath of
heart trouble (whereas Erica's are never called into question). Predictably
Harry remains the irascible rogue who can't commit (until the final
scene), and Erica becomes the obsessed cast off whose rejection fuels
her creative energies. While Harry continues to act the playboy, Erica is
unhinged by her encounter with him and regresses into cringe-worthy,
laughable scenes of weeping as she types a play about their failed affair;
she titles the work 'A Woman to Love' after the frustrating phrase Harry
had previously come up to describe her.[15] As John Patterson explains it,
as when Keaton was Annie Hall, 'she does the same old thing all over
again: ditzy, neurotic but somehow self-assured, beanpole-pretty and
good at falling on her ass.'[16] Whereas Harry immediately returns to dat-
ing younger women, Erica has to force herself to accept young Julian's
devotion which can never really distract her from her passion for Harry,
or perhaps from her need to play the more appropriate late-life role of
caregiver. Most importantly, Diane Keaton has to play the same old role
that she has always played in order to ensure Nicholson's screen virility
does not change.

In the final scenes, Harry tracks Erica down in Paris. The film is then
well set up to indulge in its last fantasy. Harry attests to having spent the
last six months tracking down every woman he has wronged in an attempt to make good. This plot device allows a last foray into misogynistic
understandings of heterosexual women's needs, depicting women slam-
ming doors until eventually one wants to pour her heart out, still reeling
from the pain her brief tryst with Harry has caused. Whether this is a
heterosexual woman's fantasy that men will one day atone for their neglect, or a heterosexual man's fantasy that he can make good by asking for
forgiveness, it bolsters the gender dynamic of the film; simply put: despite their age, women love (men) and men leave (women), with the
exception of heart attack patients and their doctors.

Similar to *About Schmidt*'s hot-tub scene, the most remarked upon
scene in *Something's Gotta Give* occurs early in the film when the disori-
ented Harry happens upon Erica naked in her bedroom. Covering his
eyes in horror, this Harry has not yet achieved the grace to comment
on Erica's naked beauty as he eventually does in their sex scene. As a

Diane Keaton and Jack Nicholson attending a gala. © Matthew Imaging / WireImage/Getty Images

disgusted David Denby puts it, 'How do these two veterans react to this unfortunate moment? Erica whoops, shrieks, and tries to desperately cover herself, while Harry throws up his arms as if to avoid an anthrax attack, shouts, "No! No!," and hurls himself against the nearest wall.'[17] Speaking of her first full frontal scene in quite some time, Keaton dismisses her image, saying 'At this point, does it really matter? Nobody is looking at me the way I once imagined people would look at me, like with deviant thoughts. I think they just go, "Huh. There it is. Intact."'[18] Though underestimating her aging body's considerable charms, Keaton's response is a more reasonable expectation of middle-aged nudity – that is, it is highly unlikely that people with Harry and Erica's experience would be so flapped by her state of undress. This is not to argue that this overall implausible film lacks verisimilitude, but rather to point to the exaggeration necessary to demean the aging female frame in order to deflect attention from the failing, heart attack ridden male body on display.

As a showcase of Nicholson's aging, *Something's Gotta Give* is disheartening. The rogue ages into the ageist rogue: afraid of his own old body and other old bodies and capable of mature actions only to assure his long-term security. While the generous interpretation of the film is that it is possible and even more likely that a person will find true love in later middle age, the more assiduous interpretation is that women – however accomplished – are drawn to misogynist patients who will, in time, if the women are lucky, accept their care. Most potently the symbol of masculinity, heterosexual intercourse can continually be achieved as long as one can find a partner careful enough of aging, frail bodies.

The Bucket List

Transforming from apparently loveable rogue in *Something's Gotta Give* to unlikeable scoundrel in *The Bucket List*, Nicholson continues to delve into the most negative interpretations of aging with little sign of respite. Cast opposite Morgan Freeman, Nicholson yet again embodies white male privilege while inhabiting an unpleasantness reserved for the very rich. Edward Cole (Nicholson) is the extraordinarily affluent owner of private hospitals in one of which he promptly lands due to the onset of terminal cancer. He is forced to share a room despite his enormous wealth because he has made his career explaining that he runs hospitals rather than country clubs: 'two to a room, no exceptions.' Of course Cole receives exceptional care despite his semi-private space and his (not quite) last-gasp year is anything but typical.

Cole rooms with his opposite, Carter Chambers (Freeman). Having had to give up his dream of becoming a history professor,[19] Chambers instead took a job as a mechanic when his wife became pregnant. He did this because job opportunities were slim for black men at the time, and this one offered him a solid income with which to support his family. Upon learning of their mutual physical demise, Cole and Chambers strike up an unlikely but unsurprising opposites-attract friendship. Callously leaving Chambers's family (Cole has none to speak of) behind, the pair concoct a boyish plan to live out their fantasies before their

Morgan Freeman and Jack Nicholson at *The Bucket List* premiere. © Dave Hogan/ Getty Images Entertainment/Getty Images

imminent deaths. Though their wishes are a mixed bag, including vague and specific plans, and the titular bucket list is continually revised throughout the film, the first exploits are stereotypical male midlife crisis dreams come true: skydiving, race car driving, and, for Cole, anonymous sex with a younger woman. The two men actively re-earn their masculinity through daredevil exploits and the will to complete a set of actions while they still can.

Chambers's past heroic struggles to make ends meet, especially the sacrifices he has made for his family, make all the more valuable Cole's spending power. In turn, Chambers's long-suffering wife, appropriately a nurse, is cast aside in order to free him up to act like a young man again. When his illness emerges from remission, interrupting their laddish pursuits, Chambers's wife once again plays the faithful companion so that Cole can continue to check items off the bucket list without feeling that he abandoned Chambers. Cole's past heroism lies more questionably in having 'taken care of' his daughter's abusive husband, so that although he himself is odious in his childish misogyny, he has acted against a worse figure of masculine ills. Following Chambers's suggestion, Cole is reunited with his daughter and meets his granddaughter. Doing so brings him, as the voice-over suggests, the joy that money cannot buy (and the film does not veer away from such clichés, relying on one ['kick the bucket'] in its title).

While the film is not focused on the slow 'ravages' of old age, and is not narratively rich enough to merit extensive discussion, the production feeds on ageist ideas that the end is near and that long, dull lives must be remedied. What is more, the film supports the tired notion that if freed from the conventional trappings of work and family, men could do what they really wanted, and that – regardless of their life experiences or means – what men of all ages really want is to jump out of planes, drive fast cars, sleep with young women, and hang out with their buddies. Of course, they can only really enjoy doing so if they have entrapments at home as a contrast, and so Chambers's wife and Cole's estranged daughter are key characters, though absent.

Conclusion: As Good as Jack Gets

The aging represented in each of *About Schmidt*, *Something's Gotta Give*, and *The Bucket List* resonates because it is conveyed by Jack Nicholson, known for always having been an adult onscreen but also for having worked outside the system to the extent that he became the system. As

McRuer explains it, compulsory able-bodiedness, like compulsory heterosexuality, uses the appearance of choice to hide the lack of choice. Of Nicholson's masculinity, Bingham argues, 'The key to Nicholson's appeal even in the films critical of male role-playing is the sense that he breaks the standards for acceptable social behavior ... Many of the films may be critical of patriarchal roles, but the childish abandon of the Nicholson figure is often suicidal ... because it leaves him open to the strictures of the symbolic, which cannot allow irresponsible behavior in grown men.'[20] To survive the 'childish abandon' of acceptable social behaviour, desired by Schmidt, indulged by Harry, and exaggerated by Cole, Nicholson plays characters who are presented as having limited choices due to the infirmities of their aging; Schmidt no longer has his wife to bear the brunt of his frustration with his dull life, Harry can't endure the rigours of youthful sex (or sex with youths), and Cole is told that he will die within months. As a result, each Nicholson character achieves an admirable capaciousness – expanding definitions of masculinity so as to always adhere to them, and each does so at the expense of other characters expected to bear the sloughed off characteristics that threaten an aging man's masculinity.

The Bucket List's Chambers is a prime example of such a holding tank. Importantly, though he is not killed off violently as Ned Logan is in Unforgiven, Chambers dies before Cole so that Chambers can narrate, as Morgan Freeman's characters so often do. I have not yet devoted a section of a chapter to Freeman's late career despite a temptation to do so. Rather, I have awkwardly placed him as the silvering screen does: in a supporting role, full of dignity but ultimately unimportant, and conveniently killed off. Even when in a celebrated lead role, Freeman plays a supporting character, as is the case in Driving Miss Daisy (USA, Bruce Beresford, 1989) and Invictus (USA, Clint Eastwood, 2009). In both films his positioning highlights the remaining power of a rich white character (Miss Daisy as played by Jessica Tandy in Driving Miss Daisy and the captain of the white rugby team played by Matt Damon in Invictus). Even when he plays such characters as God or the U.S. or South African president, Freeman is a background force. On the silvering screen, Freeman's own age is never the central premise; rather, he plays characters who reinforce the broader message about what the aging of U.S. society might mean. Judging from Ned Logan in Unforgiven, Scrap in Million Dollar Baby, and Carter Chambers in The Bucket List, the news is not good for black people in the United States, regardless of their access to money. Logan's and Chambers's deaths both drive the main character to achieve what he has pretended not to want to achieve, despite his age, infirmities, and reformations.

Freeman is neither a rebel nor an actor who easily fits in with the dominant Hollywood system, but he is necessary to imagining both. As McRuer points out, with eccentricity being the type into which Jack Nicholson is cast, the 'bad boy' becomes the new embodiment of a post-modern star system. Seeming to have reformed the classical Hollywood style by accepting experimental roles, Nicholson, especially in films about aging, has created his own formulaic style. The aging letch persona, onscreen and off, embodies the contradictions that make Hollywood appealing. That is, aging is highly gendered and the maintenance of masculinity into old age requires femininity, increased misogyny, and racism to enhance the youthfulness of aging masculinity.

Conclusion: Final Films,
The Silvering Screen Comes of Age

People assume that just because you don't stand as straight as a sapling, you're deaf. Or that your mind is pumpkin mush. The other day, when I was being led into a meeting with a bishop, one of the society ladies told another, 'We must get this woman to parliament soon. Who knows how much longer she'll be with us?' Half bent though I was, I dug my fingers into her ribs. She let out a shriek and spun around to face me. 'Careful,' I told her, 'I may outlast you!'

Aminata Diallo in The Book of Negroes[1]

They, Too, Must Die

Though mortality looms over many of the films discussed in this book, and death often precipitates the conclusion of the plot, the act of dying is usually not the main preoccupation of silvering screen films. The phrase *memento mori* certainly influences the negative depiction of aging, particularly of a late life that involves terminal illness, but death is not overtly represented as the biggest fear. Instead, *surviving* with illness or disability comes across as considerably more terrifying than the seemingly expected end of life. Despite this 'better off dead' aura, euthanasia does not thematically dominate the silvering screen. Rather than indicating a contemporary, enlightened acceptance of human fate, I would argue that the alternate focus on the horrors of living with illness and/or disability, and the possibilities for men at least to overcome both, reveals a set of values and politics that undergird the silvering screen. As a result, the films avoid the automatic association of death with old age that is so popular that there is a social prohibition on mourning a parent who dies when very old, dictated by notions that one expects an old person to die and ought to merely celebrate a long life well lived along with a 'blessed release' from suffering.[2] To complicate matters further, while we are supposed to expect elderly parents to die (and be relieved when they are freed from the pains of late life), we expect our idols to be immortal. On the silvering screen, not only are the older characters in danger of being closer to death than the younger ones, but so too are the actors who play the parts. So while perhaps audiences could imagine that the characters represented are satisfactorily close to the ends of their lives, it is nonetheless a shock when the actors are similarly near their demise.

Final Films

In this chapter, I will briefly compare two 1990s films in which the lead actor was terminally ill during shooting. In the first, *Il Postino* (Italy, Michael Radford, 1995), the actor was a relatively young man, only in his early forties, who died of natural causes. In the second, *The Straight Story* (USA, David Lynch, 1999), the actor was a relatively old man, in his late seventies, who was terminally ill, but took his own life before the illness had the chance to kill him. Because of my focus on the silvering screen, I focus more on *The Straight Story*'s depiction of aging after setting up the assumptions revealed by the unexpected backstage process of *Il Postino*. The comparison of these films demonstrates that although death can happen at any age, its meaning adjusts according to interpretations of the age of the person who dies.

While an older person is closer to death than when that same person was younger, death is not the sole province of the elderly. *Il Postino* demonstrates the fragility of the automatic relationship between age and death. The film depicts a moving and unlikely friendship between a young postman and aspiring poet Mario Ruoppolo (Massimo Troisi) and his unexpected mentor Pablo Neruda (Philippe Noiret). Despite such an immense cliché, that is, the earnest young man who strives to write poetry seductive enough to win over Beatrice (Maria Grazia Cucinotta), the script succeeds because of the type of poetry Neruda wrote, tightly tied to his communist politics. Sadly, when Ruoppolo is finally invited to read his work at a rally dedicated to Neruda, he is killed in a violent uprising. His death is visually represented by a single piece of paper floating under the feet of fleeing audience members. This devastating sight is followed by two sets of text on the screen, the first is a Neruda poem that begins, 'And it was at that age ... Poetry arrived / in search of me,' and the second is a dedication that reads, 'To our friend Massimo' (the actor's name).

In a much-cited earlier scene, after Mario accidentally succeeds in crafting a metaphor by describing himself as 'a boat tossing around on those words,' he asks Neruda whether the revered poet thinks 'the whole world is just the metaphor for something else.' Indeed the trampled piece of paper unexpectedly becomes a symbol not only for the young aspiring poet's death before his public reading, but also for the actor Massimo Troisi's death before full artistic expression. At the age of forty-one, Troisi died of a massive heart attack shortly after filming. Though no doubt his death was a shock, his heart trouble was no surprise. He had postponed a heart transplant in order to complete a film to which he had been committed for a number of years. While he agreed that filming could be adjusted to his ailing health, he refused to cancel filming.

In the introduction to this book, I cite Harrison Ford explaining that his definition of successful aging entails performing his own stunts.[3] Troisi, in his forties, was often replaced by a stuntman, certainly for scenes of him riding his bicycle up a steep incline as his character brings the mail to the poet's home, but even for stunts such as standing for long periods of time. In most scenes that don't replace Troisi with a double, his character sits and speaks softly – this understated manner comes across as an impressive and endearing humility on the part of Ruoppolo. It would likely come across differently were he in his eighties, or even sixties. As Ford implies, it would appear that the actor/character was no longer capable of strong appearance due to age.

In Ruoppolo/Troisi's case the actor was certainly not capable of 'looking the camera in the eye' while performing any physical activity, but the character was. Without the knowledge of Troisi's condition, it was entirely possible to read the film as about youthful potential: a coming of age tragically cut short by revolutionary insurrection into which a relatively innocent man is accidentally drawn. I remember coming home from seeing *Il Postino* in the theatre and immediately turning to the Internet to find out why the film had been dedicated to the young and impressive actor, Massimo Troisi. I was completely shocked to learn of his fate, and to this day have trouble reconciling his tragic death with Ruoppolo's. Similarly, a friend and colleague of mine – herself a poet – spoke to me of her experience after watching the film. She was inconsolable because the young poet hadn't even had a chance to read his poem. These reactions were age specific, and rather than simple reactions to the actor's death, they were heightened reactions to the character's death. Had the film been dedicated to Noiret, though he was only sixty-four years old at the time, our reactions, while still infused with a sadness, would have been different – not so much because of Noiret's career, but because Neruda had the chance to publish his works and express himself fully before this point in his career. It is far more narratively and experientially expectable (and therefore acceptable) that the mentor die after passing on his wisdom to a younger version of himself. The death of the apprentice intervenes in a cycle that is vital to the homogenous vision of the silvering screen.

This reading of *Il Postino* gives a context for my reading of *The Straight Story*, the last silvering screen film that I will discuss at length in this book. Like the theatre and home versions of *Il Postino*, the home version of *The Straight Story* poignantly closes with a dedication, this time to the actor Richard Farnsworth, who portrayed the main character Alvin Straight. Farnsworth shot himself in the year that followed filming. He had suffered from supposedly terminal cancer for several years and that cancer caused him great pain in his hips, similar to that suffered by Alvin Straight in the film. All reports indicate that intense pain induced Farnsworth to take his own life.[4] That he died of his own volition and not from the so-called ravages of age makes him a curious yet compelling elderly figure.

At the time of the film's theatrical release, viewers had to reconcile their understandings of aging with the spectacle of Farnsworth, an elderly and ailing man; presently, the informed viewer has an even more troubling reconciliation to establish. The dedication emphasizes the occupation of film space by an actor running out of lifetime. In the case of stars such as Farnsworth,[5] with longstanding, underappreciated Hollywood careers, physical signs of age symbolize the difficulties of remaining in or, in his case, finally obtaining centre stage in late life. In addition, the film is based on the actual experiences of an elderly man whose voyage attracted media attention in the mid-1990s. Grappling with these two old bodies, *The Straight Story* challenges viewers to re-evaluate space and time continua through a narrative and visual appeal that markedly mixes Disney production with Lynch's direction.

The Straight Story portrays an unusual journey across the Midwest atop a rider mower. David Lynch's vision of Alvin Straight's journey seems, perhaps problematically, quirky and endearing. The seventy-three-old man on a journey to see his estranged brother Lyle succeeds out of sheer determination and strict adherence to his own way. The resulting movie consists of placid rolling shots of cornfields and highways that enhance

Alvin Straight (Richard Farnsworth) tackles the highway at his own pace. ©
Christophe d'Yvoire/Sygma/Corbis

the depictions of Straight's journey and set off his encounters with others
along the road, which are shot with much less camera movement. The
people he meets continually underestimate him though he leaves a trail of
wisdom behind him. He gently convinces a young, pregnant woman to
return to her family. He tells a group of young cyclists, 'The worst part
about being old is remembering when you was young.' He shocks a well-
meaning host by responding patiently to her concerns about his safety
camping on the road side with the question: 'When I fought in the trenches
in World War I, why should I be afraid of an Iowa cornfield?' Because he is
on the road *again*, and not on the road for the first time, as so many others
seem to assume, he draws upon vast experience to succeed.

When he asks his host why he should be afraid, Straight poses a very
good question predicated on an entirely different understanding of himself than others have. As an old man on the road, he appears incongruous and incapable, and his unconventional thirty-year-old mode of
transport intensifies that supposed incongruity and incapacity. People

Alvin Straight (Richard Farnsworth) dispenses sage advice. © Getty Images/ Stringer/Getty Images Entertainment/Getty Images

want to feed him, shelter him, and drive him the rest of the way. He refuses every offer, saying he wants to finish the journey his way. In doing so, he defies underlying assumptions about what it means to be old. Whereas others assume he wants help and is just too proud to ask for it, in fact, he would rather eat his own food than accept food from a charitable pastor, and he would rather sleep in his own trailer than allow others to care for him indoors. He chooses to finish his journey on the rider mower despite offers of other rides. As he placidly rejects each offer of help, viewers witness the baffled reaction of a series of overly generous others who usually believe that he is just too proud to accept or too senile to understand.

When Alvin Straight tells his daughter Rose, a vaguely disabled character played by Sissy Spacek, 'I'm gonna go back on the road,' her immediate response is, 'But Dad *how* are you?' He responds thoughtfully, 'Well, I haven't quite got that figured yet.' Straight's 'story' as an *old* man who wishes to travel on a rider mower to visit his brother is different from what it would have been had he simply been a young or middle-aged man with painful hips who wanted to visit his brother on a rider mower.

It is precisely 'how' Straight decides to tackle the road that preoccupies the film, diegetically and visually. The long, steady tracking shots of the highway's centre dividing line emphasize his unhurried advancement and location on the shoulder (the road's periphery). The metaphorical implications are clear. His progress is slower and more precarious than that of others and, viewers are pushed to assume, more than that of his own past experience. There is even a scene that is a direct adapted copy of the crop-duster scene from Hitchcock's *North by Northwest* (USA, 1959), which demonstrates a transformation from more youthful cinema. That scene and others demonstrate the way in which Straight has to drive off to the side of the road to let bigger and more powerful vehicles pass by. Further, the journey is unpredictable. Still, he arrives in his own time and achieves his quiet goal of staring at the stars with his brother. Other people's assumptions fade in relation to his quiet determination, and careful camera work enables viewers to accompany an old man on a journey that literally succeeds and metaphorically exceeds typical conceptions of aging. When viewers witness Farnsworth's agonizing movements as he plays Alvin climbing off the tractor to retrieve a wind-swept hat, they cannot dismiss the film as un-embodied. When Alvin Straight first learns of his brother's stroke, he calmly acknowledges that time could be running out for him as well, and he sets out to occupy space. The actor Farnsworth too works against time by occupying film space in a final, critically renowned appearance.

Farnsworth's death bizarrely reinforces and simultaneously contradicts the message of *The Straight Story*. On the one hand, the suicide can be interpreted as the action of an old man determined to live and die on his own terms, much as Straight insists on making his journey in his own way and time. On the other hand, the suicide can be interpreted as a fearful reaction to the ravages of cancer, unlike the dogged determination of Straight's approach to his own and his brother's illnesses. Mario Ruoppoli's death is more narratively significant than Alvin Straight's would have been. Similarly, Massimo Troisi's death is more remarkable than Richard Farnsworth's, despite the graphic violence of the latter. While it seems obvious that death would be a key focus of the silvering screen, and that its presence would simplify the apparent meaning of old age, in fact mortality offers little to cultural understandings of aging because it is not death in old age that attracts such fear in popular discourse. Rather, the idea of dying before one's time or living while old dictates a petrified form of cinema, informative in its preoccupations and absences.

The Silvering Screen Fades to Black and White

In the early chapters of this book, I make a fairly contentious claim that the mainstream offerings among silvering screen films homogenize aging into a set of manageable, one could say cosmetic, concerns. Further, it is my position that this homogenization covers a set of more genuine, probing concerns that plague contemporary society in relation to the greying of the population, some of which poke through in the independent films that fit roughly into the category of the silvering screen. A focus on death within the silvering screen would be a focus on the death of the current socio-economic system, a phenomenon that many of the films work together to obscure, committed as they are to imagining that money should be value and that the economic system can simply reproduce itself generation after generation.

The values that support the silvering screen are commensurate with the dominant economic system. Worry about disability is (mistaken) worry about use value. Transforming late life into a set of encounters with illness, disability, and the need for care relates it to political economy rather than to moral economy. For example, fixating on the maintenance of masculinity into late life is about ongoing commitment to profit motive, the same mechanism that greases the wheels of the care system – not only in the overly privatized United States, but also in countries like Canada that purport to have socialized medicine.

The politics that support the silvering screen are not merely neo-liberal, a term which obscures much-needed conversation about the ills of capitalism, but they also are not merely identity politics according to which 'old' should be recuperated as a valid sense of self, one around which political advocacy could cohere. Further, much as I might prefer not to admit it, the Left is as ageist as the Right (and so is the 'Center,' as the recent Obama campaign illustrated).[6] There is not really a progressive political force to turn to, though the Left might be more likely to subsidize late life care. Rather, the silvering screen, in its focus on the failing, propped up body, obliterates the fundamental shift in social relations that the current demographic situation entails. These are its politics (i.e., hiding the replacement of security with contingency). An intriguing, but missing, theme that could appear in a realistic silvering screen film is the internecine struggle for employment. Boomers appear to be tenuously grasping their lucrative, always stable, jobs when they ought to move over for the next generation. However, when these older workers do choose to retire, they are typically not replaced by a replicate new generation of workers. Rather the nature of work is fundamentally transformed into contract, often offshore, labour. The silvering screen, by contrast, pretends that a younger generation, members of which may have different political values than the members of the older generation, as in *Barbarian Invasions* and *The Savages*, will nonetheless occupy the position in which they see their elders, physically pitiable as it may be. This fantasy ignores the entirely different world into which this next generation will age.

Just as its films do not graphically portray death, the silvering screen promises not to die. Whether or not the proportion of older adults to younger people diminishes, now that it has such a stranglehold the silvering screen is unlikely to dwindle. While it could transform, its current commitment to glossing over particular problems and benefits of aging makes change unlikely. Rather, the homogenization may lead to running out of new plots, and thus lead to retro plots that resurrect and remake old silvering screen plots. Thinking of *Whatever Happened to Baby Jane?* this makes a rebirth of outright horror about aging likely. As fears about technology taking over jobs and identity intensifies, the gimmicky age-based science fiction that is currently emerging will appear more frequently, so that films like *The Curious Case of Benjamin Button* (USA, David Fincher, 2008) and *Youth without Youth* (Italy, Francis Ford Coppola, 2007) will continue to transform old age onscreen into a freak show.

The silvering screen's preoccupation with health, wealth, and masculinity – essentially a preoccupation with constructing youthfulness – ignores the current global economic transformation that portends even greater inequities in financial security which will greatly affect health and disability across a person's lifespan. While seniors' groups are growing in number and in strength in the global north, the likelihood of them greatly transforming big-screen production remains slim. Documentary productions featuring the gritty reality of nursing home milieux, the heart-warming yet challenging dimensions of filial care for parents who are becoming demented, and the creative possibilities of older adults may infiltrate mainstream media, such as has already been the case on television shows such as *This American Life* and in production contexts such as the National Film Board of Canada. The seeds of hope for a different consciousness can be found in a growing awareness of the ways in which oldness is an important category for contemporary identity. However, as generative as a new awareness of old subjectivity can be, and as vital as it is to undo assumptions about identity, creativity, and Alzheimer's, these concepts do little to address the racial, gendered, economic, and aged inequities that occur on a broader scale. Until those inequities diminish, the silvering screen will persist in its black and white, lurid depictions of old age. While it seems at first glance that an increase in films about aging indicates a greater social concern about old people, in fact the films reflect an ongoing pathologization of changes associated with age. That pathologization demonstrates that the only stronger social concern relevant to old people is a fear that they impose an untenable financial and emotional burden upon 'productive' members of society.

The slave character quoted in the epigraph to this chapter, Aminata Diallo, opens the narrative that begins Lawrence Hill's novel by acknowledging the ways in which people around her assume that her body bent with age is wracked with other disabilities. Most importantly, she points to the assumed invisibility that comes with being treated as though she can no longer hear nor think. Her threat, 'I may outlast you!' cuts to the central fear promulgating the silvering screen. While a late life riddled with disabilities worries a general public, a capable older person is equally frightening. The idea that the older person might live an even longer life threatens the financial stability of the current economic system, especially when that older person is a racialized body vital to the capitalist machinery, yet supposedly expendable and easily expended. Sooner or later, the silvering screen will fade to black, either by disappearing or by at last telling stories of other aging bodies. For now, Harrison Ford can look the camera in the eye, Melanie Griffith can't get a decent part, and Morgan Freeman usually plays the decent man who dies and/or narrates.

Filmography

Included here, organized alphabetically by title, are details on all the films discussed in this book.

50 First Dates (USA, 2004)
Director: Peter Segal
Screenplay: George Wing
Cinematographer: Jack N. Green
Editor: Jeff Gourson
Music: Teddy Castellucci
Starring: Adam Sandler, Drew Barrymore, Rob Schneider, Sean Astin
Distribution: Columbia Pictures

About Schmidt (USA, 2002)
Director: Alexander Payne
Screenplay: Alexander Payne, Jim Taylor
Cinematographer: James Glennon
Editor: Kevin Tent
Music: Rolfe Kent
Starring: Jack Nicholson, Kathy Bates, Hope Davis, Dermot Mulroney
Distribution: New Line Cinema

After Life [*Wandafuru Raifu*] (Japan, 1998)
Director: Hirokazu Kore-eda
Screenplay: Hirokazu Kore-eda
Cinematographers: Masayoshi Sukita and Yutaka Yamasaki
Editor: Hirokazu Kore-eda

Music: Yasuhiro Kasamatsu
Starring: Arata, Erika Oda, Susumu Terajima, Taketoshi Naito, Kyoko Kagawa
Distribution: Artistic License Films

All About Eve **(USA, 1950)**
Director: Joseph L. Mankiewicz
Screenplay: Joseph L. Mankiewicz
Cinematographer: Milton R. Krasner
Editor: Barbara McLean
Music: Alfred Newman
Starring: Bette Davis, Anne Baxter, George Sanders, Celeste Holm, Gary Merrill
Distribution: Twentieth Century Fox

Alone **(USA, 1997)**
Director: Michael Lindsay-Hogg
Screenplay: Horton Foote
Cinematographer: Jeff Jur
Editors: Norman Buckley, Anthony Sloman
Music: David Shire
Starring: Hume Cronyn, James Earl Jones, Betty Murphy, Shelley Duvall
Distribution: Paramount Pictures

American Pie **(USA, 1999)**
Director: Paul Weitz
Screenplay: Adam Herz
Cinematographer: Richard Crudo
Editor: Priscilla Nedd-Friendly
Music: David Lawrence
Starring: Jason Biggs, Chris Klein, Thomas Ian Nicholas, Eugene Levy, Shannon Elizabeth
Distribution: Universal Pictures

Antonia's Line [*Antonia*] **(Netherlands, 1995)**
Director: Marleen Gorris
Screenplay: Marleen Gorris
Cinematographer: Willy Stassen
Editors: Wim Louwrier, Michiel Reichwein
Music: Ilona Sekacz
Starring: Willeke van Ammelrooy, Els Dottermans, Victor Löw
Distribution: Asmik Ace Entertainment

As Good as It Gets **(USA, 1997)**
Director: James L. Brooks
Screenplay: Mark Andrus, James L. Brooks
Cinematographer: John Bailey
Editor: Richard Marks
Music: Hans Zimmer
Starring: Jack Nicholson, Helen Hunt, Greg Kinnear, Cuba Gooding Jr., Shirley
Knight, Skeet Ulrich
Distribution: TriStar Pictures

Autumn Spring [*Babí léto*] **(Czech Republic, 2002)**
Director: Vladimír Michálek
Screenplay: Jirí Hubac
Cinematographer: Martin Strba
Editor: Jirí Brozek
Music: Michal Lorenc
Starring: Vlastimil Brodský, Stella Zázvorková, Stanislav Zindulka
Distribution: BKP Film

Away from Her **(Canada, 2006)**
Director: Sarah Polley
Screenplay: Sarah Polley
Cinematographer: Luc Montpellier
Editor: David Wharnsby
Music: Jonathan Goldsmith
Starring: Julie Christie, Gordon Pinsent, Olympia Dukakis, Kristen Thomson,
Michael Murphy, Wendy Crewson
Distribution: Capri Releasing, Mongrel Media

The Barbarian Invasions [*Les invasions barbares*] **(Canada, 2003)**
Director: Denys Arcand
Screenplay: Denys Arcand
Cinematographer: Guy Dufaux
Editor: Isabelle Dedieu
Music: Pierre Aviat
Starring: Rémy Girard, Stéphane Rousseau, Dorothée Berryman, Louise Portal
Distribution: Miramax Films

Bend It Like Beckham **(UK, 2002)**
Director: Gurinder Chadha

Screenplay: Gurinder Chadha, Guljit Bindra, Paul Mayeda Berges
Cinematographer: Jong Lin
Editor: Justin Krish
Music: Craig Pruess
Starring: Parminder Nagra, Keira Knightley, Jonathan Rhys Meyers, Anupam Kher, Shaznay Lewis, Archie Panjabi
Distribution: Helkon SK, Fox Searchlight Pictures

Between Strangers (**Canada & Italy, 2002**)
Director: Edoardo Ponti
Screenplay: Edoardo Ponti
Cinematographer: Gregory Middleton
Editor: Roberto Silvi
Music: Zbigniew Presiner
Starring: Sophia Loren, Mira Sorvino, Deborah Kara Unger, Pete Postlethwaite
Distribution: Equinox Entertainment

The Bucket List (**USA, 2007**)
Director: Rob Reiner
Screenplay: Justin Zackham
Cinematographer: John Schwartzman
Editor: Robert Leighton
Music: Marc Shaiman
Starring: Jack Nicholson, Morgan Freeman, Sean Hayes, Beverly Todd
Distribution: Warner Bros.

Calendar Girls (**UK, 2003**)
Director: Nigel Cole
Screenplay: Juliette Towhidi, Tim Firth
Cinematographer: Ashley Rowe
Editor: Michael Parker
Music: Patrick Doyle
Starring: Helen Mirren, Julie Walters, Linda Bassett, Annette Crosbie, Celia Imrie, Penelope Wilton
Distribution: Touchstone Pictures

Central Station [*Central do Brasil*] (**Brazil, 1998**)
Director: Walter Salles
Screenplay: Marcos Bernstein, João Emanuel Carneiro
Cinematographer: Walter Carvalho

Editors: Felipe Lacerda, Isabelle Rathery
Music: Antonio Pinto
Starring: Fernanda Montenegro, Marília Pêra, Vinícius de Oliveira, Soia Lira, Othon Bastos
Distribution: Canal+

Checking Out (USA, 2005)
Director: Jeff Hare
Screenplay: Richard Marcus
Cinematographer: Matthew Jensen
Editor: Edward R. Abroms
Music: Nicholas Pike
Starring: Peter Falk, Laura San Giacomo, Judge Reinhold, David Paymer
Distribution: Allumination FilmWorks

Club eutanasia (Mexico, 2004)
Director: Agustín Tapia
Screenplay: Agustín Tapia
Cinematographer: Javier Morón
Editors: Roberto Bolado, Agustín Tapia
Music: Leoncio Lara, Jaime Pavón
Starring: Rosita Quintana, Héctor Gómez, Lorenzo de Rodas, Ofelia Medina
Distribution: Allumination FilmWorks

Cocoon (USA, 1985)
Director: Ron Howard
Screenplay: Tom Benedek
Cinematographer: Donald Peterman
Editors: Daniel P. Hanley, Mike Hill
Music: James Horner
Starring: Don Ameche, Wilford Brimley, Hume Cronyn, Brian Dennehy, Jack Gilford, Maureen Stapleton, Jessica Tandy, Gwen Verdon, Herta Ware
Distribution: Twentieth Century Fox

The Color of Money (USA, 1986)
Director: Martin Scorsese
Screenplay: Walter Tevis, Richard Price
Cinematographer: Michael Ballhaus
Editor: Thelma Schoonmaker
Music: Robbie Robertson

Starring: Paul Newman, Tom Cruise, Mary Elizabeth Mastrantonio,
Helen Shaver, Forest Whitaker, John Turturro
Distribution: Touchstone Pictures

Cool Hand Luke (USA, 1967)
Director: Stuart Rosenberg
Screenplay: Donn Pearce, Frank R. Pierson
Cinematographer: Conrad Hall
Editor: Sam O'Steen
Music: Lalo Schifrin
Starring: Paul Newman
Distribution: Warner Bros.

The Curious Case of Benjamin Button (USA, 2008)
Director: David Fincher
Screenplay: Eric Roth
Cinematographer: Claudio Miranda
Editors: Kirk Baxter, Angus Wall
Music: Alexandre Desplat
Starring: Brad Pitt, Cate Blanchett, Taraji P. Henson, Julia Ormond,
Tilda Swinton
Distribution: Paramount Pictures, Warner Bros.

Dark Victory (USA, 1939)
Director: Edmund Goulding
Screenplay: Casey Robinson
Cinematographer: Ernest Haller
Editor: William Holmes
Music: Max Steiner
Starring: Bette Davis, George Brent
Distribution: Warner Bros.

Daybreak [*Om jag vänder mig om*] (Sweden, 2003)
Director: Björn Runge
Screenplay: Björn Runge
Cinematographer: Ulf Brantås
Editor: Lena Dahlberg
Music: Ulf Dageby
Starring: Pernilla August, Jakob Eklund, Marie Richardson, Leif Andrée,
Peter Andersson, Ann Petrén, Sanna Krepper
Distribution: Newmarket Films

The Death of Mr. Lazarescu [*Moartea domnului Lazarescu*] **(Romania, 2005)**
Director: Cristi Puiu
Screenplay: Cristi Puiu, Razvan Radulescu
Cinematographers: Andrei Butica, Oleg Mutu
Editor: Dana Bunescu
Music: Andreea Paduraru
Starring: Ion Fiscuteanu, Luminita Gheorghiu
Distribution: Tartan Films

The Decline of the American Empire [*Le déclin de l'empire américain*] **(Canada, 1986)**
Director: Denys Arcand
Screenplay: Denys Arcand
Cinematographer: Guy Dufaux
Editor: Monique Fortier
Music: François Dompierre
Starring: Dominique Michel, Dorothée Berryman
Distribution: Cineplex-Odeon Films

Driving Miss Daisy **(USA, 1989)**
Director: Bruce Beresford
Screenplay: Alfred Uhry
Cinematographer: Peter James
Editor: Mark Warner
Music: Hans Zimmer
Starring: Jessica Tandy, Morgan Freeman, Dan Aykroyd, Esther Rolle
Distribution: Warner Bros.

Easy Rider **(USA, 1969)**
Director: Dennis Hopper
Screenplay: Peter Fonda, Dennis Hopper, Terry Southern
Cinematographer: László Kovács
Editor: Donn Cambern
Music: Roger McGuinn
Starring: Peter Fonda, Dennis Hopper, Jack Nicholson
Distribution: Columbia Pictures

Elsa and Fred [*Elsa y Fred*] **(Argentina, 2005)**
Director: Marcos Carnevale
Screenplay: Marcos Carnevale, Marcela Guerty, Lily Ann Martin
Cinematographer: Juan Carlos Gómez
Editor: Nacho Ruiz Capillas

Music: Lito Vitale
Starring: Manuel Alexandre, China Zorrilla, Blanca Portillo, José Ángel Egido, Omar Muñoz
Distribution: Altafilms Grupo Alta Classics

Eternity and a Day [*Mia eoniotita ke mia mera*] **(Greece, 1998)**
Director: Theo Angelopoulos
Screenplay: Theo Angelopoulos
Cinematographers: Yorgos Arvanitis, Andreas Sinanos
Editor: Yannis Tsitsopoulos
Music: Eleni Karaindrou
Starring: Bruno Ganz, Isabelle Renauld, Fabrizio Bentivoglio
Distribution: Merchant Ivory Productions

Father of the Bride **(USA, 1991)**
Director: Charles Shyer
Screenplay: Frances Goodrich, Albert Hackett, Nancy Meyers, Charles Shyer
Cinematographer: John Lindley
Editor: Richard Marks
Music: Alan Silvestri
Starring: Steve Martin, Diane Keaton, Kimberly Williams, Martin Short
Distribution: Touchstone Pictures

Five Easy Pieces **(USA, 1970)**
Director: Bob Rafelson
Screenplay: Adrien Joyce
Cinematographer: László Kovács
Editors: Christopher Holmes, Gerald Shepard
Music: Pearl Kaufman
Starring: Jack Nicholson, Karen Black
Distribution: Columbia Pictures

The Gin Game **(USA, 2003)**
Director: Arvin Brown
Screenplay: D. L. Coburn
Cinematographer: John Simmons
Editor: Tara Timpone
Music: Mike Post
Starring: Dick Van Dyke, Mary Tyler Moore
Distribution: Public Broadcasting Service

Gran Torino **(USA, 2009)**
Director: Clint Eastwood
Screenplay: Nick Schenk
Cinematographer: Tom Stern
Editors: Joel Cox, Gary D. Roach
Music: Kyle Eastwood, Michael Stevens
Starring: Clint Eastwood, Bee Vang
Distribution: Warner Bros.

Grandfather **[Gong Gong] (Singapore, 2001)**
Director: Chee Nien Lau
Screenplay: Joon Kai Chan, Chee Nien Lau
Cinematographer: Abhijoy Gandhi
Editor: Choon Hiong Ho
Music: Lydia Leong
Starring: Raeann Heng, Roseann Heng, Poh Thiau Neo
Distribution: Ngee Ann Polytechnic

Great Expectations **(USA, 1998)**
Director: Alfonso Cuarón
Screenplay: Mitch Glazer
Cinematographer: Emmanuel Lubezki
Editor: Steven Weisberg
Music: Patrick Doyle, Ron Wasserman
Starring: Ethan Hawke, Gwyneth Paltrow
Distribution: Twentieth Century Fox

Grumpier Old Men **(USA, 1995)**
Director: Howard Deutch
Screenplay: Mark Steven Johnson
Cinematographer: Tak Fujimoto
Editors: Maryann Brandon, Seth Flaum, Billy Weber
Music: Alan Silvestri
Starring: Walter Matthau, Jack Lemmon, Ann-Margret, Sophia Loren,
Burgess Meredith
Distribution: Warner Bros.

Grumpy Old Men **(USA, 1993)**
Director: Donald Petrie
Screenplay: Mark Steven Johnson

Cinematographer: John E. Jensen
Editor: Bonnie Koehler
Music: Alan Silvestri
Starring: Walter Matthau, Jack Lemmon, Ann-Margret, Burgess Meredith,
Daryl Hannah, Kevin Pollak
Distribution: Warner Bros.

Harold and Maude **(USA, 1971)**
Director: Hal Ashby
Screenplay: Colin Higgins
Cinematographer: John Alonzo
Editors: William A. Sawyer, Edward Warschilka
Music: Cat Stevens
Starring: Ruth Gordon, Bud Cort, Vivian Pickles, Eric Christmas, Cyril Cusack,
Ellen Greer, G. Wood
Distribution: Paramount Pictures

Hombre **(USA, 1966)**
Director: Martin Ritt
Screenplay: Irving Ravetch, Harriet Frank Jr.
Cinematographer: James Wong Howe
Editor: Frank Bracht
Music: David Rose
Starring: Paul Newman, Fredric March, Richard Boone
Distribution: Twentieth Century Fox

How to Make an American Quilt **(USA, 1995)**
Director: Jocelyn Moorhouse
Screenplay: Jane Anderson
Cinematographer: Janusz Kaminski
Editor: Jill Bilcock
Music: Thomas Newman
Starring: Winona Ryder, Anne Bancroft, Ellen Burstyn, Kate Nelligan,
Alfre Woodard
Distribution: Universal Pictures

Hush ... Hush, Sweet Charlotte **(USA, 1964)**
Director: Robert Aldrich
Screenplay: Henry Farrell, Lukas Heller
Cinematographer: Joseph F. Biroc

Editor: Michael Luciano
Music: Frank De Vol
Starring: Bette Davis, Olivia de Havilland, Joseph Cotten, Agnes Moorehead
Distribution: Twentieth Century Fox

The Hustler (USA, 1961)
Director: Robert Rossen
Screenplay: Sidney Carroll, Robert Rossen
Cinematographer: Eugen Schüfftan
Editor: Dede Allen
Music: Kenyon Hopkins
Starring: Paul Newman, Jackie Gleason, Piper Laurie, George C. Scott
Distribution: Twentieth Century Fox

I'm Not Rappaport (USA, 1996)
Director: Herb Gardner
Screenplay: Herb Gardner
Cinematographer: Adam Holender
Editors: Anne McCabe, Emily Paine, Wendy Stanzler
Music: Gerry Mulligan
Starring: Walter Matthau, Ossie Davis, Amy Irving, Craig T. Nelson, Boyd Gaines
Distribution: Gramercy Pictures

Indiana Jones and the Raiders of the Lost Ark (USA, 1981)
Director: Steven Spielberg
Screenplay: Lawrence Kasdan
Cinematographer: Douglas Slocombe
Editor: Michael Kahn
Music: John Williams
Starring: Harrison Ford, Karen Allen
Distribution: Paramount Pictures

Innocence (Australia, 2000)
Director: Paul Cox
Screenplay: Paul Cox
Cinematographer: Tony Clark
Editor: Simon Whitington
Music: Paul Grabowsky
Starring: Julia Blake, Charles Tingwell, Kristine Van Pellicom, Kenny Aernouts
Distribution: Cinemavault Releasing

Invictus (**USA, 2009**)
Director: Clint Eastwood
Screenplay: Anthony Peckham
Cinematographer: Tom Stern
Editors: Joel Cox, Gary D. Roach
Music: Kyle Eastwood, Michael Stevens
Starring: Morgan Freeman, Matt Damon
Distribution: Warner Bros.

Iris (**UK, 2001**)
Director: Richard Eyre
Screenplay: Richard Eyre, Charles Wood
Cinematographer: Roger Pratt
Editor: Martin Walsh
Music: James Horner
Starring: Kate Winslet, Judi Dench, Jim Broadbent, Hugh Bonneville
Distribution: Buena Vista International, Miramax Films, Paramount Pictures

Jesus of Montreal [Jésus de Montréal] (**Canada, 1989**)
Director: Denys Arcand
Screenplay: Denys Arcand
Cinematographer: Guy Dufaux
Editor: Isabelle Dedieu
Music: Jean-Marie Benoît, François Dompierre, Yves Laferrière
Starring: Lothaire Bluteau, Catherine Wilkening, Johanne-Marie Tremblay
Distribution: Koch Lorber Films

Kotch (**USA, 1971**)
Director: Jack Lemmon
Screenplay: John Paxton
Cinematographer: Richard H. Kline
Editor: Ralph E. Winters
Music: Marvin Hamlisch
Starring: Walter Matthau, Deborah Winters, Felicia Farr, Charles Aidman,
Ellen Geer
Distribution: United Artists

Kramer vs. Kramer (**USA, 1979**)
Director: Robert Benton
Screenplay: Robert Benton

Cinematographer: Néstor Almendros
Editors: Gerald B. Greenberg, Ray Hubley, Bill Pankow
Music: Paul Gemignani, Herb Harris, John Kander, Erma E. Levin, Roy B. Yokelson, Antonio Vivaldi
Starring: Dustin Hoffman, Meryl Streep, Justin Henry, Jane Alexander
Distribution: Columbia Pictures

Ladies in Lavender (UK, 2005)
Director: Charles Dance
Screenplay: Charles Dance
Cinematographer: Peter Biziou
Editor: Michael Parker
Music: Nigel Hess
Starring: Judi Dench, Maggie Smith, Daniel Brühl, Natascha McElhone
Distribution: Lakeshore International

Last Orders (UK, 2001)
Director: Fred Schepisi
Screenplay: Fred Schepisi
Cinematographer: Brian Tufano
Editor: Kate Williams
Music: Paul Grabowsky
Starring: Michael Caine, Tom Courtenay, David Hemmings, Bob Hoskins, Helen Mirren, Ray Winstone
Distribution: Sony Pictures Classics

The Left-Handed Gun (USA, 1957)
Director: Arthur Penn
Screenplay: Leslie Stevens
Cinematographer: J. Peverell Marley
Editor: Folmar Blangsted
Music: Alexander Courage
Starring: Paul Newman, Lita Milan, John Dehner
Distribution: Warner Bros.

Letters from Iwo Jima (USA, 2006)
Director: Clint Eastwood
Screenplay: Iris Yamashita
Cinematographer: Tom Stern
Editors: Joel Cox, Gary D. Roach

Music: Kyle Eastwood, Michael Stevens
Starring: Ken Watanabe, Kazunari Ninomiya, Tsuyoshi Ihara, Ryo Kase,
Shidō Nakamura
Distribution: Warner Bros.

A Long Weekend in Pest and Buda [*Egy hét Pesten és Budán*]**(Hungary, 2003)**
Director: Károly Makk
Screenplay: Károly Makk, Mark Vlessing
Cinematographer: Elemér Ragályi
Editor: Mária Rigó
Music: László Dés
Starring: Mari Töröcsik, Iván Darvas, Eszter Nagy-Kálózy, Dezsö Garas
Distribution: Bunyik Entertainment

Lost for Words **(UK, 1999)**
Director: Alan J. W. Bell
Screenplay: Deric Longden
Cinematographer: Alan Pyrah
Editor: Janey Walkin
Music: Jim Parker
Starring: Thora Hird, Pete Postlethwaite, Penny Downie, Jennifer Luckraft,
David Shimwell, Anne Reid, Keith Clifford
Distribution: Yorkshire Television, Independent Television

Madadayo **(Japan, 1993)**
Director: Akira Kurosawa
Screenplay: Akira Kurosawa
Cinematographer: Takao Saitô, Masaharu Ueda
Editor: Akira Kurosawa
Music: Shinichirô Ikebe
Starring: Tatsuo Matsumura, Kyoko Kagawa, Hisashi Igawa, George Tokoro,
Masayuki Yui
Distribution: Toho

Million Dollar Baby **(USA, 2004)**
Director: Clint Eastwood
Screenplay: Paul Haggis
Cinematographer: Tom Stern
Editor: Joel Cox
Music: Clint Eastwood

Starring: Clint Eastwood, Hilary Swank, Morgan Freeman
Distribution: Warner Bros.

A Month of Sundays (USA, 2001)
Director: Stewart Raffill
Screenplay: Keith Murphy
Cinematographer: Jacques Haitkin
Editor: Terry Kelley
Music: John Campbell
Starring: Michelle Allsopp, Dwight Armstrong, Mary Boucher, Kevin Brief
Distribution: PorchLight Entertainment

Mrs. Brown (UK, 1997)
Director: John Madden
Screenplay: Jeremy Brock
Cinematographer: Richard Greatrex
Editor: Robin Sales
Music: Stephen Warbeck
Starring: Judi Dench, Billy Connolly, Geoffrey Palmer, Antony Sher,
Gerard Butler
Distribution: Miramax Films

Mrs. Henderson Presents (UK, 2005)
Director: Stephen Frears
Screenplay: Martin Sherman
Cinematographer: Andrew Dunn
Editor: Lucia Zucchetti
Music: George Fenton
Starring: Judi Dench, Bob Hoskins, Kelly Reilly, Will Young
Distribution: Pathe

Mrs. Palfrey at the Claremont (USA, 2005)
Director: Dan Ireland
Screenplay: Ruth Sacks
Cinematographer: Claudio Rocha
Editors: Nigel Galt, Viginia Katz
Music: Stephen Barton
Starring: Joan Plowright, Rupert Friend, Zoe Tapper, Anna Massey,
Robert Lang
Distribution: Paragon Pictures

My Kingdom (Italy & UK, 2001)
Director: Don Boyd
Screenplay: Don Boyd, Nick Davies
Cinematographer: Dewald Aukema
Editor: Adam Ross
Music: Simon Fisher-Turner, Deirdre Gribbin
Starring: Richard Harris, Reece Noi, Lynn Redgrave, Tom Bell, Emma Catherwood
Distribution: First Look International

Never Too Late (Canada, 1997)
Director: Giles Walker
Screenplay: Donald Martin
Cinematographer: Savas Kalogeras
Editor: Ion Webster
Music: Normand Corbeil
Starring: Olympia Dukakis, Jean Lapointe, Jan Rubes, Cloris Leachman, Corey Haim, Matt Craven
Distribution: MTI Home Video

Nobody's Fool (USA, 1994)
Director: Robert Benton
Screenplay: Robert Benton
Cinematographer: John Bailey
Editor: John Bloom
Music: Howard Shore
Starring: Paul Newman, Jessica Tandy, Bruce Willis, Melanie Griffith
Distribution: Paramount Pictures

Noel (USA, 2004)
Director: Chazz Palminteri
Screenplay: David Hubbard
Cinematographer: Russell Carpenter
Editor: Susan E. Morse
Music: Alan Menken
Starring: Penélope Cruz, Susan Sarandon, Paul Walker, Alan Arkin, Daniel Sunjata, Robin Williams, Chazz Palminteri
Distribution: Convex Group

The Notebook (USA, 2004)
Director: Nick Cassavetes
Screenplay: Jeremy Leven

Cinematographer: Robert Fraisse
Editor(s): Alan Heim
Music: Aaron Zigman
Starring: James Garner, Gena Rowlands, Ryan Gosling, Rachel McAdams
Distribution: New Line Cinema

The Odd Couple **(USA, 1967)**
Director: Gene Saks
Screenplay: Neil Simon
Cinematographer: Robert B. Hauser
Editor: Frank Bracht
Music: Neal Hefti
Starring: Jack Lemmon, Walter Matthau
Distribution: Paramount Pictures

On Golden Pond **(USA, 1981)**
Director: Mark Rydell
Screenplay: Ernest Thompson
Cinematographer: Billy Williams
Editor(s): Robert L. Wolfe
Music: Dave Grusin
Starring: Katharine Hepburn, Henry Fonda, Jane Fonda
Distribution: Universal Pictures

Open Hearts [*Elsker dig for evigt*] **(Denmark, 2002)**
Director: Susanne Bier
Screenplay: Anders Thomas Jensen
Cinematographer: Morten Søborg
Editors: Pernille Bech Christensen, Thomas Krag
Music: Jesper Winge Leisner
Starring: Mads Mikkelsen, Nikolaj Lie Kaas
Distribution: Nordisk Film

The Other Side of the Street [*O outro lado da rua*] **(Brazil, 2004)**
Director: Marcos Bernstein
Screenplay: Marcos Bernstein, Melanie Dimantas
Cinematographer: Toca Seabra
Editor: Marcelo Moraes
Music: Guilherme Bernstein Seixas
Starring: Fernanda Montenegro, Raul Cortez, Laura Cardoso
Distribution: Strand Releasing

Paris Blues (USA, 1961)
Director: Martin Ritt
Screenplay: Jack Sher, Irene Kamp, Walter Bernstein
Cinematographer: Christian Matras
Editor: Roger Dwyre
Music: Billy Strayhorn, Duke Ellington
Starring: Sidney Poitier, Paul Newman, Diahann Carroll, Joanne Woodward
Distribution: United Artists

Pather Panchali (India, 1955)
Director: Satyajit Ray
Screenplay: Satyajit Ray
Cinematographer: Subrata Mitra
Editor: Dulal Dutta
Music: Ravi Shankar
Starring: Kanu Bannerjee, Karuna Bannerjee, Subir Bannerjee,
Chunibala Devi
Distribution: Curzon Film Ditributors (1957), Merchant Ivory Productions
(1995), Sony Pictures Classics (1995), Columbia TriStar (2003)

Pauline and Paulette [*Pauline & Paulette*] (Belgium, 2001)
Director: Lieven Debrauwer
Screenplay: Jaak Boon, Lieven Debrauwer
Cinematographer: Michel van Laer
Editor: Philippe Ravoet
Music: Frédéric Devreese
Starring: Dora van der Groén, Ann Petersen
Distribution: Sony Pictures Classics

The Postman [*Il Postino*] (Italy, 1994)
Director: Michael Radford
Screenplay: Anna Pavignano, Michael Radford, Furio Scarpelli, Giacomo
Scarpelli, Massimo Troisi
Cinematographer: Franco Di Giacomo
Editor: Roberto Perpignani
Music: Luis Enríquez Bacalov
Starring: Philippe Noiret, Massimo Troisi, Maria Grazia Cucinotta
Distribution: Miramax Films

Rhapsody in August [*Hachi-gatsu no kyôshikyoku*] (Japan, 1991)
Director: Akira Kurosawa

Screenplay: Akira Kurosawa
Cinematographers: Takao Saitô, Masaharu Ueda
Editor: Akira Kurosawa
Music: Shinichirô Ikebe
Starring: Sachiko Murase, Richard Gere
Distribution: Shochiku Films

A Rumor of Angels **(UK, 2000)**
Director: Peter O'Fallon
Screenplay: James Eric, Jamie Horton, Peter O'Fallon
Cinematographer: Roy H. Wagner
Editor: Louise Rubacky
Music: Tim Simonec
Starring: Vanessa Redgrave, Ray Liotta
Distribution: Metro-Goldwyn-Mayer

Saraband [*Sarabande*] **(Sweden, 2003)**
Director: Ingmar Bergman
Screenplay: Ingmar Bergman
Cinematographers: Per-Olof Lantto, Sofi Stridh, Raymond Wemmenlöv
Editor: Sylvia Ingemarsson
Starring: Liv Ullmann, Erland Josephson, Börje Ahlstedt, Julia Dufvenius, Gunnel Fred
Distribution: Mongrel Media

The Savages **(USA, 2007)**
Director: Tamara Jenkins
Screenplay: Tamara Jenkins
Cinematographer: Mott Hupfel
Editor: Brian A. Kates
Music: Stephen Trask
Starring: Laura Linney, Philip Seymour Hoffman, Philip Bosco
Distribution: Fox Searchlight Pictures

The Shower [*La Douche*] **(Lebanon, 1999)**
Director: Michel Kammoun
Screenplay: Michel Kammoun
Cinematographer: Muriel Aboulrouss
Editor: Richard Nakhle
Music: Hani Siblini
Starring: Raymond Hosni

Singin' in the Rain (USA, 1952)
Directors: Gene Kelly, Stanley Donen
Screenplay: Adolph Green, Betty Comden
Cinematographer: Harold Rosson
Editor: Adrienne Fazan
Music: Nacio Herb Brown, Arthur Freed
Starring: Gene Kelly, Donald O'Connor, Debbie Reynolds, Jean Hagen
Distribution: Metro-Goldwyn-Mayer

Slap Shot (USA, 1977)
Director: George Roy Hill
Screenplay: Nancy Dowd
Cinematographer: Victor J. Kemper
Editor: Dede Allen
Music: Elmer Bernstein
Starring: Paul Newman, Strother Martin, Micheal Ontkean, Lindsay Crouse
Distribution: Universal Pictures

Slumdog Millionaire (UK, 2008)
Director: Danny Boyle, Loveleen Tandan
Screenplay: Simon Beaufoy
Cinematographer: Anthony Dod Mantle
Editor: Chris Dickens
Music: A.R. Rahman
Starring: Dev Patel, Freida Pinto, Madhur Mittal, Tanay Chheda, Ayush Mahesh Khedekar, Rubina Ali, Anil Kapoor, Irrfan Khan
Distribution: Warner Bros., Fox Searchlight Pictures

Something's Gotta Give (USA, 2003)
Director: Nancy Meyers
Screenplay: Nancy Meyers
Cinematographer: Michael Ballhaus
Editor: Joe Hutshing
Music: Hans Zimmer
Starring: Jack Nicholson, Diane Keaton, Keanu Reeves, Amanda Peet
Distribution: Columbia Pictures

Son of the Bride [El hijo de la novia] (Argentina & Spain, 2001)
Director: Juan José Campanella
Screenplay: Fernando Castets, Juan José Campanella

Cinematographer: Daniel Shulman
Editor: Camilo Antolini
Music: Ángel Illarramendi
Starring: Ricardo Darín, Héctor Alterio, Norma Aleandro, Eduardo Blanco,
Natalia Verbeke
Distribution: Patagonik Film Group

A Song for Martin [*En sång för Martin*] **(Germany, 2001)**
Director: Bille August
Screenplay: Bille August
Cinematographer: Jörgen Persson
Editor: Janus Billeskov Jansen
Music: Stefan Nilsson
Starring: Sven Wollter, Viveka Seldahl, Reine Brynolfsson, Linda Källgren
Distribution: Columbia TriStar

Spring Forward **(USA, 1999)**
Director: Tom Gilroy
Screenplay: Tom Gilroy
Cinematographer: Terry Stacey
Editor: James Lyons
Music: Hahn Rowe
Starring: Ned Beatty, Liev Schreiber. Campbell Scott
Distribution: Metro-Goldwyn-Mayer

Standing Still **(Canada, 1996)**
Director: Catherine Quinn
Screenplay: Catherine Quinn
Editor: Catherine Quinn
Starring: Ellen White
Distribution: Women Make Movies

A Storm in Summer **(USA, 2000)**
Director: Robert Wise
Screenplay: Rod Serling
Cinematographer: Albert Dunk
Editor: Jack Hofstra
Music: Cynthia Millar
Starring: Peter Falk, Andrew McCarthy, Nastassja Kinski
Distribution: Hallmark Entertainment

The Straight Story (USA, 1999)
Director: David Lynch
Screenplay: John Roach, Mary Sweeney
Cinematographer: Freddie Francis
Editor: Mary Sweeney
Music: Angelo Badalamenti
Starring: Richard Farnsworth, Sissy Spacek
Distribution: Walt Disney Pictures

Sunset Boulevard (USA, 1950)
Director: Billy Wilder
Screenplay: Charles Brackett, Billy Wilder, D.M. Marshman Jr.
Cinematographer: John F. Seitz
Editor: Arthur Schmidt
Music: Franz Waxman
Starring: William Holden, Gloria Swanson, Erich von Stroheim
Distribution: Paramount Pictures

The Sunshine Boys (USA, 1995)
Director: John Erman
Screenplay: Neil Simon
Cinematographer: Tony Imi
Editor: Jack Wheeler
Music: Irwin Fisch
Starring: Woody Allen, Peter Falk, Michael McKean, Liev Schreiber, Edie Falco, Sarah Jessica Parker, Tyler Noyes, Olga Merediz
Distribution: Hallmark Entertainment, CBS

A Thousand Acres (USA, 1997)
Director: Jocelyn Moorhouse
Screenplay: Laura Jones
Cinematographer: Tak Fujimoto
Editor: Maryann Brandon
Music: Richard Hartley
Starring: Michelle Pfeiffer, Jessica Lange, Jennifer Jason Leigh, Colin Firth, Keith Carradine
Distribution: Touchstone Pictures

Tokyo Story [Tôkyô monogatari] (Japan, 1953)
Director: Yasujiro Ozu

Screenplay: Kôgo Noda, Yasujiro Ozu
Cinematographer: Yuuharu Atsuta
Editor: Yoshiyasu Hamamura
Music: Kojun Saitô
Starring: Chishû Ryû, Chieko Higashiyama, Setsuko Hara
Distribution: Shochiku Films, Criterion Pictures

The Trip to Bountiful (USA, 1985)
Director: Peter Masterson
Screenplay: Horton Foote
Cinematographer: Fred Murphy
Editor: Jay Freund
Music: J.A.C. Redford
Starring: Geraldine Page, John Heard, Carlin Glynn, Richard Bradford, Rebecca De Mornay
Distribution: FilmDallas Pictures

Unforgiven (USA, 1992)
Director: Clint Eastwood
Screenplay: David Webb Peoples
Cinematographer: Jack N. Green
Editor: Joel Cox
Music: Lennie Niehaus
Starring: Clint Eastwood, Gene Hackman, Morgan Freeman, Richard Harris
Distribution: Warner Bros.

Unhook the Stars (USA, 1996)
Director: Nick Cassavetes
Screenplay: Helen Caldwell, Nick Cassavetes
Cinematographer: Phedon Papamichael
Editor: Petra von Oelffen
Music: Steven Hufsteter
Starring: Gena Rowlands, Marisa Tomei
Distribution: Miramax Films

The Verdict (USA, 1982)
Director: Sidney Lumet
Screenplay: David Mamet
Cinematographer: Andrzej Bartkowiak
Editor: Peter C. Frank

Starring: Paul Newman, Charlotte Rampling, Jack Warden, James Mason,
Milo O'Shea
Distribution: Twentieth Century Fox

***Vodka Lemon* (France, 2003)**
Director: Hiner Saleem
Screenplay: Hiner Saleem
Cinematographer: Christophe Pollock
Editor: Dora Mantzoros
Music: Michel Korb, Roustam Sadoyan
Starring: Romen Avinian, Lala Sarkissian
Distribution: Amka Films Productions, Arte France Cinéma, Cinéfacto, Paradise
Films, Sintra Srl

***Voyage to the Beginning of the World* [*Viagem ao Princípio do Mundo*] (Portugal, 1997)**
Director: Manoel de Oliveira
Screenplay: Manoel de Oliveira
Cinematographer: Renato Berta
Editor: Valérie Loiseleux
Music: Emmanuel Nuñes
Starring: Marcello Mastroianni, Jean-Yves Gautier, Leonor Silveira, Diogo Dória,
Isabel de Castro
Distribution: Canal+, Strand Releasing

***Waking Ned Divine* (UK, 1998)**
Director: Kirk Jones
Screenplay: Kirk Jones
Cinematographer: Henry Braham
Editor: Alan Strachan
Music: Shaun Davey
Starring: Ian Bannen, David Kelly, Fionnula Flanagan
Distribution: Twentieth Century Fox

***Whatever Happened to Baby Jane?* (USA, 1962)**
Director: Robert Aldrich
Screenplay: Lukas Heller
Cinematographer: Ernest Haller
Editor: Michael Luciano
Music: Frank De Vol
Starring: Bette Davis, Joan Crawford, Victor Buono
Distribution: Warner Bros.

Wild Strawberries [*Smultronstället*] **(Sweden, 1957)**
Director: Ingmar Bergman
Screenplay: Ingmar Bergman
Cinematographer: Gunnar Fischer
Editor: Oscar Rosander
Music: Erik Nordgren
Starring: Victor Sjöström, Bibi Andersson, Ingrid Thulin, Gunnar Björnstrand
Distribution: Svensk Filmindustri

The Winter Guest **(USA & UK, 1996)**
Director: Alan Rickman
Screenplay: Sharman MacDonald, Alan Rickman
Cinematographer: Seamus McGarvey
Editor: Scott Thomas
Music: Michael Kamen
Starring: Emma Thompson, Phyllida Law, Gary Hollywood, Arlene Cockburn, Sheila Reid, Sandra Voe, Douglas Murphy
Distribution: Capitol Films

Youth without Youth **(USA, 2007)**
Director: Francis Ford Coppola
Screenplay: Francis Ford Coppola
Cinematographer: Mihai Malaimare Jr.
Editor: Walter Murch
Music: Osvaldo Golijov
Starring: Tim Roth, Bruno Ganz, Alexandra Maria Lara, André Hennicke
Distribution: Sony Pictures Classics

Notes

Introduction

1 Ford, quoted on TheRaider.net, 'Frequently Asked Questions.'
2 Pogrebin, 'A Long Shot in *Chicago* Pays Off; for Melanie Griffith, Last Laugh Is Sweet.'
3 Starpulse.com, 'Antonio Banderas Says Wife Melanie Griffith Is 'a Victim of Aging'.'
4 Beauvoir, *Old Age*.
5 Throughout this book I distinguish between America (an ideological construction of a country whose sense of self-grandeur is indicated by adopting a moniker that more accurately refers to more than one continent) and the United States (a geographical and political location that is also determined ideologically but is more comparable to a national designation such as Canada or the UK). Thus, I use the terms America and American to tap into the vision promoted by Hollywood and other popular discourses, and United States to designate a more appropriate naming of the nation.
6 Addison, '"Must the Players Keep Young?": Early Hollywood's Cult of Youth.'
7 Gullette, *Aged by Culture*, 177.
8 Daly, 'Harrison Ford Q&A: Indy Speaks!'
9 Particularly in the 1980s, films about aging continued Bergman's road trip motif, wherein mobility becomes literalized as a plot device to signify the limitations placed on aging bodies. Examples include *The Trip to Bountiful* (USA, Peter Masterson, 1985) and *Driving Miss Daisy* (USA, Bruce Beresford, 1989).
10 Beugnet, 'Screening the Old,' 3.
11 Markson, 'The Female Aging Body through Film,' 98.

12 Notable examples include but are not limited to:

> 1995: *Antonia's Line, Grumpier Old Men, How to Make an American Quilt, Madadayo*
> 1996: *I'm Not Rappaport, Never Too Late, Standing Still*
> 1997: *Mrs. Brown, Unhook the Stars, The Winter Guest, Alone, The Sunshine Boys, A Thousand Acres*
> 1998: *Central Station, Eternity and a Day, Voyage to the Beginning of the World, Waking Ned Devine*
> 1999: *After Life, Grandfather, Lost for Words, The Straight Story*
> 2000: *A Rumor of Angels, Spring Forward, Innocence, Stormy Summer, The Shower*
> 2001: *Iris, A Song for Martin, Utsav, My Kingdom, Pauline and Paulette, Month of Sundays, Last Orders*
> 2002: *Autumn Spring, Between Strangers, About Schmidt*
> 2003: *Daybreak, Vodka Lemon, Barbarian Invasions, A Long Weekend in Pest and Buda, Something's Gotta Give, Calendar Girls, Saraband, The Gin Game*
> 2004: *Noel, The Notebook, Club Eutanasia, The Other Side of the Street*
> 2005: *Ladies in Lavender, Mrs. Palfrey at the Claremont, The Death of Mr. Lazarescu, Checking Out, Mrs. Henderson Presents, Elsa and Fred*

13 Gilleard and Higgs, *Cultures of Ageing*, 8.
14 Mitchell and Snyder, *Narrative Prosthesis*, 96 (my italics).
15 Woodward, ed., *Figuring Age*, x.
16 Gullette, *Aged by Culture*, 18 (Gullette's italics).
17 Markson, 'The Female Aging Body through Film,' 95.
18 Gilleard and Higgs, *Cultures of Ageing*, 67.
19 Faircloth, *Aging Bodies*, 3.
20 Cruikshank, *Learning to Be Old*; Gullette, *Aged by Culture*; Beauvoir, *Old Age*.
21 Markson, 'The Female Aging Body through Film.'
22 Basting, *The Stages of Age*, 6.
23 Gullette, *Aged by Culture*, 27.
24 Smith, 'Imagining from the Inside,'; Smith, *Engaging Characters*; Mulvey, *Visual and Other Pleasures*; Silverman, *Male Subjectivity at the Margins*; Silverman, *The Acoustic Mirror*.
25 Cole and Winkler, *The Oxford Book of Aging*, 7; Woodward, *Figuring Age*, xvi.
26 Gullette, *Aged by Culture*, 78 (Gullette's italics).

Chapter 1. Same Difference? Gerontology and Disability Studies Join Hands

1 Mortimer, 'The Elegance of Old Age Has Now Been Forgotten.'
2 Langan, 'Mobility Disability,' 475 (Langan's italics).

3 Linton, *My Body Politic: A Memoir*, 176.
4 Ibid., 179.
5 Gilleard and Higgs, *Cultures of Ageing*.
6 The phrase 'enforcing normalcy' is from Lennard J. Davis's foundational disability studies work; see Davis, *Enforcing Normalcy*.
7 Gilleard and Higgs, *Cultures of Ageing*, 6.
8 This is not to deny the existence of the power of the boomers, but merely to claim that particular interpretations of its significance must be challenged.
9 Katz, *Disciplining Old Age*, 6.
10 Mitchell and Snyder's foundational argument situates disability as a fundamental aspect of narratives that often functions to make human bodies appear to be 'whole': In their words, 'the effort is to make the prosthesis show, to flaunt its imperfect supplementation as an illusion.' Mitchell and Snyder, *Narrative Prosthesis*, 8.
11 Markotić, 'The Coincidence of the Page.'
12 The life expectancies (as listed by the UN and measured in years) in countries where silvering screens films appear prominently were, in the period from 2005–10: 78.2 (United States), 78.3 (Denmark), 79.2 (Belgium), 79.4 (United Kingdom), 80.7 (Canada), and 80.9 (Sweden). By contrast, corresponding life expectancies in other countries were: 43.8 (Afghanistan), 46.2 (Rwanda), and 64.7 (India).
13 Kelly and Mamo, 'Graying the Cyborg,' 99.
14 Calasanti and Slevin, eds., *Age Matters*, 3.
15 Like Anne Davis Basting (following Richard Schechner), I place the terms performance and performativity on a continuum that encompasses films about everyday life and more formal drama; Basting, *The Stages of Age*, 6.
16 Biggs, 'Age, Gender, Narratives, and Masquerades,' 52.
17 Gullette, *Aged by Culture*, 22.
18 Gilleard and Higgs, *Cultures of Ageing*, 81.
19 Beugnet, 'Screening the Old,' 4 (my italics).
20 Calasanti and Slevin, eds., *Age Matters*, 8.
21 Powell, *Social Theory and Aging*, 3–4, 7; Katz, *Disciplining Old Age*, 92; Gullette, *Aged by Culture*, 104.
22 Katz, *Disciplining Old Age*, 4.
23 Gullette, *Aged by Culture*, 29.
24 Ibid., 106.
25 Markson, 'The Female Aging Body through Film,' 93.
26 Addison, '"Must the Players Keep Young?": Early Hollywood's Cult of Youth,' 11.
27 Beugnet, 'Screening the Old,' 2.

28 Sontag, *The Double Standard of Aging*.

29 Gilleard and Higgs, *Cultures of Ageing*, 10.

30 Woodward, *At Last, the Real Distinguished Thing*.

31 Woodward, *Aging and Its Discontents*.

32 Woodward, ed., *Figuring Age: Women, Bodies, Generations*.

33 Waxman, *From the Hearth to the Open Road*; Waxman, *To Live in the Center of the Moment*.

34 Wyatt-Brown and Rossen, eds., *Aging and Gender in Literature*.

35 Gullette, *Aged by Culture*; Gullette, *Declining to Decline*; Gullette, *Safe at Last in the Middle Years*.

36 Biggs, 'Age, Gender, Narratives, and Masquerades,' 56.

37 Calasanti and Slevin, eds., *Age Matters*, 2.

38 Meyers, 'Miroir, Memoire, Mirage,' 39.

39 Ibid., 24.

40 Miller, 'The Marks of Time,' 9.

41 Ray, 'Researching to Transgress,' 176.

42 Furman, 'There Are No Old Venuses,' 7–8.

43 Sobchack, 'Scary Women,' 209.

44 Bartky, 'Unplanned Obsolescence,' 67.

45 Ford, quoted on TheRaider.net, 'Frequently Asked Questions.'

46 Keating, 'Introduction: Perspectives on Healthy Aging,' 3–4.

47 Rowe and Kahn, 'Successful Aging,' 433–40.

48 Snyder and Mitchell, 'Re-engaging the Body,' 377.

49 This argument fits with the thinking of Michael Hardt and Antonio Negri who claim that the potential for revolution lies in the refuse created by capitalist production. See McRuer, *Crip Theory*, for a discussion of the relationship between their argument and emerging paradigms in disability studies.

50 Snyder and Mitchell, *Cultural Locations of Disability*, 15.

51 Morris, 'Impairment and Disability,' 11.

52 Though I deny 'normalcy' as anything more than a prescription, I use the term 'normal' here cynically to gesture towards its popularly agreed upon and endorsed definition which comes from statistics and usually refers to conformity to a tacitly shared standard or average.

53 Wendell, *The Rejected Body*, 18.

54 Gullette, *Aged by Culture*, 113.

55 CBC News. 'New Rules Aim to Help Ontarians with Disabilities.'

56 Thomson, 'Seeing the Disabled,' 348.

57 Mitchell and Snyder, eds., *The Body and Physical Difference*, 3.

58 Davidson, *Concerto for the Left Hand*, 168.

59 Wendell, 'Unhealthy Disabled,' 21.

60 Smith and Hutchison, 'Introduction,' 1.

61 Woodward, 'Against Wisdom.'

62 Thomson, *Extraordinary Bodies*, 5.

63 Wendell, *The Rejected Body*, 12–3.

64 Couser, *Recovering Bodies.*

65 Norden, *The Cinema of Isolation.*

66 As Michelle Putnam explains, 'From the theoretical standpoint of social models of disability, a person does not *have* a disability, a person *experiences* disability. This distinction has the net effect of removing from the person the exclusive burden of accommodating him- or herself to the environment that contributes to disability by sharing the responsibility with the environment to create a more balanced situation. In social models of disability, both the person and the environment have adaptive capabilities.' 'Linking Aging Theory and Disability Models,' 804 (Putnam's italics).

67 Asch, 'Critical Race Theory, Feminism, and Disability,' 18.

68 Siebers, *Disability Theory*, 73–5.

69 Snyder and Mitchell, *Cultural Locations of Disability*; Bhabha, *The Location of Culture.*

70 Katz, *Disciplining Old Age*, 6–7.

71 Bell, 'Introducing White Disability Studies,' 275.

72 Gullette, *Aged by Culture*, 107.

73 Steinem, 'Women Are Never Front-Runners'; Myrie, 'Race or Sex Shouldn't Decide Who Wins.'

74 Brown, 'A Vote of Allegiance?'; Neal, 'Barack Obama and the African-American Vote.'

75 Morrison, 'Comment.'

76 Graham-Felsen, 'Toni Morrison Endorses Barack Obama.'

77 Harper, 'Campaign Fatigue or Old Age'; Kurtz, 'Is McCain's Age Showing? Tongues Wag over Flubs.'

78 Reagan's one-liner was: 'Thomas Jefferson once said, "We should never judge a president by his age, only by his works." And ever since he told me that, I stopped worrying.' Quoted in Martin, 'Poll: Age Trumps Race among Voters.'

79 Buckley, 'The Age Thing,' 60.

80 Michaels, 'Against Diversity,' 33.

81 Ibid., 36.

82 For example, in a pre-inaugural *Globe and Mail* article, Sarah Boesveld refers to 'the Yes We Can youth who shot Mr Obama to power.' Boesveld, 'Whippersnappers in the Workplace.'

83 Scheiber, 'Race against History,' 25.
84 Shear, 'Obama Takes First Campaign Trip South.'
85 Quoted in Dickerson, 'Obama's South Carolina Debut.'
86 Obama, Barack. 'Obama Victory Speech.'
87 Blackburn, *Age Shock*, 12.
88 Chris Bell died in December, 2009, shocking the disability community into a sudden acute awareness of the importance of his already valued work. In my own reaction, I was only too aware that part of the shock to me was that he was so young (born in 1974) and I had always anticipated many future opportunities to get to know him and his work better. Though I reject the edict forbidding the mourning of extremely old parents and grandparents, I can't help recognizing the extreme sorrow accompanying the loss of one who didn't have the chance to live as many years. Not only has his work jarred me out of complacency about the whiteness of age studies, but his death has unsettled me in the realization of my own age-based assumptions, a fact I can only hope he would have found satisfying.

Chapter 2. Baby Jane Grew Up: The Horror of Aging in Mid-Twentieth-Century Hollywood

1 Quoted in Norden, *The Cinema of Isolation*, 218.
2 Corber, 'Joan Crawford's Padded Shoulders,' 1.
3 People, 'Gloria Steinem.'
4 Shingler and Gledhill, 'Bette Davis,' 67.
5 Russo, 'Aging and the Scandal of Anachronism.'
6 Ibid., 20.
7 Ibid., 27.
8 Ibid., 21.
9 Ibid. (Russo's italics).
10 With the term 'crip' I am picking up on Robert McRuer's usage in *Crip Theory*. Specifically, I mean that the actresses must politically adopt a critically disabled position. McRuer, *Crip Theory*.
11 Fischer, 'Sunset Boulevard: Fading Stars,' 164.
12 Markson, 'The Female Aging Body through Film,' 99.
13 Gullette, *Aged by Culture*, 170.
14 Kaplan, 'Trauma and Aging,' 174.
15 Fischer, 'Sunset Boulevard: Fading Stars,' 173.
16 Quoted in Vermilye, *Bette Davis*, 122.
17 Quoted in ibid.
18 Brooks, 'Performing Aging/Performance Crisis,' 236.
19 Russo, 'The Scandal of Anachronism,' 25.

20 Brooks, 'Performing Aging/Performance Crisis,' 233.
21 For example, in the final scene of *Dark Victory*, Bette Davis's character (a young woman who has been tamed into heterosexual domesticity) has gone blind and is about to die. She tells her friend, 'I'm the lucky one; I don't have to grow old.'
22 Goodley and Lawthom, 'Epistemological Journeys in Participatory Action Research,' *Disability & Society*, 164.
23 Thomson, 'Feminist Theory, the Body, and the Disabled Figure,' 279.
24 Ibid., 287.
25 Mulvey, *Visual and Other Pleasures*; Quoted in Thomson, 'Feminist Theory, the Body, and the Disabled Figure,' 287.
26 Norden, *The Cinema of Isolation*, 218.

Chapter 3. Grey Matters: Dementia, Cognitive Difference, and the 'Guilty Demographic' on Screen

 1 Quoted in Rhoades, '*The Savages* Tackles the Grim Reality of an Aging Parent.'
 2 Dementia here functions as an umbrella term for many forms of cognitive dissonance: Alzheimer's, Vascular dementia, Parkinson's disease, Pick's disease, and other related conditions.
 3 Basting, 'Looking Back from Loss,' 87.
 4 Ibid.
 5 Eakin, 'What Are We Reading When We Read Autobiography?' 123.
 6 Ibid.
 7 Basting, '"God Is a Talking Horse": Dementia and the Performance of Self,' 79.
 8 Eakin, 'What Are We Reading When We Read Autobiography?' 123.
 9 Basting, '"God Is a Talking Horse": Dementia and the Performance of Self.'
10 Ibid., 92. I would propose that this ideology extends far beyond the United States, though perhaps is believed most vehemently in the United States.
11 Basting, 'Looking Back from Loss,' 97.
12 Thomson, *Extraordinary Bodies*.
13 Ibid.
14 Ibid., 7.
15 Here and throughout this book, I have supplied quotations from non-English movies in English from the translations provided in the subtitles of the film.
16 Woodward, 'Performing Age, Performing Gender,'; Howell, 'Film Review.'
17 Holden, 'Film Review: When Love and Disease Both Strike out of the Blue.'
18 Jenkins, 'Northern Lites; New Canadian Documentaries; *A Song for Martin*.'

19 The full lyrics are:

> I don't want to play in your yard,
> I don't like you anymore.
> You'll be sorry when you see me
> Sliding down our cellar door.
>
> You can't holler down our rain barrel,
> You can't climb our apple tree,
> I don't wanna play in your yard,
> If you can't be good to me.
>
> You can't holler down our rain barrel,
> You can't climb our apple tree,
> I don't wanna play in your yard,
> If you can't be good to me.

20 Taylor, 'Review of *The Savages*.'
21 Williams, 'Savagely Funny.'
22 Ibid.

Chapter 4. 'Sounds Like a Regular Marriage': Monogamy and the Fidelity of Care

1 McRuer, *Crip Theory*, 31.
2 Holden, 'Film Review: When Love and Disease Both Strike out of the Blue.'
3 Kauffmann, 'Review of *Iris*,' 26.
4 Showalter, 'An "Iris" Stripped of Her Brilliance.'
5 Grabinski, 'Review of *Iris*,' 426 (my italics).
6 Adams, 'Marriage Made in Heaven.'
7 Polley, 'Foreword,' xi-xii.
8 Ibid., xviii.
9 Ibid.
10 Burns, 'Now Come the Night.'
11 Morgenstern, 'Review of *Away from Her*.'
12 Axmaker, 'Poignant *Away* Paints a Painful Portrait of Loss.'
13 Burns, 'Now Comes the Night.'
14 Pevere, '*Away from Her*: A Marriage Adrift.'
15 Munro, *Away from Her*, 37.
16 Ibid., 16.
17 Ibid., 13.
18 Ibid., 17.

19 A Canadian love poem that features infidelity prominently and viscerally.
20 Quoted in Victoria Times Colonist, 'Christie Quip Irks Alzheimer's Group.'
21 Polley, 'Foreword,' xviii.
22 Munro, *Away From Her*, 3, 6.
23 Ibid., 5.
24 Ibid., 7.
25 Ibid., 25.
26 Ibid., 23.
27 Ibid., 18.
28 Ibid., 61.
29 Bradshaw, 'Review of *Away from Her*.'
30 *Away from Her* drops many hints about the location of shooting.
31 Imboden, 'Review of *The Barbarian Invasions*,' 49.
32 Kermode, 'The Last Rites.'
33 Castle, 'A Couple's Journey with Alzheimer's Disease.'

Chapter 5. Yes, We Still Can: Paul Newman, Clint Eastwood, Aging Masculinity, and the American Dream

1 Mortimer, 'The Elegance of Old Age Has Now Been Forgotten.'
2 Holden, '*Grumpier Old Men*: 2 Short Fuses Pressing Their Luck.'
3 Pevere, 'Review of *Grumpy Old Men*.'
4 Ebert, 'Review of *Grumpy Old Men*.'
5 Taylor, 'Grumpier Old Men Ogle Loren.'
6 Holden, 'Grumpier Old Men: 2 Short Fuses Pressing Their Luck.'
7 Shakespeare, 'The Sexual Politics of Disabled Masculinity,' 59.
8 King, 'Film Star Paul Newman Dies at 83.'
9 Silverman, 'Screen and Real-Life Hero Paul Newman Dies at 83.'
10 Groen, 'Review of *Nobody's Fool*.'
11 James, 'Review of *Nobody's Fool*.'
12 Guthmann Edward. 'Everybody Is Family in "Fool's" Paradise.'
13 Kempley, 'Review of *Nobody's Fool*.'
14 As Kempley puts it, 'Tandy, luminous to the last as Sully's landlady, Miss Beryl, has a line that was sadly prophetic: 'I've got a feeling God's creeping in on me. I've got a feeling this is the year he lowers the boom.'
15 Kempley, 'Review of *Nobody's Fool*.'
16 James, 'Review of *Nobody's Fool*.'
17 Ibid.
18 Groen, 'Review of *Nobody's Fool*.'
19 Guthmann, 'Everyone Is Family in 'Fool's' Paradise.'

20 Groen, 'Review of *Nobody's Fool.*'
21 James, 'Review of *Nobody's Fool.*'
22 In addition to eliminating Ruth, the film eliminates another minor character from the novel – the token black man, a prep cook at the local café.
23 Johnson, *Make Them Go Away*, 2.
24 Ibid.
25 Quoted in Ibid., 150.
26 Quoted in Ibid., 242.
27 Bingham, *Acting Male.*
28 Jeffords, *Hard Bodies.*
29 Ibid.
30 Scott, 'Review of *Unforgiven.*'
31 Salamon, 'Eastwood as Reformed Gunslinger.'
32 Freeman, 'Black, American History.'
33 I would like to think that my experience viewing the film in Peterborough was vastly different from elsewhere, but I suspect that other audiences also laughed harder the more racist Kowalski became.
34 Denby, 'Review of *Gran Torino.*'
35 Foundas, 'Clint Eastwood Finds Salvation in *Gran Torino.*'
36 Canby, 'Review of *Unforgiven.*'
37 Headlam, 'Interview with Clint Eastwood.'
38 Dargis, 'Review of *Gran Torino.*'
39 Ibid.
40 Quoted in Headlam, 'Interview with Clint Eastwood.'
41 Quoted in Ibid.
42 Goldstein, 'Clint Eastwood's *Gran Torino* Is Hollywood's Coolest Car.'

Chapter 6. As Old as Jack Gets: Nicholson, Masculinity, and the Hollywood System

1 Carson, 'Ten Things You Can't Say About the Movies.'
2 Stacey, *Star Gazing.*
3 Bingham, *Acting Male*, 117.
4 McRuer, *Crip Theory*, 8.
5 Ibid., 20.
6 Bingham, *Acting Male*, 109.
7 Bradshaw, 'Review of *About Schmidt.*'
8 Bingham, *Acting Male*, 6.

9 Indeed, when I rented the film to review it, the young man behind the counter 'warned' me that I would see Kathy Bates naked. I was bemused by his gallant desire to protect me from I'm not sure what.

10 Scott, 'Weep, and the World Laughs Hysterically.'

11 Ebert, 'Review of *About Schmidt.*'

12 The only woman of colour featured in the film is the final doctor Harry sees, who, though young enough that she compares him to her father, does not seem to attract him in the least.

13 While Harry is sixty-three years old and Erica is in her fifties, they are presented as though they are the same age, in part because of the drastic age difference between Marin and Harry and in part because women are perceived to age more rapidly than men.

14 The film doesn't allow for same-sex desire even in order to make fun of it. The opening lines are Harry saying, 'Ah, the sweet uncomplicated satisfaction of the younger woman; that fleeting age when everything just falls into place. It's magic time, and it can render any man, anywhere, absolutely helpless.'

15 Reviewer A.O. Scott affirms, 'At the sneak preview I attended last week, the harder Erica cried, the harder the audience laughed, which I might have found disturbing if I had not been laughing so helplessly myself.' Scott, 'Weep, and the World Laughs Hysterically.'

16 Patterson, 'Puttin' on the Ditz.'

17 Denby, 'Star Season.(Movie Review).'

18 Quoted in Patterson, 'Puttin' on the Ditz.'

19 His aptitude is conveyed by his intricate and irritating knowledge of trivial information about anything that could be a question on *Jeopardy*.

20 Bingham, *Acting Male*, 150.

Conclusion: Final Films, The Silvering Screen Comes of Age

1 Hill, *The Book of Negroes*, 1.

2 Russo, 'The Scandal of Anachronism.'

3 TheRaider.net, 'Frequently Asked Questions.'

4 Guthmann, 'Richard Farnsworth's Dignity and Grace,'; Ebert, 'Grey Fox a Suicide at Age 80.'

5 Jessica Tandy is another example of an actor with a long-standing film career but who rarely gained the spotlight. As she aged, and could play older characters, her apparently physical frailty accentuated the place she had long taken onscreen.

6 I credit here a graduate course paper by my research assistant David Hugill who notes the aggressive youth and masculinity of heroes of the left: Guevera, Castro, Marx, et al.

Works Cited

Adams, Tim. 'Marriage Made in Heaven.' *The Observer*, 18 March 2001.

Addison, Heather. '"Must the Players Keep Young?": Early Hollywood's Cult of Youth.' *Cinema Journal* 45 (2006): 3–25.

Andrus, Mark, and James L. Brooks. *As Good As It Gets*, DVD. Directed by James L. Brooks. USA: TriStar Pictures, 1997.

Arcand, Denys. *Les invasions barbares* [Barbarian Invasions], DVD. Directed by Denys Arcand. Canada: Miramax Films, 2003.

– *Le déclin de l'empire américain* [The Decline of the American Empire], DVD. Directed by Denys Arcand. Canada: Cineplex Odeon Films, 1986.

Asch, Adrienne. 'Critical Race Theory, Feminism, and Disability: Reflections on Social Justice and Personal Identity.' In *Gendering Disability*, edited by Bonnie G. Smith and Beth Hutchison, 9–44. Rutgers, NJ: Rutgers University Press, 2004.

August, Bille. *En sång för Martin* [A Song for Martin], DVD. Directed by Bille August. Germany: Columbia TriStar, 2001.

Axmaker, Sean. 'Poignant *Away* Paints a Painful Portrait of Loss.' *Seattle Post-Intelligencer*, 10 May 2007.

Bandyopadhyay, Bibhutibhushan, and Satyajit Ray. *Pather Panchali*, DVD. Directed by Satyajit Ray. India: Government of West Bengal, 1955.

Bartky, Sandra Lee. 'Unplanned Obsolescence: Some Reflections on Aging.' In *Mother Time: Women, Aging, and Ethics*, edited by Margaret Urban Walker, 61–74. Lanham, MD: Rowman & Littlefield Publishers, 2000.

Basting, Anne Davis. '"God Is a Talking Horse": Dementia and the Performance of Self.' *TDR: The Drama Review* 45 (2001): 78–94.

– 'Looking Back from Loss: Views of the Self in Alzheimer's Disease.' *Journal of Aging Studies* 17 (2003): 87–99.

– *The Stages of Age: Performing Age in Contemporary American Culture*. Ann Arbor: University of Michigan Press, 1998.

Beauvoir, Simone de. *Old Age*. London: Penguin Books, 1977.

Bell, Chris. 'Introducing White Disability Studies: A Modest Proposal.' *The Disability Studies Reader*. 2nd ed., edited by Lennard J. Davis, 275–82. New York: Routledge, 2006.

Benton, Robert. *Nobody's Fool*, DVD. Directed by Robert Benton. USA: Paramount Pictures; Capella International, 1994.

Bergman, Ingmar. *Smultronstället* [Wild Strawberries], DVD. Directed by Ingmar Bergman. Sweden: Svensk Filmindustri, 1957.

Beugnet, Martine. 'Screening the Old: Femininity as Old Age in Contemporary French Cinema.' *Studies in the Literary Imagination* 39, no. 2 (2006): 1–20.

Bhabha, Homi K. *The Location of Culture*. London: Routledge, 1994.

Biggs, Simon. 'Age, Gender, Narratives, and Masquerades.' *Journal of Aging Studies* 18, no. 1 (2004): 45–59.

Bingham, Dennis. *Acting Male: Masculinities in the Films of James Stewart, Jack Nicholson and Clint Eastwood*. New Brunswick, NJ: Rutgers University Press, 1994.

Blackburn, Robin. *Age Shock: How Finance Is Failing Us*. London: Verso, 2006.

Boesveld, Sarah. 'Whippersnappers in the Workplace.' *Globe and Mail*, 12 January 2009, L1.

Boon, Jaak, and Lieven Debrauwer. *Pauline and Paulette*, DVD. Directed by Lieven Debrauwer. Belgium: Sony Pictures Classics, 2001.

Brackett, Charles, D.M. Marshman Jr., Billy Wilder. *Sunset Boulevard*, DVD. Directed by Billy Wilder. USA: Paramount, 1950.

Bradshaw, Peter. Review of *About Schmidt*. *Guardian*, 23 January 2003.

– Review of *Away from Her*. *Guardian*, 27 April 2007.

Brooks, Jodi. 'Performing Aging/Performance Crisis.' In *Figuring Age: Women, Bodies, Generations*, edited by Kathleen Woodward, 232–47. Bloomington: Indiana University Press, 1999.

Brown, DeNeen L. 'A Vote of Allegiance?' *Washington Post*, 24 March 2008.

Buckley, Christopher. 'The Age Thing.' *National Review* 60, no. 15 (18 August 2008): 60.

Burns, Sean. 'Now Comes the Night.' *Philadelphia Weekly*, 16 May 2007.

Calasanti, Toni M., and Kathleen F. Slevin, eds. *Age Matters: Realigning Feminist Thinking*. New York: Routledge, 2006.

Canby, Vincent. Review of *Unforgiven*. *New York Times*, 7 August 1992, B1.

Carson, Tom. 'Ten Things You Can't Say About the Movies.' *Esquire*, 31 March 1999.

Castle, Emery. 'A Couple's Journey with Alzheimer's Disease: The Many Faces of Intimacy.' *Generations* 25, no. 2 (2001): 81.

CBC News. 'New Rules Aim to Help Ontarians with Disabilities.' 1 January 2010. http://www.cbc.ca/canada/story/2010/01/01/ont-accessbility-customer-service-disabilities.html

Chivers, Sally. *From Old Woman to Older Women: Contemporary Culture and Women's Narratives.* Columbus: Ohio State University Press, 2003.

'Christie Quip Irks Alzheimer's Group.' *Victoria Times-Colonist*, 2008, C11.

Cole, Thomas R., and Mary G. Winkler. *The Oxford Book of Aging.* New York: Oxford University Press, 1994.

Comden, Betty, and Adolph Green. *Singin' in the Rain*, DVD. Directed by Stanley Donen. Metro-Goldwyn-Mayer, 1952.

Corber, Robert J. 'Joan Crawford's Padded Shoulders: Female Masculinity in *Mildred Pierce.*' *Camera Obscura* 62 (2006): 1–31.

Couser, G. Thomas. *Recovering Bodies: Illness, Disability, and Life Writing.* Wisconsin Studies in American Autobiography. Madison: University of Wisconsin Press, 1997.

Cruikshank, Margaret. *Learning to Be Old: Gender, Culture, and Aging.* Lanham, MD: Rowman & Littlefield Publishers, 2003.

Daly, Steve. 'Harrison Ford Q&A: Indy Speaks!' *Entertainment Weekly*, 14 March 2008.

Dargis, Manohla. Review of *Gran Torino. New York Times*, 12 December 2008.

Davidson, Michael. *Concerto for the Left Hand: Disability and the Defamiliar Body.* Corporealities. Ann Arbor: University of Michigan Press, 2008.

Davis, Lennard J. *Enforcing Normalcy: Disability, Deafness, and the Body.* New York: Verso, 1995.

Denby, David. Review of *Gran Torino. New Yorker*, 5 January 2009.

– 'Star Season.' *New Yorker*, 22 December 2003.

Dickerson, John. 'Obama's South Carolina Debut.' *Slate.com*, 17 February 2007.

Eakin, Paul John. 'What Are We Reading When We Read Autobiography?' *Narrative* 12, no. 2 (2004): 121–32.

Ebert, Roger. 'Grey Fox a Suicide at Age 80.' *Windsor Star*, October 11, 2000, B10.

– Review of *About Schmidt. Chicago Sun-Times*, 20 December 2002. http://rogerebert.suntimes.com/apps/pbcs.dll/article?AID=/20021220/REVIEWS/212200301/1023.

– Review of *Grumpy Old Men. Chicago Sun-Times*, 24 December 1993. http://rogerebert.suntimes.com/apps/pbcs.dll/article?AID=/199.

Eyre, Richard, and Charles Wood. *Iris*, DVD. Directed by Richard Eyre. USA: Miramax Films, 2001.

Faircloth, Christopher A. *Aging Bodies: Images and Everyday Experience.* Walnut Creek, CA: AltaMira Press, 2003.

Farrell, Henry, and Lukas Heller. *Hush... Hush, Sweet Charlotte*, DVD. Directed by Robert Aldrich. USA: Twentieth Century Fox, 1965.

Fischer, Lucy. '*Sunset Boulevard*: Fading Stars.' In *The Other within Us: Feminist Explorations of Women and Aging*, edited by Marilyn Pearsall, 163–76. Boulder, CO: Westview Press, 1997.

Foote, Horton. *The Trip to Bountiful*, DVD. Directed by Peter Masterson. USA: Island Pictures, 1985.

Foundas, Scott. 'Clint Eastwood Finds Salvation in *Gran Torino*.' *The Village Voice*, 9 December 2008. http://www.villagevoice.com/2008-12-10/film/clint-eastwood-finds-salvation-in-gran-torino/.

Freeman, Morgan, interviewed by Mike Wallace. 'Black, American History.' *60 Minutes*, CBS, 15 December 2005. http://www.cbsnews.com/video/watch/?id=1131887n.

Furman, Frida Kerner. 'There Are No Old Venuses: Older Women's Responses to Their Aging Bodies.' In *Mother Time: Women, Aging, and Ethics*, edited by Margaret Urban Walker, 7–22. Lanham, MD: Rowman & Littlefield Publishers, 2000.

Gilleard, C.J., and Paul Higgs. *Cultures of Ageing: Self, Citizen, and the Body*. Harlow, England: Prentice Hall, 2000.

Glazer, Mitch. *Great Expectations*, DVD. Directed by Alfonso Cuarón. USA: Twentieth Century Fox, 1998.

Goldstein, Patrick. 'Clint Eastwood's *Gran Torino* Is Hollywood's Coolest Car.' *Los Angeles Times*, 12 January 2009. http://latimesblogs.latimes.com/the_big_picture/2009/01/clint-eastwoods.html.

Goodley, Dan, and Rebecca Lawthom. 'Epistemological Journeys in Participatory Action Research: Alliances between Community Psychology and Disability Studies.' *Disability & Society* 20, no. 2 (2005): 135.

Grabinski, C. Joanne. Review of *Iris. The Gerontologist* 43, no. 3 (2003): 426.

Graham-Felsen, Sam. 'Toni Morrison Endorses Barack Obama.' 28 January 2008. http://my.barackobama.com/page/community/post/samgrahamfelsen/CGVRG.

Groen, Rick. Review of *Nobody's Fool. Globe and Mail*, 13 January 1995, C1.

Gullette, Margaret Morganroth. *Aged by Culture*. Chicago: University of Chicago Press, 2004.

– *Declining to Decline: Cultural Combat and the Politics of the Midlife*. Age Studies. Charlottesville, VA: University Press of Virginia, 1997.

– *Safe at Last in the Middle Years: The Invention of the Midlife Progress Novel – Saul Bellow, Margaret Drabble, Anne Tyler, and John Updike*. Berkeley: University of California Press, 1988.

Guthmann, Edward. 'Everybody Is Family in "Fool's" Paradise.' *San Franscisco Chronicle*, 13 January 1995. http://www.sfgate.com/cgi-bin/article.cgi?f=/c/a/1995/01/13/DD20646.DTL.

– 'Richard Farnsworth's Dignity and Grace.' *San Francisco Chronicle*, 14 October 2000. http://www.sfgate.com/cgi-bin/article.cgi?file=/chronicle/archive/2000/10/14/DD40242.DTL&type=printable.

Harper, Tim. 'Campaign Fatigue or Old Age?' *Guelph Mercury*, 30 October 2008, A11.

Headlam, Bruce. 'Interview with Clint Eastwood.' *New York Times*, 14 December 2008, L1.

Heller, Lukas. *Whatever Happened to Baby Jane?*, DVD. Directed by Robert Aldrich. Warner Bros., 1962.

Higgins, Colin. *Harold and Maude*, DVD. Directed by Hal Ashby. USA: Paramount, 1971.

Hill, Lawrence. *The Book of Negroes*. Toronto: HarperCollins, 2007.

Holden, Stephen. 'Film Review: When Love and Disease Both Strike out of the Blue.' *New York Times*, 28 June 2002, 13.

– '*Grumpier Old Men*: 2 Short Fuses Pressing Their Luck.' *New York Times*, 22 December 1995. http://movies.nytimes.com/movie/review?res=9F02E3D F1539F931A15751C1A963958260.

Howell, Peter. 'Film Review: Much More Than the Sam of Its Parts.' *Toronto Star*, 3 May 2002. http://search.ebscohost.com/login.aspx?direct=true&db=rch&A N=6FP3056591454&site=ehost-live.

Imboden, Roberta. Review of *The Barbarian Invasions (Les Invasions Barbares)*. *Film Quarterly* 58, no. 3 (2005): 48–52.

James, Caryn. Review of *Nobody's Fool*. *New York Times*, 23 December 1994. http://movies.nytimes.com/movie/review?res=9800E3DF1F38F930A15751 C1A962958260.

Jeffords, Susan. *Hard Bodies: Hollywood Masculinity in the Reagan Era*. New Brunswick, NJ: Rutgers University Press, 1994.

Jenkins, Mark. 'Northern Lites; New Canadian Documentaries; *A Song for Martin*. *Washington City Paper*, 18 July 2003, 46. http://proquest.umi.com/pqd web?did=506868131&Fmt=7&clientId=29618&RQT=309&VName=PQD.

Jenkins, Tamara. *The Savages*, DVD. Directed by Tamara Jenkins. USA: Fox Searchlight Pictures, 2007.

Jensen, Anders Thomas. *Elsker dig for evigt* [Open Hearts], DVD. Directed by Suzanne Bier. New Market Films, 2002.

Johnson, Mark Steven. *Grumpier Old Men*, DVD. Directed by Howard Deutch. Warner Bros., 1995.

Johnson, Mary. *Make Them Go Away: Clint Eastwood, Christopher Reeve and the Case against Disability Rights.* Louisville: Advocado Press, 2003.

Joyce, Adrien. *Five Easy Pieces,* DVD. Directed by Bob Rafelson. USA: Columbia Pictures, 1970.

Kaplan, E. Ann. 'Trauma and Aging.' In *Figuring Age: Women, Bodies, Generations,* edited by Kathleen Woodward, 171–94. Bloomington: Indiana University Press, 1999.

Katz, Stephen. *Disciplining Old Age: The Formation of Gerontological Knowledge.* Knowledge, Disciplinarity and Beyond. Charlottesville: University Press of Virginia, 1996.

Kauffmann, Stanley. Review of *Iris. New Republic,* 11 February 2002, 26–8.

Keating, Norah. 'Introduction: Perspectives on Healthy Aging.' *Canadian Journal on Aging/Revue canadienne du vieillissement* 24, no. 1 (2005): 3–4.

Kelly, Joyce, and Laura Mamo. 'Graying the Cyborg: New Directions in Feminist Analyses of Aging, Science, and Technology.' In *Age Matters: Realigning Feminist Thinking,* edited by Toni M. Calasanti and Kathleen F. Slevin, 99–122. New York: Routledge, 2006.

Kempley, Rita. Review of *Nobody's Fool. Washington Post,* 13 January 1995. http://www.washingtonpost.com/wp-srv/style/longterm/movies/videos/nobodys-foolrkempley_c0049d.htm.

Kermode, Mark. 'The Last Rites: Mark Kermode Basks in the Ethereal Glow of a French-Canadian Gem.' *New Statesman,* 23 February 2004.

King, Kyle. 'Film Star Paul Newman Dies at 83.' *Voice of America,* 27 September 2008. www.voanews.com.

Kurtz, Howard. 'Is McCain's Age Showing? Tongues Wag over Flubs' *Washington Post,* 23 July 2008, C1

Langan, Celeste. 'Mobility Disability.' *Public Culture* 13, no. 3 (2001): 459–84.

Linton, Simi. *My Body Politic: A Memoir.* Ann Arbor: University of Michigan Press, 2006.

Mankiewicz, Joseph L. *All About Eve,* DVD. Directed by Joseph L. Mankiewicz. USA: Twentieth Century Fox Home Entertainment, 1950.

Markotić, Nicole. 'Coincidence of the Page.' *Tessera* 27 (1999): 6–15.

Markson, Elizabeth. 'The Female Aging Body through Film.' In *Aging Bodies: Images and Everyday Experiences,* edited by Christopher Faircloth, 77–102. Walnut Creek, CA: AltaMira Press, 2003.

Martin, Michel. 'Poll: Age Trumps Race among Voters.' *Tell Me More,* NPR, 25 June 2008. http://search.ebscohost.com/login.aspx?direct=true&db=rch&AN=6XN200806250801&site=ehost-live.

McRuer, Robert. *Crip Theory: Cultural Signs of Queerness and Disability.* Cultural Front. New York: New York University Press, 2006.

Meyers, Diana Tietjens. 'Miroir, Mémoire, Mirage: Appearance, Aging, and Women.' In *Mother Time: Women, Aging and Ethics*, edited by Margaret Urban Walker, 23–44. Lanham, MD: Rowman & Littlefield Publishers, 2000.

Meyers, Nancy. *Something's Gotta Give*, DVD. Directed by Nancy Meyers. USA: Columbia Pictures, 2003.

Michaels, Walter Benn. 'Against Diversity.' *New Left Review* 52 (2008): 33–6.

Miller, Nancy K. 'The Marks of Time.' In *Figuring Age: Women, Bodies, Generations*, edited by Kathleen M. Woodward, 3–19. Bloomington: Indiana University Press, 1999.

Mitchell, David T., and Sharon L. Snyder. *Narrative Prosthesis: Disability and the Dependencies of Discourse*. Corporealities: Discourses of Disability. Ann Arbor: University of Michigan Press, 2001.

– eds. *The Body and Physical Difference: Discourses of Disability*. The Body, in Theory: Histories of Cultural Materialism. Ann Arbor: University of Michigan Press, 1997.

Morgenstern, Joe. Review of *Away from Her. Wall Street Journal*, 4 May 2007. http://online.wsj.com/article/SB117823237455091453.html.

Morris, Jenny. 'Impairment and Disability: Constructing an Ethics of Care That Promotes Human Rights.' *Hypatia* 16, no. 4 (2001): 1–16.

Morrison, Toni. 'Comment.' *New Yorker*, 5 October 1998. http://www.newyorker.com/archive/1998/10/05/1998_10_05_031_TNY_LIBRY_000016504?currentPage=2.

Mortimer, John. 'The Elegance of Old Age Has Now Been Forgotten.' *Observer*, 18 January 2009. http://www.guardian.co.uk/commentisfree/2009/jan/18/john-mortimer-final-column-old-age.

Mulvey, Laura. *Visual and Other Pleasures*. London: Macmillan, 1989.

Munro, Alice. *Away from Her*. Toronto: Penguin Canada, 2007.

Myrie, Evelyn. 'Race or Sex Shouldn't Decide Who Wins.' *Hamilton Spectator*, 31 January 2008. http://www.thespec.com/article/317536.

Neal, Conan. 'Barack Obama and the African-American Vote.' In *Talk of the Nation*, NPR, 31 January 2008. http://search.ebscohost.com/login.aspx?direct=true&db=rch&AN=6XN200801311401&site=ehost-live.

Norden, Martin F. *The Cinema of Isolation: A History of Physical Disability in the Movies*. New Brunswick, NJ: Rutgers University Press, 1994.

Obama, Barack. 'Obama Victory Speech.' *Huffington Post*, 4 November 2008. http://www.huffingtonpost.com/2008/11/04/obama-victory-speech_n_141194.html.

Patterson, John. 'Puttin' on the Ditz.' *Guardian*, 31 January 2004. http://www.guardian.co.uk/film/2004/jan/31/features.johnpatterson.

Pavignano, Anna, Michael Radford, Furio Scarpelli, Giacomo Scarpelli, Massimo Troisi. *Il Postino*, DVD. Directed by Michael Radford. Italy: Miramax, 1995.

Payne, Alexander, Jim Taylor. *About Schmidt*, DVD. Directed by Alexander Payne. USA: New Line Cinema, 2002.

People. 'Gloria Steinem.' 8 May 1995. http://www.people.com/people/archive/article/0,,20105690,00.html.

Peoples, David Webb. *Unforgiven*, DVD. Directed by Clint Eastwood. USA: Warner Bros., 1992.

Pevere, Geoff. '*Away from Her*: A Marriage Adrift.' *Toronto Star*, 4 May 2007. http://www.thestar.com/entertainment/article/210290.

– Review of *Grumpy Old Men*. *Globe and Mail*, 31 December 1993, C3.

Pogrebin, Robin. 'A Long Shot in *Chicago* Pays Off; for Melanie Griffith, Last Laugh Is Sweet.' *New York Times*, 18 September 2003. http://query.nytimes.com/gst/fullpage.html?res=9C04E5DE153AF93BA2575AC0A9659C8B63.

Polley, Sarah. *Away from Her*, DVD. Directed by Sarah Polley. Canada: Pulling Focus Pictures, 2006.

– 'Foreword.' In *Away from Her*, by Alice Munro. Toronto: Penguin Canada, 2007.

Powell, Jason L. *Social Theory and Aging*. Lanham, MD: Rowman & Littlefield Publishers, 2006.

Price, Richard. *The Color of Money*, DVD. Directed by Martin Scorsese. USA: Touchstone Pictures, 1986.

Putnam, M. 'Linking Aging Theory and Disability Models: Increasing the Potential to Explore Aging with Physical Impairment.' *Gerontologist* 42, no. 6 (2002): 799–806.

Ray, Ruth E. 'Researching to Transgress: The Need for Critical Feminism in Gerontology.' *Journal of Women and Aging* 11, no. 2/3 (1999): 171–84.

– 'Toward the Croning of Feminist Gerontology.' *Journal of Aging Studies* 18 (2004): 109–21.

Rhoades, Shirrel. '*The Savages* Tackles the Grim Reality of an Aging Parent.' *Solares Hill*, 2008, 17.

Roach, John, Mary Sweeny. *The Straight Story*, DVD. Directed by David Lynch. USA: Disney, 1999.

Robinson, Casey. *Dark Victory*, DVD. Directed by Edmund Goulding. USA: Warner Bros., 1939.

Rowe, John W., and Robert L Kahn. 'Successful Aging.' *Gerontologist* 37, no. 4 (1997): 433–40. http://www.proquest.com.cat1.lib.trentu.ca:8080/.

Russo, Mary. 'The Scandal of Anachronism.' In *Figuring Age: Women, Bodies, Generations*, edited by Kathleen Woodward, 20–33. Bloomington: Indiana University Press, 1999.

Salamon, Julie. 'Eastwood as Reformed Gunslinger.' *Wall Street Journal*, 6 August 1992, A1.

Scheiber, Noam. 'Race against History.' *New Republic* 230, no. 20 (2004): 21–6.

Schenk, Nick. *Gran Torino*, DVD. Directed by Clint Eastwood. USA: Warner Bros., 2009.

Scott, A.O. 'Weep, and the World Laughs Hysterically.' *New York Times*, 12 December 2003. http://movies.nytimes.com/movie/review?_r=1&res= 9C0DEFD9173CF931A25751C1A9659C8B63&scp=3&sq=something%27s%20 gotta%20give&st=cse.

Scott, Jay. Review of *Unforgiven*. *Globe and Mail*, 7 August 1992, C1.

Shakespeare, Tom. 'The Sexual Politics of Disabled Masculinity.' *Sexuality and Disability* 17, no. 1 (1999): 53–64.

Shear, Michael D. 'Obama Takes First Campaign Trip South.' *Washington Post*, 18 February 2007. http://search.ebscohost.com/login.aspx?direct=true&db= rch&AN=WPT120688795707&site=ehost-live.

Shingler, Martin, and Christine Gledhill. 'Bette Davis: Actor/Star.' *Screen* 49, no. 1 (2008): 67–76.

Showalter, Elaine. 'An "Iris" Stripped of Her Brilliance.' *Chronicle of Higher Education* 48, no. 23 (2002): B18.

Siebers, Tobin. *Disability Theory*. Corporealities. Ann Arbor: University of Michigan Press, 2008.

Silverman, Kaja. *Male Subjectivity at the Margins*. New York: Routledge, 1992.

– *The Acoustic Mirror: The Female Voice in Psychoanalysis and Cinema*. Theories of Representation and Difference. Bloomington: Indiana University Press, 1988.

Silverman, Stephen M. 'Screen and Real-Life Hero Paul Newman Dies at 83.' *People*, 27 September 2008. http://www.people.com/people/package/ article/0,,20229386_20199694,00.html.

Smith, Bonnie G., and Beth Hutchison. 'Introduction.' In *Gendering Disability*, edited by Bonnie G. Smith and Beth Hutchison, 1–8. Rutgers, NJ: Rutgers University Press, 2004.

Smith, Murray. *Engaging Characters: Fiction, Emotion, and the Cinema*. New York: Oxford University Press, 1995.

– 'Imagining from the Inside.' In *Film Theory and Philosophy*, edited by Richard Allen and Murray Smith, 412–30. New York: Oxford University Press, 1997.

Snyder, Sharon L., and David T. Mitchell. *Cultural Locations of Disability*. Chicago: University of Chicago Press, 2006.

– 'Re-engaging the Body: Disability Studies and the Resistance to Embodiment.' *Public Culture* 13, no. 3 (2001): 367–90.

Sobchack, Vivian. 'Scary Women: Cinema, Surgery, and Special Effects.' In *Figuring Age: Women, Bodies, Generations*, edited by Kathleen M. Woodward, 200–11. Bloomington: Indiana University Press, 1999.

Sontag, Susan. *The Double Standard of Aging*. Toronto: The Women's Kit, 1972.

Stacey, Jackie. *Star Gazing: Hollywood Cinema and Female Spectatorship*. London: Routledge, 1994.

Starpulse.com 'Antonio Banderas Says Wife Melanie Griffith Is "a Victim of Aging".' http://www.starpulse.com/news/index.php/2007/06/25/antonio _banderas_says_wife_melanie_griff.

Steinem, Gloaria. 'Women Are Never Front-Runners.' *New York Times*, 8 January 2008. http://www.nytimes.com/2008/01/08/opinion/08steinem.html.

Taylor, Ella. 'Review of *The Savages*.' *Houston Press*, 2007. http://proquest.umi.com/pqdweb?did=1410461971&Fmt=7&clientId=29618&RQT=309&VName =PQD.

Taylor, Noel. 'Grumpier Old Men Ogle Loren.' *Ottawa Citizen*, 22 December 1995, C10.

TheRaider.net. 'Frequently Asked Questions.' http://www.theraider.net/films/indy4/faq.php#ford2old.

Thompson, Ernest. *On Golden Pond*, DVD. Directed by Mark Rydell. USA: Universal Pictures, 1981.

Thomson, Rosemarie Garland. *Extraordinary Bodies: Figuring Physical Disability in American Culture and Literature*. New York: Columbia University Press, 1997.

– 'Feminist Theory, the Body, and the Disabled Figure.' In *The Disability Studies Reader*, edited by Lennard J. Davis, 279–92. New York: Routledge, 1997.

– 'Seeing the Disabled: Visual Rhetorics of Popular Disability Photography.' In *The New Disability History: American Perspectives*, edited by Paul Longmore and Lauri Umansky, 335–74. New York: New York University Press, 2000.

Uhry, Alfred. *Driving Miss Daisy*, DVD. Directed by Bruce Beresford. USA: Warner Bros., 1989.

Vermilye, Jerry. *Bette Davis*. A Pyramid Illustrated History of the Movies. New York: Pyramid Publications, 1973.

Waxman, Barbara Frey. *From the Hearth to the Open Road: A Feminist Study of Aging in Contemporary Literature*. Contributions in Women's Studies. New York: Greenwood Press, 1990.

– *To Live in the Center of the Moment: Literary Autobiographies of Aging*. Age Studies. Charlottesville: University Press of Virginia, 1997.

Wendell, Susan. *The Rejected Body: Feminist Philosophical Reflections on Disability*. New York: Routledge, 1996.

– 'Unhealthy Disabled: Treating Chronic Illnesses as Disabilities.' *Hypatia* 16, no. 4 (2001): 17–33.

Williams, John C. 'Savagely Funny.' *Arkansas Times*, 17 January 2008. http://proquest.umi.com/pqdweb?did=1426861971&Fmt=7&clientId=29618&RQT =309&VName=PQD.

Woodward, Kathleen M., ed. *Figuring Age: Women, Bodies, Generations*, Theories of Contemporary Culture, vol. 23. Bloomington: Indiana University Press, 1999.

Woodward, Kathleen M. 'Against Wisdom: The Social Politics of Anger and Aging.' *Cultural Critique* 51 (2002): 186–218.

– *Aging and Its Discontents: Freud and Other Fictions.* Theories of Contemporary Culture. Bloomington: Indiana University Press, 1991.

– *At Last, the Real Distinguished Thing: The Late Poems of Eliot, Pound, Stevens, and Williams.* Columbus: Ohio State University Press, 1980.

– 'Performing Age, Performing Gender.' *NWSA Journal* 18, no. 1 (2006): 162–89.

Wyatt-Brown, Anne M., and Janice Rossen, eds. *Aging and Gender in Literature: Studies in Creativity.* Feminist Issues. Charlottesville: University Press of Virginia, 1993.

Zackham, Justin. *The Bucket List*, DVD. Directed by Rob Reiner. USA: Warner Bros., 2007.

Index

able-bodiedness, 6, 123; compulsory, 75, 122, 137; threats to, 75

ableism, 95; ageism via, 31, 40

About Schmidt (Payne), 5, 37, 124–9, 136–7, 176n12

accessibility, 3–5, 9

After Life, 176n12

age: acting against one's, 41, 49, 50, 57; acting one's, 41, 45, 49, 51, 53, 119; instability of, 50

age cohort definitions, 6–7

age identity, 11; normative, 62; ravages of on mind, 59; relational quality of, 49

ageism, xii, 47, 66, 104, 119, 130, 134, 136; via ableism, 31, 40; of Left and Right, 146; presidential candidates and, 31

agency: female, 88; sexual, 91

age studies, 9; aging studies vs., 15; critical gerontology and, 15–16; feminist, 16–19; white, 28–9

aging: acceptance of, 41; ambivalence towards, 56; assumptions about, 144; burdensomeness of, 6–7, 9, 148; cultural locations for, 28; cultural views of, xii, xxi, 73; death and, xix, 14, 24, 37, 48, 49, 139, 140; decay and, xviii, 14; decline and, xix, 6, 14, 21, 49; deformity and, xii; dependency and, 25; disability and, 6, 19–23, 24, 35, 39, 41, 42, 49, 53, 55, 56, 58, 148; as disease, 14, 19; 'double standard' of, 16; empowerment and, 15; extreme, 59; failed, tragedy of, 51; femininity and, xviii, 39, 57; gendered nature of, 138; graceful, developmental models of, 41; growing old vs. looking old, 8; healthy, 8, 20; homogenization of, 146; horror of, 73; images of, xix–xxi; invisibility of, 99; masculinity and, 29, 99–120; mental ability and, xii, xvii, 48; natural, 7; normative, 62; pathologization of, 48, 57, 148; physical ability and, xii, xviii; race and, 28–9; into senescence, xix; social and cultural understandings of, 43; as state of life to be embraced, 19; 'successful,' 20–1, 141; unification of experience of, 7; visibly, 8; with